# Fuzzy and Uncertain Object-Oriented Databases

## Concepts and Models

T0320633

# ADVANCES IN FUZZY SYSTEMS — APPLICATIONS AND THEORY

**Honorary Editor:** Lotfi A. Zadeh (*Univ. of California, Berkeley*)
**Series Editors:** Kaoru Hirota (*Tokyo Inst. of Tech.*),
George J. Klir (*Binghamton Univ.–SUNY*),
Elie Sanchez (*Neurinfo*),
Pei-Zhuang Wang (*West Texas A&M Univ.*),
Ronald R. Yager (*Iona College*)

Advances in Fuzzy Systems — Applications and Theory   Vol. 13

# Fuzzy and Uncertain Object-Oriented Databases
## Concepts and Models

*With a Foreword by Ronald R. Yager*

Editor
## Rita De Caluwe
*University of Ghent, Belgium*

**World Scientific**
*Singapore • New Jersey • London • Hong Kong*

*Published by*

World Scientific Publishing Co. Pte. Ltd.

P O Box 128, Farrer Road, Singapore 912805

*USA office:* Suite 1B, 1060 Main Street, River Edge, NJ 07661

*UK office:* 57 Shelton Street, Covent Garden, London WC2H 9HE

**Library of Congress Cataloging-in-Publication Data**

Fuzzy and uncertain object-oriented databases : concepts and models /
    editor, Rita de Caluwe ; with a foreword by Ronald R. Yager.
        p.    cm. -- (Advances in fuzzy systems ; vol. 13)
    Includes bibliographical references.
    ISBN 9810228937
    1. Object-oriented databases.    2. Fuzzy systems.    I. Caluwe, Rita de.
II. Series.
QA76.9.D3F893    1997
005.75'7--dc21                                              97-28478
                                                                CIP

**British Library Cataloguing-in-Publication Data**

A catalogue record for this book is available from the British Library.

Printed in Singapore.

# CONTENTS

# FOREWORD

The theory of fuzzy sets was initiated in 1965 in the pioneering work of L.A. Zadeh. During the following two decades the theoretical underpinnings of this theory were developed and refined. During the last decade, beginning in about 1985, fuzzy set theory began finding its way into a large number of applications. This is especially true in the area of control where fuzzy logic combined with other soft computing technologies such as neural networks and genetic algorithms have provided a very powerful paradigm. As we enter the last stages of the twentieth century, fuzzy set methods are poised to make even greater contributions to the improved quality of life. With the rapid development of the internet, a medium based upon the confluence of computing and communication technologies, the stage is set for a decade marked by an explosive expansion of an information based culture throughout the world. Here we shall see agents traveling through the internet gatheringinformation and making decisions on behalf of their owners. In order to realize this promise we need methodologies for the intelligent representation and manipulation of information. Fuzzy sets clearly provides a tool that can help in this task.

An important component of this information society are databases, which enable us to store large amounts of information in a structure that provides for easy access through querying. One contribution fuzzy sets is making to database theory is in the area of flexible querying systems. Here we are able to represent questions to databases involving the types of soft concepts human beings use in a form that can be easily implemented in the SQL environment. A significant direction in databases is the development of object-oriented databases. Object-oriented databases allow for a higher order of abstraction in the data model. In this environment we are able to include class type objects and allow specific objects of a class to inherit various properties associated with the classes to which they belong. This volume focuses on an important extension of this object-oriented paradigm which allows for the inclusion of vagueness, imprecision and uncertainty in this paradigm. The editor of this book has gathered papers from the leading researchers in the field of fuzzy object-oriented databases to provide a pioneering volume that will be useful to future researchers and practitioners as a source of many ideas and paradigms for the inclusion of uncertainty in object-oriented databases. Each of the contributors to this volume is a highly regarded researcher who has made numerous contributions to fuzzy information engineering. The editor of this volume is to be complimented for her efforts to provide a guiding light in this new direction.

Ronald R. YAGER
New York, April 1997

# PREFACE

Enriching database models so as to allow the user to deal with fuzzy and uncertain information has been of scientists' concern for years. This resulted in numerous contributions, mainly with respect to the popular relational model or to some related form of it. The experience was instructive, although still far away from concrete applications.

Time has come that the advantages of object-oriented databases are acknowledged outside the research and academic worlds and a breakthrough of new commercial software is observed. Lately research has been devoted to the endowment of this type of databases with more real world reflecting semantics. It proved that the object-oriented paradigm lends itself extremely well to it. This is very promising and opens new perspectives for the availability of new generation database products in a near future.

The book presents the latest research results in dealing with fuzziness and uncertainty in object-oriented databases. The different chapters have been contributed by different authors. Each chapter is self-contained. However, an introductory chapter has been added to provide more background information.

I am very grateful for the spirit of kind cooperation and understanding which I experienced in my contacts with all the co-authors of the book. Among them I specially wish to mention Nancy VAN GYSEGHEM and Valerie CROSS, who have been collaborating with me also outside the frame of this book, Nancy already for many years. I am also indebted to Ronald YAGER for the kind foreword, which he accepted to write for the book. Finally I wish to acknowledge the valuable help of all the members of our research team, especially of Guy DE TRE and Patricia MAESFRANCKX, and of our former assistant Pieter MOERMAN, who all, with youthful enthusiasm, took care of numerous details like checking language, style and lay-out.

Rita DE CALUWE
Ghent (Belgium), April 1997

# BASIC NOTIONS AND RATIONALE OF THE INTEGRATION OF UNCERTAINTY MANAGEMENT AND OBJECT-ORIENTED DATABASES

R. DE CALUWE

*Computer Science Laboratory, University of Ghent,*
*Sint-Pietersnieuwstraat 41, B-9000 Ghent, Belgium*

N. VAN GYSEGHEM

*Department of Mathematics and Computer Science,*
*Centenary College of Louisiana,*
*P.O. Box 41188 Shreveport La 71134-1188, U.S.A.*

V. CROSS

*Systems Analysis, Miami University,*
*Oxford, OH 45056, U.S.A.*

The field of databases is a very vast field which has been studied by many researchers for many years. Countless books and papers have been published that reflect the increasing importance of this field. The present book contributes to this research by focusing on the integration of the object-oriented database theory with the theory of uncertainty modelling, which is another rapidly developing field. Combining the advantages of both theories permits the design of databases which are semantically far more powerful and user-friendly than the traditional ones. This chapter of the book explains the reasons for this and introduces the basic concepts an terminology of the underlying theories.

## 1 Data and Databases

The purpose of a database application is to store data, information or knowledge about the application.

The terms "data" and "database", "information" and "knowledge" appear in all chapters of this book, and although they are considered common basic concepts within the field of databases, they deserve some attention here.

1

- The term data covers a broad scope in meaning, ranging from crude figures and strings, as used for input and output, to their counterparts, which carry specific semantics. For instance, a number can be considered as a mere mathematically defined structure, or can represent an age or a salary.
- A database is a structured collection of data, which are intentionally brought together and made persistent and suited for querying.
- In the context of this book, information means semantically meaningful data which can be derived from a database by querying it in a more or less intelligent way.
- Facts and their logical interrelations are termed knowledge. Knowledge can also be kept in a database, for instance represented in the form of logical rules or via an equivalent formalism. In this case the database is generally called a knowledge base.

From the foregoing, it is clear that a database comprises more than just data and hence, that modelling a database is more complex than modelling data. A database model uses a data model for the description part of its data. The concepts of data modelling and of database modelling are both descriptive, indicating the existence of an underlying structure, in which the static as well as the dynamic aspects are included. The way in which these aspects are addressed is very different between different models.

## 2   Uncertainty

It is probably impossible to capture all of the semantics of real world information, a fortiori to model it in a perfect way. Frequently, the observation of and the knowledge about the real world are deficient and, as a consequence, its modelling and hence its representation is imperfect in some way.

In written English literature, a deficiency in the knowledge of information is most frequently termed "uncertainty", regardless of the application field [Klir 1995].

Although our world is filled with a wide variety of different kinds of uncertainty, science has typically ignored most uncertainty in its models, and preferred most of the time to consider uncertain information as lacking information. Admitting the use of uncertain information is admitting to take into account the individual interpretation of knowledge. This is not an obvious policy. A very strong tradition in science strives for absolute objectivity and certainty, based on facts and figures of common understanding and by the evaluation and approval of the community, which is so characteristic of our twentieth century lifestyle. At the eve of the third millennium, this tradition seems to be changing, and the handling of uncertainty is being acknowledged as essential to science [Korth 1997]. The interested reader can find such common observations further developed and put in their historical perspective in [Klir 1995], a standard reference work for fuzzy sets and fuzzy logic, and in a very basic French text, [Arago 1994], which also serves as a reference text for fuzzy sets and fuzzy logic.

## 2.1 The nature of uncertainty

Focusing on the application field of databases, it is of interest to study the different kinds of uncertainty which can exist about the data, about the way to structure data, about the facts involving or relating data and about the meaning of data, taking into account that data eventually can draw their meaning from the comparison with other data through their mutual or supposed proximity or similarity. Therefore, the data model as well as the database model can be affected by the different kinds of uncertainty.

[Motro 1995] gives a classification of uncertainty with respect to database applications, and assumes that uncertainty permeates the models of the real world, but not the real world itself. He uses the term uncertainty to refer to any element of the model that cannot be asserted with complete confidence. He distinguishes:

- uncertainty (when it is not possible to determine whether an assertion in the model is true or false),
- imprecision (when the information available in the model is not as specific as it should be),
- vagueness (when the model includes elements that are inherently vague),
- inconsistency (when the model contains two or more assertions that cannot be true at the same time) and
- ambiguity (when some elements of the model lack complete semantics, leading to several possible interpretations).

The first three kinds of uncertainty in the classification, i.e. uncertainty in its specific meaning, imprecision and vagueness, are explained in more detail here, as they are addressed in the following chapters. The concept of vagueness, which is also called fuzziness, is associated with the inability to define sharp or precise borders for some domain (of information) and therefore represents an inherent uncertainty. The concepts of uncertainty and imprecision cover the deficiency of the information due to a lack of knowledge about the database application. Although there exists a certain affinity among these three concepts, they are orthogonal. They can appear side by side or simultaneously within a database environment.

Some examples should clarify the distinction between the three notions of uncertainty. To start with, consider the concept of "young ages". It is a multi-valued concept, as a number of different ages can be considered as young, and it is a vague (fuzzy) concept, because the borderline between the "young ages" and "not young ages" is not uniquely or well defined. For instance, 1 year, 2 years, 3 years ... are definitely young ages, 30 years and older are definitely not young ages, while 20 years, 21 years, ... are not really young nor really old ages : they are considered young ages to a lesser extent than the ages 1, 2, 3, ...

Technically speaking, a fuzzy concept, such as young ages, has an "and-semantics" : all ages ranging from 1 to 30 years correspond (to some extent) to "young ages".

The former example contrasts with the example of a statement such as "John is between 15 and 25 years old." Every person has a unique and well-defined age, which in this case is not precisely known or is not expressed in a precise way : John's age can be 15 years or 16 years or ... or 25 years old. In this example, the use of "is between 15 and 25 years old" illustrates the concept of imprecision.

Imprecision has an "or-semantics" : among the given ages only one age is the right one, but there is no certainty about which one.

Similarly, a statement such as "the age of John is young" expresses imprecision in the description of John's age. Here, John's age belongs to the vague concept of "young ages", or stated otherwise, John can be 1 year old or 2 years or 3 years or ... or (to a lesser extent) 20 years or 21 years ..., but he definitely is not 30 years or older. Frequently, this kind of imprecise information is also referred to as vague information, because it uses a vague concept to express the imprecision.

Finally, a statement such as "it is highly possible that John is 25 years old" illustrates an uncertainty in a very specific meaning : here it expresses doubt about the information that "John is 25 years old", but not about the use of "25". Such uncertainty can also qualify imprecise information, as in the statements "it is highly possible that John is between 15 and 25 years old" and "it is highly possible that John is young".

## 2.2    Modelling uncertainty

The existence of different kinds of uncertainty results in different ways to model uncertainty, some of which are discussed here.

A substantial part of the discussion is devoted to the fuzzy set theory as a means to model the concept of fuzziness. Another part treats the related possibility theory, as this theory offers a suitable formalism to model imprecision and uncertainty in its specific meaning. The discussion is completed with the notions of similarity and of typicality, which are used to establish degrees of uncertainty.

The fuzzy set and possibility theories have experienced rapid advances over the last decades. Only a limited number of mathematical concepts are discussed here since the contributions of the different authors mainly deal with how uncertainty handling can be part of the powerful capabilities of object-oriented databases, and not per se with the use of the most advanced mathematical novelties in the theories.

## 2.3    The fuzzy set theory and related possibility theory

The existence of a very extensive literature on fuzzy set theory witnesses its ongoing development since its introduction by L. Zadeh in the mid sixties [Zadeh 1965]. Looking for a standard reference text the reader can refer to [Klir 1995].

The concept fuzzy set can be seen as a generalization of the concept crisp set.

A fuzzy set $F$ on a universe $U$ is defined as a set of ordered pairs $(x,y)$, where $x$ is an element of the universe of discourse and $y$ is an element of the closed interval $[0,1]$:

$$F = \{ (x,y) \mid x \in U, 0 \leq y \leq 1 \}$$

The value $y$ is called the membership degree associated with $x$ by the fuzzy set $F$. A membership degree 1 indicates full membership of $x$ in $F$, a membership degree 0 indicates no membership in $F$, and a membership degree $0 < y < 1$ indicates partial membership of $x$ in $F$. Partial membership means that the element $x$ belongs to the fuzzy set only up to some degree, which is indicated by the membership degree.

A crisp set can be viewed as a special case of a fuzzy set, for which only the membership degrees 0 and 1 are associated with elements of the universe.

Similar to the characteristic function $\chi_S$ of a crisp set $S$ - which is a function $\chi_S : U \rightarrow \{0,1\}$ so that : $\chi_S(x) = 1$ if $x \in S$ and $\chi_S(x) = 0$ if $x \notin S$

for every element $x$ of the universe $U$ - the membership function $\mu_F$ of a fuzzy set $F$ is defined as a function $\mu_F : U \rightarrow [0,1]$, which associates with each element $x \in U$ the membership degree $y$ of $x$ in $F$ : $\mu_F(x) = y$.

The actual membership degree of an element in a fuzzy set does not have an absolute meaning. A membership degree $\mu_F(x)$ draws its meaning from a comparison with the membership degrees $\mu_F(u)$ of other elements $u \in U$ : if $\mu_F(x) > \mu_F(u)$, i.e. if $x$ has a higher membership degree in $F$ than $u$, then $x$ belongs to the fuzzy set $F$ with a higher degree than $u$. If $F$ describes a vague notion, such as the notion of young age, then it is said that the element $x$ resembles this notion better than $u$.

The support of a fuzzy set $F$ is a subset of the universe $U$, which contains all elements having a full or partial membership in $F$ : $supp_F = \{ x \in U \mid \mu_F(x) > 0 \}$

The core of $F$ is a subset of $U$ containing only the elements having a full membership in $F$ :

$$core_F = \{ x \in U \mid \mu_F(x) = 1 \}$$

The fuzzy set $F$ is normalized if the core is a non-empty set.

The support and the core are two special cases of (strict) $\alpha$-cuts. An $\alpha$-cut, respectively a strict $\alpha$-cut, of a fuzzy set $F$ is a subset of $U$ containing all elements having a membership degree $\geq \alpha$, respectively $> \alpha$, where $\alpha \in [ 0, 1 ]$ :

$$F_{\alpha} = \{ x \in U \mid \mu_F(x) \geq \alpha \}$$

$$F_{\bar{\alpha}} = \{ x \in U \mid \mu_F(x) > \alpha \}$$

Commonly used shapes of the membership function $\mu_F$ of a fuzzy set $F$ on the universe of real numbers $\mathbb{R}$ are trapezoidal membership functions. A trapezoidal membership function, shown in Figure 1 is determined by four parameters $(a,b,\alpha,\beta)$ :

$$x < a-\alpha \ : \ \mu_F(x) = 0$$

$$a-\alpha < x < a \ : \ \mu_F(x) = 1 - \frac{a-x}{\alpha}$$

$$a < x < b \ : \ \mu_F(x) = 1$$

$$b < x < b+\beta \ : \ \mu_F(x) = 1 - \frac{x-b}{\beta}$$

$$b+\alpha < x \ : \ \mu_F(x) = 0$$

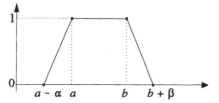

Figure 1 : trapezoidal membership function

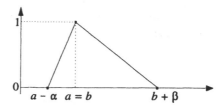

Figure 2 : triangular membership function

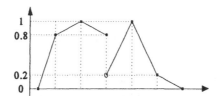

Figure 3 : piecewise linear membership function

If $a = b$ , $\mu_F$ is a triangular membership function, shown in Figure 2. Another, more general shape for the membership function of a fuzzy set on $\mathbb{R}$ is a piecewise linear membership function, shown in Figure 3. Such membership function $\mu_F$ is determined by an ordered list of breaking points. Each breaking point is represented as a quadruple $(x_i, l_i, f_i, r_i)$, where $x_i$ is the real number at which $\mu_F$ changes its slope, where $f_i$ is the membership degree of $x_i$, and where $l_i$, resp. $r_i$, are the left limit, resp. right limit of the membership function at $x_i$:

$$\{(x_1, l_1, f_1, r_1), ..., (x_i, l_i, f_i, r_i), ..., (x_n, l_n, f_n, r_n)\}$$

The membership degree associated with a real number $x$ in between two consecutive breaking points $x_i$ and $x_{i+1}$ is calculated using linear interpolation :

$$\mu_F(x) = r_i + \frac{(l_{i+1} - r_i)(x - x_i)}{(x_{i+1} - x_i)}$$

Operations defined for crisp sets are extended for fuzzy sets. However, such extensions are not unique. The most stringent condition imposed, is that an extended operation equals the regular operation when it is executed against crisp sets. A general discussion of several definitions for extended operations can be found in [Kli95]. The most frequently used, and most simple extension of set operations was originally proposed by Zadeh :

(regular) inclusion :     $F_1 \subseteq F_2 \leftrightarrow \forall x \in U: \mu_{F_1}(x) \leq \mu_{F_2}(x)$

strong inclusion :     $F_1 \sqsubset F_2 \leftrightarrow supp_{F_1} \subseteq core_{F_2}$

(regular) equality :     $F_1 = F_2 \leftrightarrow \forall x \in U: \mu_{F_1}(x) = \mu_{F_2}(x)$

complement :     $\forall x \in U: \mu_{co(F)}(x) = 1 - \mu_F(x)$

intersection :     $\forall x \in U: \mu_{F_1 \cap F_2}(x) = \min(\mu_{F_1}(x), \mu_{F_2}(x))$

union :     $\forall x \in U: \mu_{F_1 \cup F_2}(x) = \max(\mu_{F_1}(x), \mu_{F_2}(x))$

A fuzzy set of level two is a fuzzy set of fuzzy set, i.e. if $\mathscr{F}(U)$ is the universe of fuzzy sets on $U$, then a fuzzy set of level two is an element of $\mathscr{F}(\mathscr{F}(U))$.

A fuzzy relationship between the universes $U_1, ..., U_n$ is defined as a fuzzy set on the Cartesian product of the universes $U_1 \times ... \times U_n$. A similarity relationship $s$ is a fuzzy binary relationship, defined as a fuzzy set on $U \times U$ which satisfies the properties of reflexivity, symmetry and transitivity :

$$\forall x \in U: \mu_s(x,x) = 1$$

$$\forall x, y \in U: \mu_s(x,y) = \mu_s(y,x)$$

$$\forall x, y \in U: \mu_s(x,y) \geq \max\{\min(\mu_s(x,z),\mu_s(z,y)) \mid \forall z \in U\}$$

The formal definition of a fuzzy measure is beyond the scope of this introductory chapter. What is of interest, is that a fuzzy measure is used to model the uncertainty encountered when determining whether or not an element $x \in U$ is a member of a number of crisp sets. A special fuzzy measure is the possibility measure $\Pi$. For any set $S$ on the universe $U$, $\Pi(S)$ denotes the degree in which $S$ is considered "possible". A possibility measure satisfies the following properties for any set $S_1$, $S_2$ and $S$ on $U$ :

$$\Pi(S_1 \cap S_2) = \max\{\Pi(S_1), \Pi(S_2)\}$$

$$\max\{\Pi(S), \Pi(\text{co}(S))\} = 1$$

The last property indicates that at least $S$ or its complement are completely "possible", but, when $S$ is completely possible, it does not prevent its complement from also being completely possible.

For a finite universe $U$, a possibility measure can be defined by means of a possibility distribution $\pi$, which is a function $\pi: U \rightarrow [0,1]$ so that for any set $S$ on $U$ and any element of $U$ :

$$\Pi(S) = \max\{\pi(u) \mid \forall u \in S\}$$

$$\pi(x) = \Pi(\{x\})$$

A set can impose a constraint on the value of a variable $A$ by stating that the value of $A$ must belong to this set. Similarly, a (normalized) fuzzy set $F$ can impose an "elastic" constraint on the value of a variable $A$. When the membership function $\mu_F$ indicates the degrees to which the elements of the universe correspond to a real-world concept, it can be used to restrict the possible values of a variable $A$ :

$$\forall x \in U: \pi_A(x) = \mu_F(x)$$

In this case, the membership degree of $x$ in $F$ determines the possibility degree $\pi_A(x)$ in which the variable $A$ equals $x$. Such elastic constraint is also used to model the possible values of a variable $A$ of which the exact value is not precisely known. For instance, the value of $A$ can be described using a fuzzy concept or vague linguistic term, resulting in the imprecise value. This fuzzy concept is modelled as a fuzzy set, which then determines the possibility distribution $\pi_A$ modelling the value of $A$.

The regular operations which operate on crisp, precise values need to be extended to also account for imprecise values. Again, such extension is not unique, but the most frequently used, and most simple extension was originally proposed by Zadeh through the extension principle, which explains how an operation can be extended to fuzzy sets :

if :

$$f: \ U_1 \times ... \times U_n \ \rightarrow \ U_{n+1}$$
$$(x_1, ..., x_n) \ \rightarrow \ x_{n+1}$$

then:

$$f': \ \mathcal{F}(U_1) \times ... \times \mathcal{F}(U_n) \ \rightarrow \ \mathcal{F}(U_{n+1})$$
$$(X_1, ..., X_n) \ \rightarrow \ X_{n+1}$$

where for $1 \leq i \leq n+1$, $X_i$ are fuzzy sets on $U_i$, so that :

if :

$$f: \ U_1 \times ... \times U_n \ \rightarrow \ U_{n+1}$$
$$(x_1, ..., x_n) \ \rightarrow \ x_{n+1}$$

then :

$$f': \ \mathcal{F}(U_1) \times ... \times \mathcal{F}(U_n) \ \rightarrow \ \mathcal{F}(U_{n+1})$$
$$(X_1, ..., X_n) \ \rightarrow \ X_{n+1}$$

where for $1 \leq i \leq n+1$, $X_i$ are fuzzy sets on $U_i$, so that :

$$\mu_{X_{n+1}} : U_{n+1} \rightarrow [0,1]$$

$$x_{n+1} \rightarrow 0 \qquad \text{if } \nexists (x_1,...,x_n) \in U_1 \times ... \times U_n : x_{n+1} = f(x_1,...,x_n)$$

$$x_{n+1} \rightarrow \max\{\min\{\mu_{X_1}(x_1),...,\mu_{X_n}(x_n)\} \mid \forall (x_1,...,x_n) \in U_1 \times ... \times U_n : x_{n+1} = f(x_1,...,x_n)\}$$

otherwise

The original formulation of this extension principle is given for fuzzy sets without any imposed semantics. When the semantics is taken into account, it is obvious that such extended operation is useful primarily for imprecise values, i.e. for values restricted by an elastic constraint defined by fuzzy sets, or stated otherwise, for values modelled by possibility distributions.

Theories other than the fuzzy set theory and the related possibility theory have been developed to support the handling of inexactness in information. We mention for instance the rough set theory, which can support the modelling of indiscernability or ambiguity; this theory has even been used in combination with the fuzzy set theory for the same purpose [Dubois 1992], [Pawlak 1996]. We also mention the early efforts to explicitly represent the absence of information in a database environment, using the concept of null values and default values, to represent existing standard information. An interesting discussion of some of these more traditional methods is given in [Abiteboul 1995]. For the particular case of object-oriented databases, we refer to [Zicari 1990].

## 3   Object-Oriented Databases

[Cattell 1992] refers to [Ullman 1989] to state that there exist three kinds of database needs : data management, object management and knowledge management. Only data management is addressed by relational database management systems. Object management is concerned with the requirements for more complex data structures, and is addressed now by object-oriented databases. Knowledge management refers to the broader scope of deriving information about a domain through an inference system; the object-oriented technology is a breeding ground for developing this kind of systems. For instance, integrating objects and rules has already been extensively addressed in [Kim 1990].

The successive development of database models which meet these needs, demonstrates the increasing ability of database systems to master the complexity in database applications.

The older, but still successful, relational database model was first specified in [Codd 1970], the more recent object-oriented database model was first specified in the Object-Oriented Database System Manifesto [Atkinson 1990].

The shift from relational to object-oriented databases went along with the development of other data and database models, each contributing in their own way, but none of them being materialized in fully-fledged commercial products. Indeed, numerous extensions of the relational model paved the way to more powerful functional and semantic models. However, none of the new models has proved to be powerful enough to supplant the relational model as a basis for the leading market products.

Another test for the new models is dictated by economic reasons : for the vendor companies, the return on investment is very important, and for the users, the necessary cost of rewriting applications needs to be as low as possible. Object-oriented technology seems on its way to become successful in meeting this challenge. For sure, the present profusion of scientific and technical books and papers which are devoted to the bridging of the gap between relational and object-oriented database models and products is a good omen. Research on object-oriented and object-relational databases has already been recognized as leading to major achievements in the last five years [Silberschatz 1996]. An in-depth discussion is found in [Kim 1995a].

The difficulty of catching the right moment for the very transition, undoubtedly related to the accomplishments with respect to standardization [Thompson 1995], is once more painfully experienced.

The object-oriented paradigm, dating from the sixties, at first served as a basis for the development of new programming languages. Later on it became the supporting mechanism for much more complex software engineering tools, if not the essence of modern software engineering itself. A historical overview is found in [Graham 1991]. From the database perspective, a seamless integration of programming language and data handling can be achieved, which makes object-oriented database programming less cumbersome and hence, greatly improves the productivity of the programmer.

Object-oriented systems have a significant advantage over their predecessors in that more complex underlying data models can be used and, therefore, a higher level of data abstraction and thus, data independence, is provided. They are suited for more sophisticated applications and more naturally support these kinds of applications in their entirety, as the whole software environment can be built on the same principles, using the same programming tools. Authorization control, transaction management, portability, interoperability, ... all of them can be realized with the same means.

Textbooks and papers which provide the details of using object-oriented systems are abundant. Among the recent reference works on object-oriented databases we wish to mention [Graham 1991] and [Loomis 1995].

A proposal for standardization of object-oriented databases has emerged [Cattell 1994] and was revised shortly after, already including possible further extensions in the same report [Cattell 1996]. The ODMG proposal was sparked by the efforts of the OMG-group, to standardize the object model by defining an architecture in view of creating portable applications, and by the X3/SPARC/DBSSG/OODB Task Group, which describes an object-oriented database as a collection of characteristics. The ODMG group proposal has been established by a consortium of object-oriented database vendors, and is backed by industrial input and academic reviewing, but stands outside of the traditional standard bodies. Nowadays it can be considered as a de facto standard awaiting approval from the standard committees.

### 3.1   The Object-Oriented Paradigm

Central to the object-oriented paradigm is the notion of an object. Objects stand for real world or abstract entities and consist of encapsulated data structures, possibly of great complexity, having behavioural capacities. Based on their properties of structure and behaviour, objects belong to classes, which can be related to each other in subclass-superclass hierarchies endowed with inheritance. In practice, classifying objects can be a very difficult problem [Booch 1991].

Object-oriented database systems fully exploit the notions of object, class and inheritance; when only the structural part of object-orientation is taken into account, the term object-centered database systems is used. In short, object-oriented databases are sometimes called object databases.

Some of the following chapters study object-centered models, others study additional aspects, up to the treatment of full object-oriented models.

Only a limited number of concepts are essential to all object-oriented modelling. The concepts which are useful for the understanding of the next chapters are introduced hereafter. Unfortunately, sometimes there is a lack of agreement on the terminology.

In the object model, each object has a unique object identifier (OID) which is used to distinguish it from all other objects.

Each object is of a particular type, generally called a class in object-oriented programming languages. The term type is preferred here, since the term class has been used to define both object intent (structure and behaviour) and object extent (set of like objects). The term class has also been loosely used to refer to the implementation of a type since a type can have more than one implementation specification.

Some types known as abstract types are intended as supertypes for other subtypes and may not have objects directly created from them.

Collection types are predefined data organization methods such as sets, bags, lists, and arrays. Objects may be grouped into named instances of one of these collection types.

The extent of an object type is a system-maintained set collection for all the objects of the object type. This extent includes the objects of all subtypes of the type and is also referred to as the maximal extent.

The object type defines the properties, i.e., attributes and relationships, and the operations that make up objects of this type. Each attribute has a type. Attributes are classified as simple attributes or complex attributes. Simple attributes take on literal values. Complex attributes are categorized as reference attributes and collection attributes. Reference attributes hold references to objects, i.e., object identifiers. Collection attributes hold collection object identifiers. Attribute signatures define the attribute name and the type of its legal values.

The other kind of property, a relationship, defines an association between types of objects. In [Cattell 1994] and likewise in [Cattell 1996] only binary relationships are supported. A relationship is also referred to as a reference attribute. The relationship signature specifies the cardinality, i.e., one-to-one, one-to-many or many-to-many, the related object type, and the inverse attribute which refers to an attribute in the related object type.

The inverse attribute is essential to ensure referential integrity. The declaration of an inverse attribute represents the implicit specification of a traversal path. With binary relationships, traversal paths must exist in pairs, one for each direction of traversal of the relationship.

Operations are functions that can be applied on or by objects; they define the behaviour of objects. An operation is defined in two parts: by its external and by its internal characteristics, called the interface and its implementation. They are specified as a set of operation signatures and methods. An operation signature defines the name of the operation, the name and type of any parameters, the name and type of any returned values, and the names of any exceptions which the operation might cause to occur. A method for an operation specifies the implementation of the operation. An object's methods are used to encapsulate the semantics of the object.

Object types are linked to other object types in subtype/supertype hierarchies. The main purpose of subtype/supertype hierarchies is to permit generalization which is also referred to as inheritance, subtyping or subclassing. Generalization may be considered as one of the following: specialization, specification, and classification. In specialization, the subtype inherits the properties and operations of the supertype and may choose to override certain properties of the supertype and/or extend its properties when additional properties are required by the subtype. Specification permits a subtype to be defined for a supertype by testing a predicate defined over a set of attributes. Distinguishing between different subtypes might be necessary, for example, if different methods are required for them. In classification, subtypes are simply used as sets to categorize objects. Specification includes classification as a trivial case since a specific attribute could be defined to indicate to which subtype the object belongs. Although these different kinds of generalization exist, database systems and programming languages use the same subtyping mechanism to realize each kind of generalization. This practice may be a reason for some of the confusion existing among object-oriented systems.

Multiple inheritance occurs when a subtype has multiple supertypes. Multiple inheritance is useful when more than one orthogonal classification hierarchy exists.

Database objects which have to outlive the execution of the application programs, are made persistent, in contrast to the other objects which are only transient.

The object model concepts and terminology just reviewed are part of a rapidly changing object technology. The rapid change is being brought about partly by the needs of the applications and by the promises of the database vendors. The object model may serve as a unifying framework for supporting multimedia and complex applications and for integrating with developers' increasingly object-based tools.


## 4   Uncertainty in Object-Oriented Databases


Uncertainty handling is not frequently addressed in a database environment. This contrasts with other application areas, such as engineering applications, decision problems, control systems, rule based knowledge systems and so on, where uncertainty management has been incorporated and has lead to new and interesting solution methods. These application areas have in common the emphasis of data handling and are much less demanding than database environments which model the information itself.

The majority of the papers concerning fuzzy databases treat formal aspects related to relational databases; practical realizations seem exceptional and either have been developed as prototypes or are the result of private initiatives. Even the most leading references in the literature about uncertainty, such as [Klir 1995], are very brief in their treatment of database applications, at best referring to research about uncertainty in relational databases and not mentioning the efforts of the last decade with respect to object-oriented databases. Moreover, the very few books on fuzziness and databases [Bosc 1995], [Petry 1996] are barely concerned with object-orientation. However, in [Graham 1991], inheritance under uncertainty is briefly considered.

In fact, up to now, only a limited number of research groups have investigated the problem of modelling fuzziness and uncertainty in the context of object-oriented databases. Nevertheless, combined fuzzy and uncertain object-oriented databases offer the power of object-orientation and the availability of a richer semantic expressiveness. The development of theoretical fuzzy and uncertain object-oriented database models is now approaching the point that useful products can begin their initial development.

Of course, as always, research is continuing; at present the definition of a unifying framework for a fuzzy object model is being investigated [Cross 1997].

The next chapters describe proposals for integrating uncertainty in object-oriented database models.

The earlier attempts to endow object-centered models, semantic networks and frame-based models, with fuzzy semantics, are addressed by Rossazza et al. in chapter 2. The proposed model is based on the notion of typicality modelled by fuzzy sets. The model is a static one since all the crisp and fuzzy information is contained in the attributes of the objects themselves. The hierarchical links are based on inclusion definitions related to different implication definitions. As this model is able to handle default knowledge, exceptions can be represented in the model.

In chapter 3 by George et al., the approach of modelling imprecision is based on the similarity concept. The uncertainty in classification and in the inheritance hierarchies in class/subclass relationships, as a consequence of the allowed imprecision in data, is modelled by using fuzzy set theory. An algebra for the defined data model is presented. The practical interest of the theory is illustrated by the development of an extensive example and the discussion of further possible applications.

Extending a graph-based object-oriented data model is presented by Bordogna et al. in chapter 4. The graphical representation goes along with a formal definition of the model, which uses the fuzzy set and possibility theories to represent uncertainty. Uncertainty is investigated here at the schema level as well as at the instance level.

The model of Van Gyseghem et al. is presented in chapter 5. The model is an extension of an object-oriented database model, based on the fuzzy set and possibility theories. It considers uncertainty at the data level as well as the schema level and also discusses the dynamic aspects of object-orientation.

Na et al. present in chapter 6 a fuzzy object data model and a fuzzy association algebra. Fuzzy associations are defined at the metalevel for relationships between classes and at the object level for relationships between objects. Next, patterns of fuzzy associations are defined, and by the algebra, operations on the patterns. The result of the pattern matching operation can be interpreted as the extent to which the retrieved data meet the requirements expressed by the corresponding formulated query.

## References

[Abiteboul 1995]    Abiteboul, S., Hull, R., and Vianu V., *Foundations of Databases*, Addison-Wesley Publishing Company, Reading, Massachusetts (USA), 1995

[Arago 1994]    Observatoire Français des Techniques Avancées (rapport Arago 14) *Logique floue*, Masson, Paris (France), 1994

[Atkinson 1990]    Atkinson, M., Bancilhon. F., DeWitt, D., Dittrich, K., Maier, D., Zdonik, S., *The Object-Oriented Database System Manifesto*, in [Kim 1990]

[Booch 1991]    Booch, G., *Object-Oriented Design with Applications*, The Benjamin/Cummings Publishing Company, Inc., Redwood City, California (USA), 1991

[Bosc 1995]    Bosc, P., and Kacprzyk, J., eds., *Fuzziness in Database Management Systems*, Physica-Verlag, Heidelberg (Germany), 1995

[Cattell 1992]    Cattell, R.G.G., *Object Data Management, Object-Oriented and Extended Relational Database Systems*, Addison-Wesley Publishing Company, Reading, Massachusetts (USA), 1991 (reprinted with corrections in 1992)

[Cattell 1994]    Cattell, R.G.G., ed., *The Object Database Standard : ODMG-93*, Morgan Kaufmann Publishers Incorporation, San Francisco, California (USA), 1994

[Cattell 1996]    Cattell, R.G.G., ed., *The Object Database Standard : ODMG-93, version 1.2*, Morgan Kaufmann Publishers Incorporation, San Francisco, California (USA), 1996

[Codd 1970]    Codd, E., *A relational model for large shared data banks*, Communications of the ACM, Vol. 13, No. 6, pp. 377-387, ACM, 1970

[Cross 1997]        Cross, V., De Caluwe, R., Van Gyseghem, N., A *Perspective from the Fuzzy Object Data Management Group*, Proceedings of the FUZZ-IEEE'97 Conference, Barcelona, July 1997, IEEE, 1997

[Dubois 1992]       Dubois, D., and Prade, H., *Putting Rough Sets and Fuzzy Sets Together*, in [Slowinski 1992]

[Graham 1991]       Graham, I., *Object-Oriented Methods*, Addison-Wesley Publishing Company, Wokingham, England, 1991

[Kim 1990]          Kim, W., Nicolas J.-M., Nishio S., eds., *Deductive and Object-Oriented Databases*, Elsevier Science Publishers, North-Holland, Amsterdam (the Netherlands), 1990

[Kim 1995a]         Kim, W., *Object-Oriented Database Systems : Promises, Reality and Future*, in [Kim 1995b]

[Kim 1995b]         Kim, W., ed., *Modern Database Systems, The object model, interoperability and beyond*, Addison-Wesley, Publishing Company,, Reading Massachusetts (USA), 1995

[Klir 1995]         Klir, G.J. and Yan, B., *Fuzzy Sets and Fuzzy Logic, Theory and Application*, Prentice Hall P T R, Upper Saddle River, New Jersey (USA), 1995

[Korth 1997]        Korth, H.F. and Silberschatz, A., *Database Research Faces the Information Explosion*, Communications of the ACM, Vol. 40, No. 2, pp. 139-142, ACM, 1997

[Loomis 1995]       Loomis, M., *Object Databases, The Essentials*, Addison-Wesley Publishing Company, Reading, Massachusetts (USA), 1995

[Motro 1995]        Motro, A., *Management of Uncertainty in Database Systems*, in [Kim 1995]

[Pawlak 1996]       Pawlak, Z., *Why Rough Sets ?*, Proceedings of the Fifth IEEE, International Conference on Fuzzy Systems, New-Orleans, Sept. 8-11, 1996, Volume 2, pp. 738-743

[Petry 1996]        Petry, F., *Fuzzy Databases, Principles and Applications*, Kluwer Academic Publishers, Boston (USA), 1996

20

[Silberschatz 1996]  Siberschatz, A., Stonebraker M. and Ullman J., eds., *Database Research : Achievements and Opportunities into the 21st Century*, SIGMOD Record, Vol. 25, No. 1, March 1996, pp. 52-63, ACM 1996

[Slowinski 1992]  Slowinski, R., ed., *Intelligent Decision Support : Handbook of Applications and Advances of Rough Set Theory*, Kluwer Academic Publishers, Boston (USA), 1992

[Thompson 1995]  Thompson, C., *The Changing Database Standards Landscape*, in [Kim * 1995]

[Ullman 1989]  Ullmann, J., *Principles of Database and Knowledge-Based Systems, Volumes 1 and 2*, Computer Science Press, Rockville, Maryland (USA), 1989

[Zadeh 1965]  Zadeh, L., *Fuzzy Sets, Information and Control*, 1965, Volume 8 pp. 338-353

[Zicari 1990]  Zicari, R., *Incomplete Information in Object-Oriented Databases*, SIGMOD Record, Vol. 19, No. 3, September 1990, pp. 5-16, ACM 1990

# A HIERARCHICAL MODEL OF FUZZY CLASSES

Jean-Paul ROSSAZZA, Didier DUBOIS and Henri PRADE

*Institut de Recherche en Informatique de Toulouse (IRIT)*
*Université Paul Sabatier, 118 Route de Narbonne, 31062 Toulouse Cedex, France*

The chapter presents an object-centered representation, where both a range of allowed values and a range of typical values can be specified for the attributes describing a class. These ranges may be fuzzy. Then various kinds of (graded) inclusion relations can be defined between classes. Inheritance mechanisms are discussed in this framework, as well as other kinds of reasoning tasks such as classification. Updating is also discussed.

## 1. Introduction

This chapter investigates a representation framework where the description of a class of objects can be pervaded with vagueness and where typical values of an attribute for an object in a class can be set apart. We thus try to remain close to human being's representations. This article studies more particularly how fuzzy sets theory can be mixed with object-centered representations (O.C.R.) and used for expressing typicality, and thus handling exceptions.

The object-centered representations stem from the notion of frames expressed by Minsky[18] and the concept of object defined in Smalltalk[12]. They model knowledge as explicit entities named objects (or frames) rather than by means of relations bearing on entities, as in predicative and relational formalisms. An object may be an abstract concept (for example the concept "bird") or a real entity (the living bird named Tweety). So in an O.C.R. the objects have an explicit existence inside the knowledge base: all the information concerning an object is gathered at the same place and forms this object. The pieces of information are not scattered in the base as they are in predicative and relational formalisms. The objects having the same properties are gathered into classes which are organized into hierarchies. This organization allows an object to inherit properties from its class (if the object is an instance) or from its superclasses (if the object is a class) thus simplifying the specification of the knowledge base. Moreover a system using such an organization can easily access its knowledge and so explain its reasoning. An O.C.R. may be used in association with production rules or as one among different representation methods the user can choose.

From a cognitive point of view an O.C.R. is interesting because the human being seems to use both the notions of hierarchy and class in his reasoning. By using such hierarchies we can hope on the one hand that the system will be able to reason in a way closer to the human mind and on the other hand that the knowledge base will be more understandable and easier to model. But the reasoning process of a human being is much more complex than the simple use of class hierarchies: a human being can plausibly answer questions even if he has not all the necessary information for a sure answer. He can do that because he uses different kinds of reasoning patterns (see e.g., Collins and Michalski[6]): generalization, specialization, analogy and default reasoning and because he can handle vagueness, uncertainty and typicality.

So, in order to accommodate various forms of plausible reasoning we need an O.C.R. allowing to cope with typicality, uncertainty and vagueness. Although object-centered representations and possibility theory can get along quite easily, there have been only a few attempts to mix them: let us mention Rundensteiner and Bandler[23] who rather study fuzzy semantic networks, Vignard[27] who introduces fuzzy-valued attributes in classes, Graham and Jones[14,15] who propose a generalization of the notion of frame allowing for partial inheritance, Granger[16] who solves classification problems, using a class hierarchy with fuzzy thresholds and weighted attributes and Torasso and Console[24] who define a frame-based representation with three kinds (necessary, sufficient and supplementary) of weighted attributes.

The contents of this chapter is essentially based on works made by the authors in the early nineties. It extends a previous paper[9] on the basis of the PhD thesis of one of the authors[22]. Since this time, an increasing interest for fuzzy object-oriented models and languages has appeared in the fuzzy database literature. These works introduce some fuzzy features in the object-oriented database model. In particular, George et al.[11] use fuzzy similarity relations for defining fuzzy class schema. Bordogna et al.[3] consider a fuzzy class hierarchy with fuzzy inheritance relation, just as Van Gyseghem et al.[25,26] who also accommodate fuzzy data. Gonzalez-Gomez et al.[13] also allow for fuzzy data and fuzzy classes and propose a classification mechanism which at a global level makes use of, rather empirical, measures of compatibility, incompatibility and typicality, based on some cognitive science motivations. Recently, Na and Park[19] have presented a fuzzy object-oriented data model (allowing for objects with fuzzy attribute values) and a fuzzy association algebra for query handling. In contrast, the work reported in this chapter is primarily motivated by knowledge representation and inference issues, and not directly by object-oriented databases. It utilizes possibility theory extensively, as a framework for modelling the uncertainty of data, and fuzzy sets for modelling classes with unsharp boundaries. On the basis of the fuzzy descriptions of classes and their prototypes, some inheritance mechanisms are proposed. However, such plausible inference mechanisms should deserve a more systematic study for themselves, as initiated by Yager[30] and should be related in the future with the works developed in default reasoning, especially in the possibilistic setting (e.g., Benferhat et al.[2]).

In the approach proposed in this chapter, classes are intensionally described in terms of attributes for which we distinguish between the range of *allowed* values and the range of *typical* values, as explained in the following section. These ranges are described by fuzzy sets[31] in the most general case. The existence of two kinds of range for each attribute induces four basic types of possible inclusion between two classes.

Section 2 presents the proposed model. Section 3 describes how the updating of the model can be handled, and Section 4 deals with inference issues in this framework.

## 2. The proposed object-centered model

We aimed at defining an object-centered model with the following characteristics:

- A descriptive semantics: any real object of the model is represented through its description in terms of attribute values.
- The ability to deal with fuzzy descriptions. This will lead to the definition of fuzzy classes and fuzzy instances.
- An internal consistency: Any link between objects must be supported by a relationship between the objects descriptions.
- A distinction between necessary properties and typical properties.This will allow the model to handle exceptions and to deal with classification.
- A distinction between necessary properties of instances and their "credible" (or if we prefer, plausible) properties. This will allow the model to perform default reasoning.

### 2.1. Object description

The distinction between classes and prototypes is a key feature of the proposed model. Classes are basically viewed as sets of instances and not as prototypes of instances as they often are in OCR. In order to be able to deal with the prototype point of view, we will however introduce the notion of 'typical class'.

### 2.1.1. Attribute description

An object is described by a set of attributes. An attribute is defined on a domain which contains all the values that the attribute may take for all objects. The attribute domain does not depend on the class. Only single-valued attributes are considered in this chapter.

A property is defined as a triple (object, attribute, value). We will however use the phrase 'object property', although this is redundant.

### 2.1.2. Class description

A class can theoretically be considered from two different points of view:

- an extensional one where the class is defined by the list of its members;
- an intensional one where the class is defined by a set of attributes and their admissible values. Practically only the intensional definition is possible. We cannot know all the instances of a class in general.

As different kinds of properties are needed for representing commonsense knowledge[24,20] we propose to distinguish the typical properties of an object from its necessary properties by specifying two different set of values (named ranges) for a considered attribute: the typical range and the (necessary) range. A necessary property is represented by a triple (object, attribute, range) and a typical property by a triple (object, attribute, typical range). These two ranges are said to be associated, in the following.

#### 2.1.2.1. The range and the typical range of an attribute

The Range $R(a,c)$ of an attribute $a$ of a class $C$ is the set of allowed values that a member of $C$ can take for the attribute $a$. The range of an attribute may be fuzzy because some of its values are regarded as *atypical* (because less possible or feasible than other values); then an atypical value of the range will be assigned a membership degree strictly less than 1. However a nonatypical value will not be necessarily a somewhat typical value. We want here to point out that a class is fuzzy not because of a lack of information but in order to allow for flexibility and encompasss borderline cases.

The Typical Range $T(a,C)$ of an attribute $a$ of a class $C$ is the set of the more or less typical values that a member of $C$ can take for $a$. The typical range can be naturally represented by a fuzzy set because the notion of typicallity in intrinsically gradual. Moreover, before being somewhat typical a value must be not atypical, that is if we write $Su(T(a,C))$ for the support of $T(a,C)$ and $Co(R(a,C))$ for the core of $R(a,C)$, we should have

$$Co(R(a,C)) \supseteq Su(T(a,C)); \tag{1}$$

where the core refers to the set of elements of a fuzzy set with membership equal to 1 and where the support gathers the elements with a non-zero membership grade.

In practice, an equality rather than an inclusion will often be assumed since it might be difficult to imagine a nontypical value (not belonging whatsoever to $T(\mathbf{a},C)$) that is at the same time not atypical (belonging to $Co(R(\mathbf{a},C))$). When a typical range is not explicitly stated, we will implicitly consider, in order to be coherent with the above requirement, that the core of the range is the typical range. Let us consider a simple example:

| | |
|---|---|
| class | Birds |
| attribute | way_of_locomotion |
|    domain | {fly, walk, swim, crawl, ...} |
|    range | {fly, 0.6/walk, 0.2/swim} |
|    typical range | {fly} |
| ... | |

Here, as it has been said, the attribute way_of_locomotion is considered as being single-valued (in fact we consider the main way of locomotion). Some values of the range have received a membership degree different from 1 in order to point out their atypicality. Note that we write 'fly' instead '1/fly' for simplicity. Here the nonatypical value is the typical value. When none of the ranges of the attributes of a class is fuzzy, we have an ordinary class. Clearly, we are free to allow or not to allow the ranges or the typical ranges of attributes to be fuzzy. This is a matter of option; in practice it is perhaps not necessary to allow both for fuzzy ranges and fuzzy typical ranges.

### 2.1.2.2. Class and typical class

A class is formally defined as the Cartesian product of its possible ranges:

$$C = \{R(a_1,C) \times ... \times R(a_n,C) \mid a_i \in C, i = 1, ..., n\}.$$

The notion of typical class is defined in a similar way as the Cartesian product of the typical ranges of the class:

$$T(C) = \{T(a_1,C) \times ... \times T(a_n,C) \mid a_i \in C, i = 1, ...,n\}$$

We have seen that $R(a_i,C)$ may exist while $T(a_i,C)$ may not exist. This can be a problem for the definition of $T(C)$. This does not mean that typical attribute values do not exist strictly speaking, but that no specific typical range is available for some attribute $a_i$. This leads us to take $T(a_i,C) = Co(R(a_i,C))$, that is to say the largest fuzzy set (in terms of inclusion) compatible with condition (1).

Note that a typical class is different from a class. It has no actual existence in the database. It is only a way of describing typical properties. The typical class notion is very interesting for representing the prototypical view of the concept that the class represents. With our representation, we are able to handle and use both the general view and the prototypical view of a concept.

### 2.1.3. Instances

We call instances, the terminal objects of the hierarchy which are not able to generate other objects. As we just explained, classes are modelled in terms of fuzzy sets assessing the more or less typical and the more or less atypical values of an attribute **a** (via T(**a**,C) and R(**a**,C) respectively), for describing the variability of attribute values for the instances in a class. This contrasts with the use of fuzzy sets interpreted in terms of possibility distributions for describing *ill-known* attribute values of a given instance. Then fuzzy sets are just expressing restrictions on the possible values of *single*-valued attributes, according to the available information about the considered instance. Like classes, instances are described in terms of attributes. The available knowledge, possibly incomplete about an instance x is represented for an attribute **a** by a *possible* range P(**a**,x) and a *credible* range Cred(**a**,x). Unlike a class range, P(**a**,x) (or C(**a**,x)) is a set of mutually exclusive values: the real value of the (single-valued) attribute **a** for the instance x is in Su(P(**a**,x)) but we do not know precisely where.

P(**a**,x) is the (fuzzy) set of all the more or less possible values of the attribute **a** for the instance x. It is supposed to be a sure information (since given by the operator or obtained by inheritance).

Cred(**a**,x) denotes a range obtained in an *uncertain* way (i.e., by a plausible reasoning technique whose validity is not guaranteed). In particular, it will allow for default reasoning. In order to be coherent with the possible range, the credible range has to satisfy the following relation (which is weaker than (1)):

$$Su(P(\mathbf{a},x)) \supseteq Co(Cred(\mathbf{a},x)) \qquad (2)$$

that is to say each completely credible value is at least a little possible.

Note that (2) is a very weak relation: as we know that no value outside P(**a**,x) is allowed, a stronger relation could be Su(P(**a**,x)) $\supseteq$ Su(Cred(**a**,x)). However this latter inclusion cannot always hold, since a plausible reasoning may produce uncertain credible ranges which would not satisfy this relation (indeed an uncertain fuzzy value has a membership function which is not zero anywhere: since nothing is certain, everything remains somewhat possible, may be with a low degree).

The uncertainty of a credible range arises from the fact that it has been produced as a default range, whereas the uncertainty of a possible range denotes the uncertainty of the piece of information itself. Thus in the following example

Tweety
Way_of_locomotion:          Possible range {fly, 0.6/walk, 0.2/swim}
                            Credible range {fly}

the possible range comes from the knowledge that Tweety is a bird, and the credible range is obtained by default reasoning. If the source of information only asserts that it is 0.8 certain that Tweety is a bird, the possible range would be {fly, 0.6/walk, 0.2/swim 0.2/crawl, 0.2/...} since any value of the domain remains in this case possible at the degree $1 - 0.8 = 0.2$ (since in possibility theory, the certainty or necessity of p is such that Possibility(p) = 1 − Certainty(not p), and since here we are assessing the largest possibility degrees compatible with the certainty level). Hence the approach distinguishes between plausible values whose uncertainty is due to default reasoning (the credible ranges) and plausible values whose uncertainty is due to the lack of reliability of the source that provides the information (uncertain possible ranges supplied by the user).

## 2.2. Hierarchical links

As in an inheritance system, objects of our model are linked together with hierarchical links. These links correspond to the classical links 'is a kind of' (between two classes) and 'is a' (between an instance and a class). However, in order to be able to justify each link in the database, we are led to compute the relations between objects using their description. The use of fuzzy attributes value will lead to a gradation of these links in [0,1]. A class will be more or less a subclass of another, instead of being, or not being, a subclass.

### 2.2.1. The links 'is a kind of'

In classical O.C.R. a subclass $C_2$ is defined from its superclass $C_1$ by specialization of its ranges (i.e., the subclass ranges must be included in the corresponding ranges of $C_1$) or by addition of new attributes. In our representation the subclasses are going to be defined in a similar way once we have specified what does 'included' mean for fuzzy ranges. Moreover the distinction between range and typical range induces the existence of four types of inclusion depending if we are comparing the ranges or the typical ranges of $C_1$ with the ranges or the typical ranges of $C_2$. Obviously this comparison may be limited to the context corresponding to a subpart of the attributes involved in the descriptions of $C_1$ and $C_2$.

### 2.2.1.1. Inclusion of two fuzzy ranges

The degree of inclusion $N(B \mid A)$ of a fuzzy set A into a fuzzy set B can be defined by the expression

$$N(B \mid A) = \text{Inf}_u \{\mu_A(u) *\!\!\to \mu_B(u)\} \tag{3}$$

where $*\!\!\to$ denotes a fuzzy implication. We have four main inclusion degrees obtained by considering the following fuzzy implications: Gödel's, Dienes', Lukasiewicz' and the reciprocal of Gödel's implication (see the annex for their different properties). The minimal relation we demand between the fuzzy ranges $A = R(\mathbf{a},C_2)$ and $B = R(\mathbf{a},C_1)$ in order to say that the inclusion of A into B holds to some extent is the following

$$Su(R(\mathbf{a},C_1)) \supseteq Su(R(\mathbf{a},C_2)) \tag{4}$$

i.e., there are no values of **a** which somewhat belong to A (i.e., which are somewhat allowed in $C_2$) and which do not at all belong to B (i.e., which are forbidden in $C_1$). This property is ensured by the degree of inclusion based on Gödel implication ($a *\!\!\to b = 1$ if $a \leq b$, $a *\!\!\to b = b$ if $a > b$, see the annex). It is why this degree of inclusion, denoted $N_G$ in the following, is chosen for defining the inclusions between classes. Note that

$$N_G(B \mid A) = 1 \Leftrightarrow \mu_A \leq \mu_B \text{ and } N_A(B \mid A) > 0 \Rightarrow \exists u, \mu_A(u) > 0 \text{ and } \mu_B(u) = 0;$$

i.e., (4) holds, as expected.

### 2.2.1.2. Inclusion between classes

Since a class is defined through the conjunction of its attributes (and of their ranges), we define the inclusion degree between two classes as a conjunctive aggregation of the inclusion degrees of their ranges. The attributes are supposed to be non-interactive[32] (i.e., any n-tuple of values on the Cartesian product of the ranges is (at least somewhat) allowed for an instance of the class). To perform the conjunction we have to choose two associative conjunctive operations $\times$ and $*$ verifying

$$N_G(B_1 \times \ldots \times B_n \mid A_1 \times \ldots \times A_n) = * \{N_G(B_i \mid A_i) \mid i \in <1,n>\} \tag{5}$$

where $\times$ stands for the Cartesian product and $*$ for the conjunction of the degrees; $*\{a_i \mid i \in I\}$ is the result of combining the $a_i$'s by operation $*$. It can be proved (see the annex) that if the Cartesian product is defined by means of min operation (in order to be in agreement with the non-interactivity of the attributes[32]) we should have $* = \min$ in (5), provided that $A_1, \ldots, A_n$ are normalized (i.e., $\forall i, \exists u_i \, \mu_{A_i}(u_i) = 1$), so we can define the inclusion degree $N_G(C_1 \mid C_2)$ of $C_2$ in $C_1$ with respect to the ranges as

$$N_G(C_1 \mid C_2) = \min\{N_G(R(\mathbf{a}, C_1) \mid R(\mathbf{a}, C_2)) \mid \mathbf{a} \text{ is an attribute of } C_2\} \qquad (6)$$

where $\min\{f(a) \mid a \in A\}$ denotes the value of the smallest of the $f(a)$'s when $\mathbf{a}$ ranges in $\mathbf{A}$. Here we consider that all the attributes of $C_2$ which are not explicitly mentioned as attributes of $C_1$ can always be implicitly considered as attributes of $C_1$ with ranges equal to their domain (for these ranges Gödel's inclusion degree is equal to 1) so the minimum in (6) can be taken on the attributes of $C_1$. Note that

$$N_G(C_1 \mid C_2) > 0 \Leftrightarrow \forall \mathbf{a}, N_G(R(\mathbf{a}, C_1) \mid R(\mathbf{a}, C_2)) > 0. \qquad (7)$$

Given a collection of classes described in terms of ranges and typical ranges of attributes, it is then possible to build a valued-graph expressing the different inclusion relationships between classes and their degrees. The definitions of the inclusion degrees can be restricted to a context expressed by only a subpart of the attributes involved in the description of classes. It can be checked (see the annex) that $N_G$ satisfies the following transitivity property

$$N_G(C \mid A) \geq \min(N_G(C \mid B), N_G(B \mid A)). \qquad (8)$$

### 2.2.1.3. The four inclusion degrees

We can define four different links 'is a kind of' by substituting $T(\mathbf{a}, C_i)$ for $R(\mathbf{a}, C_i)$ (the typical ranges for the ranges) in (6). The three other degrees are:

- $N_G(T(C_1) \mid C_2)$ which estimates the extent to which the instances of $C_2$ are typical $C_1$'s;
- $N_G(C_1 \mid T(C_2))$ which estimates the extent to which the typical instances of $C_2$ are $C_1$'s;
- $N_G(T(C_1) \mid T(C_2))$ which estimates the extent to which the typical instances of $C_2$ are typical $C_1$'s.

The notation $T(C_i)$ means that we substitute $T(\mathbf{a}, C_i)$ for $R(\mathbf{a}, C_i)$ in (6).

It is clear that the following inequalities hold due to (1)

$$N_G(C_1 \mid T(C_2)) \geq N_G(C_1 \mid C_2) \geq N_G(T(C_1) \mid C_2) \qquad (9)$$

$$N_G(C_1 \mid T(C_2)) \geq N_G(T(C_1) \mid T(C_2)) \geq N_G(T(C_1) \mid C_2) \qquad (10)$$

that is to say, if $C_2$ elements are typical $C_1$ then $C_2$ elements are $C_1$ and typical $C_2$ elements are typical $C_1$. Moreover typical $C_2$ elements are then $C_1$.

Transitivity property (8) still holds when we sustitute $T(C_i)$ to $C_i$. For example, if we have $N_G(T(Bird) \mid T(African\ Bird)) = \alpha$ and $N_G(T(African\ Bird) \mid T(Ostrich)) = \beta$, we can deduce that

$$N_G(T(Bird) \mid T(Ostrich)) \geq \min(\alpha, \beta).$$

Note that $N_G(T(Bird) \mid T(African\ Bird)) = 1$ would mean that *all* typical African birds are typical birds and thus fly; this would forbid to consider ostriches (which cannot fly) as typical African birds.

The way the classes are described, as well as the various kinds of inclusion relations which can be computed from the descriptions or declared by the user, enables us to handle typicality. A statement like "typically, students are adults" can be understood as $Adu \supseteq T(Stu)$, while a statement like "typically adults are employees" may rather mean $T(Emp) \supseteq T(Adu)$, where Stu, Adu and Emp denote the classes of students, adults and employees respectively, and $T(C)$ is the subclass of typical elements of class C. These statements are for instance compatible with the following descriptions

| | Stu | Adu | Emp |
|---|---|---|---|
| *Age* | R: $\geq 15$ | R: $\geq 18$ | R: [16,65] |
| | T: [18,25] | T: [25,60] | T: [20,60] |
| *Income* | R: {scholarship, parents' money, salary} | R: <any kind> | R: {salary} |
| | T: {scholarship, parents' money} | T: {salary} | T: {salary} |

Note that the description blocks undesirable transitivity effects since $Adu \supseteq T(Stu)$, $Adu \not\subseteq T(Adu)$, $T(Emp) \supseteq T(Adu)$; thus we cannot deduce that a typical student is an employee.

### 2.3. The links 'is a'

The links 'is a kind of' are based on an inclusion degree. Links 'is a' are graded in terms of a membership degree.

## 2.3.1. Membership degree of an object in a class

When the value $P(\mathbf{a},x)$ of an attribute $\mathbf{a}$ for an object $x$ is precisely known (i.e., corresponds to a singleton of the domain of $\mathbf{a}$), its membership degree to the range $R(\mathbf{a},C)$ of the class C is given by $\mu_{R(\mathbf{a},C)}(P(\mathbf{a},x))$. More generally, when $P(\mathbf{a},x)$ is imprecisely or fuzzily known, i.e., $P(\mathbf{a},x)$ is represented by a possibility distribution which does not restrict a unique possible value. Then, we only have a bracketing of this degree; see Cayrol et al.[4] on this point. Therefore we want to be sure that the real value of the attribute for the considered object is in the range of the class even if the corresponding instance value is fuzzily known. This leads to use Dienes' inclusion degree (see the annex) since

$$N(R(\mathbf{a},C) \mid P(\mathbf{a},x)) = 1 \Leftrightarrow Co(R(\mathbf{a},C)) \supseteq Su(P(\mathbf{a},x)) \qquad (11)$$

i.e., we conclude in favor of a full membership of $x$ to C if and only if all the more or less possible values of $P(\mathbf{a},x)$ are among the values which undisputedly belong to the range. We will be at least slightly certain that $P(\mathbf{a},x)$ belongs to $R(\mathbf{a},C)$ when

$$N(R(\mathbf{a},C) \mid P(\mathbf{a},x)) > 0.$$

which implies

$$Su(R(\mathbf{a},C)) \supseteq Co(P(\mathbf{a},x))$$

that is, the completely possible values of $x$ must belong at least a little to the range.

The membership degree evaluation of an object $x$ to a class C is defined as the conjunction of the membership degree evaluations with respect to ranges defining C. Dienes' inclusion degree can be factorized[8] as Gödel's inclusion degree, provided that each $P(\mathbf{a},x)$ is normalized, i.e.,

$$N(C \mid x) = \min\{N(R(\mathbf{a},C) \mid P(\mathbf{a},x)) \mid \mathbf{a} \text{ is an attribute of } C\} \qquad (12)$$

$N(C \mid x)$ represents the certainty for $x$ to be in C, in spite of the ill-known description of $x$.

Note that $N(C \mid x)$ is generally not a true degree of membership (except if $x$ is precisely described and/or $N(C \mid x) = 1$). It is rather a degree of certainty of membership. We will however use the phrase 'membership degree' instead of 'the degree of certainty of membership'.

We can distinguish three cases:

- $N(C \mid x) = 1$: we are certain that $x$ belongs to C.
- $0 < N(C \mid x) < 1$: here either $x$ is with no doubt an atypical value of C and $N(C \mid x) < 1$ because of the atypicality of $x$ with respect to C, or $N(C \mid x) < 1$ expresses a real uncertainty on the membership of $x$ to C.

- $N(C \mid x) = 0$: it does not mean that x does not belong to C, but only that there is total ignorance about it. However it seems better to memorize links in the database only when we are at least a bit sure of them $(0 < N(C \mid x))$. We say by convention that
- x is a not-atypical instance of C if $N(C \mid x) = 1$,
- x is an atypical instance of C if $0 < N(C \mid x) < 1$,
- x is not a (considered) instance of C if $N(C \mid x) = 0$.

### 2.3.2. Instance and subclass

It can be checked that we have a transitivity property analogous to (8):

$$N(C_1 \mid x) \geq \min(N(C_2 \mid x), N_G(C_1 \mid C_2)). \tag{13}$$

This implies that given $N(C_1 \mid x) > 0$ and $N_G(C_1 \mid C_2) > 0$, we have $N(C_2 \mid x) > 0$. As attended, an instance of a class is also an instance of its superclasses. Moreover, if $N_G(C_1 \mid C_2) = 1$ ($C_2$ is not an atypical subclass of $C_1$) then $N(C_1 \mid x) \geq N(C_2 \mid x)$ (the membership degree of x for a superclass is at least equal to the membership degree for the subclass).

### 2.3.3. The four membership degrees

$N(C \mid x)$ represents the certainty for x to be in C, in spite of the ill-known description of x. To know to what extent x is a typical instance of the class C, we can compute $N(T(C) \mid x)$. It is estimated by $\min\{N(T(\mathbf{a},C) \mid P(\mathbf{a},x)) / \mathbf{a}$ is an attribute of C$\}$. Note that we have not $N(T(C) \mid x) > 0 \Rightarrow N(C \mid x) = 1$, as it could be expected. We only have a weaker property:

$$N(C \mid x) \geq N(T(C) \mid x) \tag{14}$$

that is to say the membership degree to a class is always greater than the membership degree to its associated typical class.

We may also compute credibility degrees by using the credible ranges of x:

- $N(C \mid Cred(x)) = \min\{N(R(\mathbf{a},C) \mid Cred(\mathbf{a},x)) / \mathbf{a}$ is an attribute of C$\}$.
- $N(T(C) \mid Cred(x)) = \min\{N(T(\mathbf{a},C) \mid Cred(\mathbf{a},x)) / \mathbf{a}$ is an attribute of C$\}$.

It may happen that some credible ranges are not specified in the instance description. We propose then to use the possible ranges.

## 2.4. Inheritance and instanciation

We just explained how different degrees (links) could be computed from the objects description. In the following, we are interested in computing an object description knowing its links to classes of the hierarchy, whose descriptions are already known.

### 2.4.1. Inheritance

As our model uses valuated 'a kind of' links, it is tempting to define a weighted inheritance mechanism: the user defines to which extent a class inherits from another. But then two problems arise:

- the subjectivity of the weighting: the user cannot easily justify his/her estimate;
- the validity of the weighting: the number given by the user must at end be consistent with the descriptions of all the classes involved in the inheritance process, especially when new properties are defined in the new subclasses.

Thus the proposed model does not support weighted inheritance. It however supports three kinds of inheritance: typical inheritance, atypical inheritance and 'normal' inheritance. The weighting of the specified links will be computed after having inherited the whole description of the new subclass. Of course the inheritance can be either simple or multiple.

Let us first consider the simple inheritance case. We want here to define a class C knowing that C is somewhat more specific than D. We can do it using one of the three following ways. We can say that

- C's are typical D's:     C's possible ranges inherit then from D's typical ranges;
- C's are D's:     C's possible ranges inherit then from D's ranges;
- C's are atypical D's:     C's possible ranges inherit then from
  - the intersection of D's possible ranges with the complement of D's typical ranges if the latter are known;
  - D's possible ranges if D's typical ranges are unknown.

Describing $C_2$ as a typical subclass of $C_1$ implies that $C_2$'s possible ranges inherit $C_1$'s typical ranges. Describing $C_2$ as a 'normal' subclass of $C_1$ implies that $C_2$'s possible ranges inherit $C_1$'s possible ranges and $C_2$'s typical ranges inherit $C_1$'s typical ranges. The atypical inheritance is a bit more complex: describing $C_2$ as an atypical subclass of $C_1$ means that at least one attribute of $C_2$ is atypical, but not necessarily all of them. So atypical inheritance requires to specify which attributes are atypical. For each of these attributes, $C_2$'s possible range inherits the intersection of $C_1$'s possible range and of the complement of $C_1$'s typical range (the complement

¬F of a fuzzy set F is defined by $\mu_{\neg F} = 1 - \mu_F$ as usual). Other attributes of $C_2$ inherit in a 'normal' way.

Consider, for example, the "Mammal" class below

### Mammal

| | | |
|---|---|---|
| way_of_birth | Range | {1/viviparous, 0.2/not_viviparous} |
| | Typical range | {1/viviparous} |
| way_of_locomotion | Range | {0.2/fly, walk, jump, 0.5/swim} |
| | Typical range | {walk} |
| skeletton | Range | {1/yes} |
| | Typical range | |
| suckle | Range | {1/yes, 0.5/no} |
| | Typical range | {1/yes} |

Saying "Dogs are typical mammals" will cause

### Dogs

| | | |
|---|---|---|
| way_of_birth | Range | {1/viviparous} |
| | Typical range | |
| way_of_locomotion | Range | {walk} |
| | Typical range | |
| skeletton | Range | {1/yes} |
| | Typical range | |
| suckle | Range | {1/yes} |
| | Typical range | |

whereas "African mammals are mammals" will cause

### African Mammals

| | | |
|---|---|---|
| way_of_birth | Range | {1/viviparous, 0.2/not_viviparous} |
| | Typical range | {1/viviparous} |
| way_of_locomotion | Range | {0.2/fly, walk, jump, 0.5/swim} |
| | Typical range | {walk} |
| skeletton | Range | {1/yes} |
| | Typical range | |
| suckle | Range | {1/yes, 0.5/no} |
| | Typical range | {1/yes} |

and "cetaceans are atypical mammal due to way_of_locomotion" will imply

**Cetacean**

| | | |
|---|---|---|
| way_of_birth | Range | { 1/viviparous, 0.2/not_viviparous} |
| | Typical range { 1/viviparous} | |
| way_of_locomotion | Range | {0.2/fly, jump, 0.5/swim} |
| | Typical range | |
| skeletton | Range | { 1/yes} |
| | Typical range | |
| suckle | Range | { 1/yes, 0.5/no} |
| | Typical range { 1/yes}. | |

We can see that the user will have to refine this description by specifying the actual way of locomotion of cetaceans. The consistency of any such additional information must obviously be checked. This consistency is carried out by the strict positivity of the inclusion degree.

Note that an inherited range in a typical or normal way does not affect the inclusion degree. Indeed, if we name H the inherited range, we have to compute $N_G(H \mid H)$ whose value is 1 by definition. This is in accordance with the intuition that the inclusion degree must at end depend on the properties differentiating the subclass from the superclass. The inclusion degree may be affected in an atypical inheritance if the inherited range has to be renormalized.

The multiple inheritance problem is performed in a simple way: the subclass ranges inherit the intersection of the super-classes ranges. Each super-class range is inherited according to the nature of inheritance. According to the types of inheritance different conditions must be satisfied for the amount of overlapping of the ranges or typical ranges of the involved superclasses. For instance if C inherits from $C_1$ and $C_2$ in a normal way, then for each attribute **a** $R(\mathbf{a},C_1) \cap R(\mathbf{a},C_2)$ must be normalized. Otherwise it would mean that only atypical elements of $C_1$ or $C_2$ belong to C. Similarly $T(\mathbf{a},C_1) \cap T(\mathbf{a},C_2)$ should not be empty. When C is a typical subclass of both $C_1$ and $C_2$, then $T(\mathbf{a},C_1) \cap T(\mathbf{a},C_2)$ should be normalized. In case of double atypical inheritance however, $T(\mathbf{a},C_1) \cap T(\mathbf{a},C_2)$ may be empty, and $R(\mathbf{a},C_1) \cap R(\mathbf{a},C_2)$ must not be empty although not necessaritly normalized. All these conditions are consistency requirements whose violations should be notified to the user. Lastly, note that multiple inheritance can be dissymmetric; C can be a typical subclass of $C_1$ and an atypical subclass of $C_2$, which leads to still another kind of coherence condition, as suggested by the following example.

Let us suppose we want to create the 'Bat' class as an atypical subclass of 'Mammal' and as a normal subclass of 'Flying Animal'. Considering only the 'way of locomotion' attribute, we have:

**Mammal**

| | |
|---|---|
| way of locomotion | Range {0.2/fly, walk, jump, 0.5/swim} |
| | Typical Range {walk} |

**Flying Animal**

| | |
|---|---|
| way of locomotion | Range {fly} |

We find first by intersection

**Bat**

| | |
|---|---|
| way of locomotion | Range {0.2/fly} |

and after normalization

**Bat**

| | |
|---|---|
| way of locomotion | Range {fly}. |

### 2.4.2. Instanciation

The instanciation process is similar to the inheritance process. In the same way as we have three kinds of inheritance for a class, we can define three kinds of instanciation for an instance:

- x is a typical D: x's possible ranges inherits D's typical ranges.
- x is a D: x's possible ranges inherits D possible ranges and x's credible ranges inherit D's typical ranges.
- x is an atypical D: x's possible ranges inherits D's possibles ranges if the associated typical ranges are unknown, or otherwise the intersection of D's possible ranges with the complement of their associated typical ranges.

When x is simply described as a C, its typical ranges may be viewed as more precise but more uncertain than x's possible ranges. That's why they are inherited as x's credible ranges. Note that by doing this we perform a kind of default reasoning.

Note also that the atypical instanciation favours atypical values in the class, but also prevent hazardous resoning by blocking the inheritance of credible properties.

In case of multiple instanciations, again we perform the intersection of the involved ranges and again the consistency of any additional information has to be checked.

### 2.4.3. Instanciation and ambiguity

In semantic networks an ambiguity arises when we can deduce the membership and the non-membership of an element to a class at the same time, as in the following example (figure 2.1) :

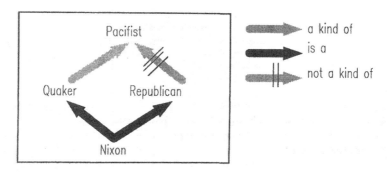

Figure 2.1: Nixon's Diamond

Two strategies are possible: to conclude nothing (the semantic network is said skeptic), or to generate the two contradictory extensions (results) (the semantic network is said to be credulous). In our model Nixon's Diamond can be represented as

**Quaker**                              **Republican**
pacifist  Range {yes, no}              pacifist  Range {yes, no}
          Typical Range {yes}                    Typical Range {no}

that is to say typical quakers are pacifist and typical republican are not pacifist. We obtain then

**Nixon**
pacifist  Range {yes, no}
          Credible Range { }

This description contains the two strategies of semantic networks: the credulous point of view corresponds to the possible ranges and the skeptical point of view corresponds to the typical ranges. Note that with the following definitions

**Pacifist**                            **Non-Pacifist**
pacifist  Range {yes}                   pacifist  Range {no}

we have $N_G$(Pacifist | Nixon) = 0 and $N_G$(Non-Pacifist | Nixon) = 0. Nixon is neither an instance of the Pacifist class, neither an instance of the Non-Pacifist Class.

The use of fuzzy sets allows to refine the description, for example by specifying that being not pacifist is more atypical of a Quaker than being pacifist for a Republican. For example, with the following definitions

|  | **Quaker** |  | **Republican** |
|---|---|---|---|
| pacifist | Range {yes, 0.2/no} | pacifist | Range {0.4/yes, no} |
|  | Typical Range {yes} |  | Typical Range {no} |

we obtain

**Nixon**
pacifist  Range {0.4/yes, 0.2/no}
Credible Range { }

After normalization

**Nixon**
pacifist  Range {yes, 0.5/no}
Credible Range { }

that is to say, Nixon is more possibly pacifist than non-pacifist.

### 2.4.4. Specificity issue

In semantic networks, problems arise when two links point to two different classes, with one being a subclass of (thus being more specific than) the other. Consider the following example (figure 2.2) :

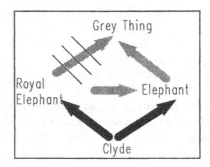

Figure 2.2: Is Clyde grey?

'Clyde is not a grey thing' is a conclusion that must be preferred to 'Clyde is a grey thing' because it is deduced from the 'Royal Elephant' class which is more specific than the 'Elephant' one.

Such problems are well handled in our model because of the way we perform multiple inheritance or instanciation. As we compute the intersection of inherited values, the specificity problem does really not exist. If C is a subclass of D then we have $N_G(D \mid C) > 0$. So we have $Su(D) \supseteq Su(C)$ and then $Su(C) \cap Su(D) = Su(C)$, that is to say, the support of the more specific class, i.e., C.

Consider the following descriptions:

| **Elephant** | | **Royal Elephant** | |
|---|---|---|---|
| color | Range {grey, 0.2/white} | color | Range {white} |
| | Typical Range {grey} | | |

we obtain using a normal instanciation mechanism

**Clyde**
color Range {0.2/white}
Credible Range { }

and after normalization

**Clyde**
color Range {white}
Credible Range { }.

### 2.4.5. Contexts

The inheritance and instantiation processes described above consider all the class attributes. But in many cases, the specified relations are only partial, that is to say are valid for subsets of attributes. For example, we want to say that 'dolphins are a kind of fish' due to their way of locomotion. This is why we introduce the notion of context here. A context is simply a subset of class attributes. In order to define a class, we have then to specify the actual superclass(es) and the partial superclass(es) with their context. Thus, in the dolphin example, we can define the Dolphin class as a subclass of Mammal and a subclass of Fish in the context of the way of locomotion.

### 2.4.6. Bottom-up inheritance

A class $C_1$ can be defined, or its description refined by pointing out a prototypical subclass $C_2$, as suggested by Kayser[17], assuming $C_2$ is already present in the system or intensionally described by the user. Then the description of $C_1$ is partially obtained from $C_2$, namely the attribute ranges of $C_2$ become the typical ranges of its superclass $C_1$. For instance, it corresponds to defining "birds" by means of "blackbirds" as being typical birds. But what do we do if an attribute of $C_1$ has already a not empty typical range? Considering that 'a blackbird is a kind of typical bird' does not mean that 'blackbirds are the only typical birds'. We have chosen to understand it (and translate it) as an inclusion of blackbird's properties in the Bird's typical properties. The new description of $T(C_1)$ is then computed by performing for each attribute the union operation (with the fuzzy set operator max) between the typical range and the subclass range. The new typical range is consistent with the possible range since we can show that —$R_1$ is short for $R(a_i,C_1)$, $R_2$ for $R(a_i,C_2)$, $T_1$ for $T(a_i,C_1)$—:

$$N_G(R_1 \mid T_1 \cup R_2) \geq \min \{N_G(R_1 \mid T_1), N_G(R_1 \mid R_2)\}.$$

Thus since we have $N_G(R_1 \mid T_1) = 1$ and $N_G(R_1 \mid R_2) = 1$, we deduce

$$N_G(R_1 \mid T_1 \cup R_2) = 1.$$

So we have only to check that $N_G(R_1 \mid R_2) = 1$ in order to be allowed to perform bottom-up inheritance.

## 3. Updating the hierarchy

In our model when a class is created, the inherited properties are copied from the superclass(es) into this new class. The inheritance is said static because the inheritance mechanism is only performed when creating the class. It allows a fast access to ranges because the inherited ranges of the objects are explicitly in the database. The proposed model differs here from classical OCR since inherited ranges are not computed at each access.

In the following paragraphs we are going to describe and explain the different updating mechanisms. We also give a brief algorithm for each type of updating of the database in order to show how these updating mechanisms could be implemented.

### 3.1. Class insertion

We are interested here in inserting a new class in an existing hierarchy. Let us suppose that we know the description of the future class C, of its future superclasses $D_1$, ..., $D_n$ and of each subclasses $D_{ij}$, $i = 1, ..., n$ of the $D_i$'s. The insertion mechanisms consists in computing the new inclusion degrees of C into $D_1, ..., D_n$, and of each $D_{ij}$ into C. If $N_G(C \mid D_{ij}) = 0$, $D_{ij}$ remains a subclass of $D_i$. Otherwise $D_{ij}$ becomes a subclass of C.

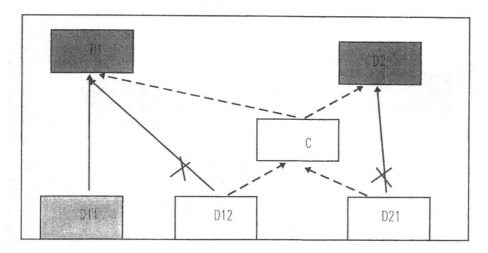

Figure 3.1: Insertion of a class in the hierarchy

In the above example (figure 3.1), the insertion of C under $D_1$ et $D_2$ implies the deletion of the links from $D_{12}$ to $D_1$ and from $D_{21}$ to $D_2$, and the creation of links from $D_{12}$ and $D_{21}$ to C. The link from $D_{11}$ to $D_1$ remains unchanged.

<u>Algorithm</u>
For each class $D_i$
       For each subclass $D_{ij}$ of $D_i$
           Compute $N_G(C \mid D_{ij})$
           If $N_G(C \mid D_{ij}) > 0$ then
                Add the link $D_{ij} \rightarrow C$ and delete the link $D_{ij} \rightarrow D_i$
       Add the link $C \rightarrow D_i$.

Note that such an insertion may imply the updating of links 'is a'. This is not considered here, but the process is similar to the updating of links 'is a kind of'.

42

## 3.2. Class deletion

The deletion of a class C implies to classify the subclasses $C_i$ of C as direct subclasses of the superclasses $D_j$ of C. The instances of C have also to be moved up in the superclasses $D_j$ as in the following figure 3.2.

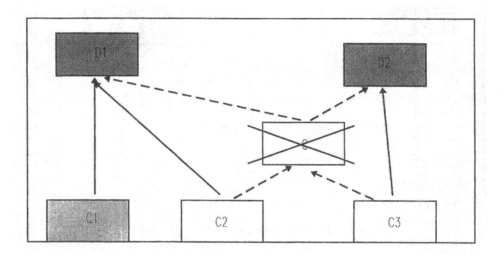

Figure 3.2: Deletion of a class in the hierarchy

<u>Algorithm</u>
For each subclass $C_i$ of C
  Delete the link $C_i \rightarrow C$
  For each superclass $D_j$ of C
    Add the link $C_i \rightarrow D_j$ (if non existing)
For each superclass $D_j$ of C
  Delete the link $C \rightarrow D_j$.
Delete C.

## 3.3. Class updating

The class updating process is more complex than insertion or deletion. Updating the description of a class may break the database consistency. The links between classes may then become no longer valid. To preserve the database consitency, we have to perform deeper modifications in the database. Such modifications can be handled in two ways:

- by updating some links in the database;
- by updating some objects descriptions.

Each way has advantages and drawbacks, so both should be offered to the user who will choose the more appropriate for what he/she wants to do.

### 3.3.1. Adding a new attribute

Adding a new attribute **a** does not affect the links between the class C and its superclasses $D_j$, since adding an attribute to C implies that it does not exist in the superclasses. But it does affect the links between C and its subclasses $C_i$.

### 3.3.1.1. Preserving the consistency by updating links

If a subclass $C_i$ of C has already the attribute **a** in its description, we have to compute $N_G(R(\mathbf{a},C) \mid R(\mathbf{a},C_i))$. If the result equals 0, $C_i$ is no longer allowed to be a subclass of C. It must become a subclass of the superclasses $D_j$. If the result is strictly positive, the hierarchy remains without updatings; we just need to compute the new value of the links $C_i \rightarrow C$ that is $\min\{N_G(R(\mathbf{a},C) \mid R(\mathbf{a},C_i)), N_G(C \mid C_i)\}$.

If $C_i$ has not attribute **a** in its description, $C_i$ can no longer be a subclass of C since C, has **a** in its description (unless $R(\mathbf{a},C)$ is the domain of **a**). Hence $C_i$ must be moved up in the hierarchy.

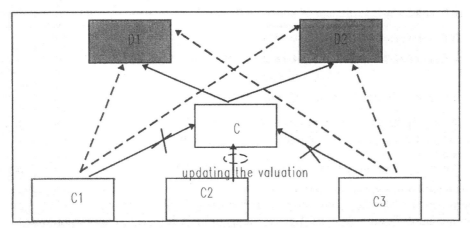

Figure 3.3: Adding a new attribute and updating links

In the above example (figure 3.3) (where only $C_1$ and $C_2$ contain the attribute **a**), $C_1$ and $C_3$ must be classified, while $C_2$ is still a C's subclass (at a new degree).

<u>Algorithm</u>
For each subclass $C_i$ of C

    If **a** belongs to the description of $C_i$ then

        If $N_G(R(\mathbf{a},C) \mid R(\mathbf{a},C_i)) > 0$ then

            Update the link $C_i \rightarrow C$

        else    delete the link $C_i \rightarrow C$

            For each superclass $D_j$ of C

            Create the link $C_i \rightarrow D_j$

    else    delete the link $C_i \rightarrow C$

        For each superclass $D_j$ of C

        Create the link $C_i \rightarrow D_j$.

The process is similar for the instances of C. The new membership degree is computed. If it equals zero, the instance is moved up by computing its membership degree to C's superclasses.

### 3.3.1.2. Preserving the consistency by updating descriptions

Adding a new attribute **a** to C must be propagated to all the subclasses descriptions. If a subclass $C_i$ has not **a** in its description, it must be added to the description of $C_i$. $R(\mathbf{a},C_i)$ and $T(\mathbf{a},C_i)$ will depend on the hierarchical link between $C_i$ and C:

- If $C_i$'s are typical C's, $R(\mathbf{a},C_i) \leftarrow T(\mathbf{a},C)$;
- If $C_i$'s are atypical C's:  if $T(\mathbf{a},C)$ exists then $R(\mathbf{a},C_i) \leftarrow \neg T(\mathbf{a},C) \cap R(\mathbf{a},C)$

                otherwise $R(\mathbf{a},C_i) \leftarrow R(\mathbf{a},C)$;
- If $C_i$'s are C's, $R(\mathbf{a},C_i) \leftarrow R(\mathbf{a},C)$ and $T(\mathbf{a},C_i) \leftarrow T(\mathbf{a},C)$.

Note that in the first and third cases, the weights of the links remain unchanged. In the second case, the new weight must be computed (but we are sure that the link still exists).

If $C_i$ has attribute **a** in its description, the type of the link $C_i \rightarrow C$ may have to be changed (from typical to normal for example). If not, we just have to compute the new weight of the link. Otherwise, we prefer trying to preserve the nature of the link by updating $C_i$'s description. Thus we compute $C_i$'s inherited value for attribute **a**, from all its superclasses (not only C). If the inherited value is empty, there is a consistency problem. Then $C_i$'s description must remained unchanged, the link $C_i \rightarrow$ C is deleted and the user is warned. If the inherited values are consistent, it becomes the new range of $C_i$ for **a**, and all the links between $C_i$ and its superclasses must be computed.

The propagation of the initial updating is a recursive process. Each subclass whose description is compatible with its superclass's description stops the recursion. The recursion goes on on subclasses whose description has been updated.

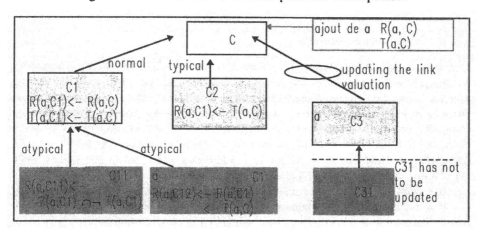

Figure 3.4: Adding a new attribute and updating descriptions

In figure 3.4 $C_1$ and $C_2$ do not have the attribute **a** in their description. Hence they inherit the ranges of C with regard to the kind of hierarchical link between them and C. $C_3$ has a description compatible with the adding of attribute **a**. Hence only the weight of the link $C_3 \rightarrow$ C has to be updated. $C_3$'s subclasses do not need to be updated whereas the process has to be performed on $C_1$'s and $C_2$'s subclasses.

The process is similar for the instances of C given that we have to consider the membership degree instead of the inclusion degree.

<u>Algorithm</u>
—C, D and **a** are the parameters of the function. C is the current class to be modified. D is the superclass of C which has called the Update-Class function for C.—
Function Update-Class (C D **a**)
If the new link nature is the same as the old one
        then    compute the new weight of the link C → D
        else    compute the inherited value from C's superclasses
               If the possible range in empty

then      delete the link $C \rightarrow D$
             warn the user
else      modify C's description with the inherited value
             for each superclass $D_i$ of C

                compute the link $D_i \rightarrow C$

             for each subclass $C_i$ of C

                Update-Class ($C_i$ C **a**).

### 3.3.2. *Deleting an attribute*

The deletion of an attribute **a** of a class C does not allow to keep the hierarchy unchanged by just modifying the descriptions. Indeed such a deletion can be viewed as considering the range and the typical range of **a** equal to the domain. A change of the nature of the links between C and its subclasses may then happen. These changes cannot be avoided by modifying the subclasses descriptions. In order to maintain the hierarchy consistent, we have to compute the new weights of the links between C and its subclasses. Note that the inclusion of C's subclasses in C is not questioned, since the deletion of attribute **a** in C makes C larger than before.

In a similar way, the membership degrees of C instances will have to be updated.

If a superclass of C contains **a** in its description, C once modified will be no longer included in it. This problem can be handled in two different ways:

• by allowing for the deletion of the attribute, only if this attribute does not appear in the superclasses of C.
• by modifying the hierarchy in searching the nearest C's ancestors in which C is included.

The user will choose the best way for the modification he/she wants to do. Here is the algorithm for the second way.

<u>Algorithm</u>
For each subclass $C_i$ of C

      Compute the new link $C_i \rightarrow C$
Compute the superclasses of C list L
While L is not empty
      D ← The first element of L
      If **a** belongs to the description of C
            Delete the link $C \rightarrow D_i$
            Search-Ancestor-And-Link(C D)
      Delete $D_i$ from L.

The function Search-Ancestor-And-Link(C D) searches for the nearest ancestors of D in which C is included and creates inclusion links between C and them.

### 3.3.3. Updating a range

Updating a range can only be done if the new range is consistent with the associated range and with the superclasses description. The inclusion degrees will have to be updated. Otherwise the user has to be warned that the modification cannot be done. If a subclass description is compatible with this new range (no change of the nature of the link), its inclusion degree in the modified class will be updated. If the subclass description is not compatible, we can update the hierarchy by modifying links or modifying classes descriptions (cf. Section 3.3.1.1 and Section 3.3.1.2).

Instances of C will be updated in the same way: if their new membership degree equals 0 they will be either moved up, or their description modified in accordance to the nature of their link to the class. If the new membership degree is positive, these instances will still be instances of C, with these new degrees.

### 3.4. Updating an instance

An instance is a leaf in the hierarchical tree. So an instance modification (attribute insertion, deletion, modification) only affects its own links. Their new weights are updated if they are positive. Otherwise the user has to be warned that the updating is not possible.

## 4. Reasoning with the proposed model

The proposed model allows various reasoning modes. Its hierarchical part allows to perform deductions as in a semantic network. Its descriptive part allows the search of new links, the search of similarities and allows for classification.

### 4.1. Reasoning in a semantic network

Every hierarchical representation has an underlying semantic network. The underlying semantic network of our model can be easily obtained by disregarding the objects description and focusing on hierarchical links.

### 4.1.1. The underlying semantic network

Disregarding the objects descriptions leads us to an underlying semantic network composed of:

- Nodes corresponding to necessary classes.
- Typical nodes corresponding to typical classes.
- Links 'is a kind of' and 'is a' between nodes and typical nodes.

This network does not contain negative links, since they are not memorized. They could be however computed using the class descriptions.

This semantic network can be qualified as being:

- *Homogeneous* since, it does not distinguish between links and typical links.
- *Monotonous* since links admit no exeption. We can see that the notion of typical class allows the underlying semantic network to deal with exceptions without using defeasible links.
- *Unipolar* since it does not contain negative links such as 'Royal Elephants are not Grey Things'. This feature is a consequence of the choice of not memorizing negative links in the database. We may regret the lack of expressivity it induces for the semantic network. But remember that the negative links implicitly exist through the objects descriptions and can be computed if needed.

### 4.1.2. Necessary classes and credible classes

The main purpose of semantic networks is to deduce the classes to which an instance (a class) belongs (is included in). As they mix multiple inheritance and exceptions, some problems of consistency and ambiguity appear. We will see that they won't appear in our model due to the unipolarity of the underlying semantic network.

As in some semantic networks[7,20] we define a deduction process which give two sets of classes. We distinguish:

- the set of necessary (certain) classes, obtained by following a path composed of links 'is a kind of';
- the set of credible classes, obtained by 'jumping' at least once from a necessary class to its associated typical class.

Consider the following example (figure 4.1).

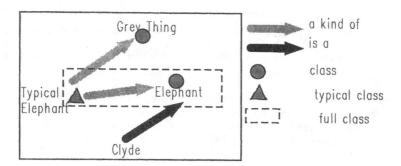

Figure 4.1: Is Clyde grey?

Knowing that Clyde is an elephant makes credible the fact that Clyde is grey because typical elephants are grey.

### 4.1.3. Weighting the certainty of a class for an instance and ranking its credible classes

The relation (13), namely $N(C_1 \mid x) \geq \min\{N(C_2 \mid x), N_G(C_1 \mid C_2)\}$ allows us to get a weight for each necessary class of an instance. Knowing the membership degree of x to $C_1$ enables us to get an estimate of the certainty of membership of x to a superclass $C_1$ of $C_2$. Unfortunately, this weight is only a lower estimate. But, if there are two paths to a class $C_1$, i.e., we get $N(C_1 \mid x) \geq \alpha$ and $N(C_1 \mid x) \geq \beta$ with $\alpha \geq \beta$, we have to keep the greatest lower bound, that is to say $N(C_1 \mid x) \geq \alpha$. In the example of Figure 4.2, we deduce

$$N(\text{Elephant} \mid \text{Clyde}) \geq \max\{\min\{1, 0.2\}, \min\{0.1, 1\}\} \geq 0.2.$$

Unsurprizingly, what we get is consistent with the fact that Clyde is an atypical elephant.

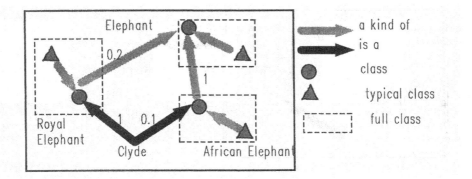

Figure 4.2: Deduction with multiple paths

Such a process does not require that the instance actually exists in the database. But then the membership degrees used for starting the computation are unknown. The user has to provide them in spite of all the problems of validity and justification of these values. However let us point out that entering $N(C \mid x) = \alpha$ would not produce better results than only assessing $N(C \mid x) \geq \alpha$. Hence, only lower bounds have to be provided.

We cannot compute a valuation for the credible classes of an instance x in the same way, because it would require the evaluation of the 'jump' from a necessary class to its typical class. It would be possible to count the 'jumps' along the reasoning paths. Of course, the more jumps that have to be done, the less credible the obtained conclusion is. In the example of Figure 4.3 'Bill is an employee' is thus less credible than 'Bill is an Adult'. If we have to choose between these two conclusions, the first one should be preferred.

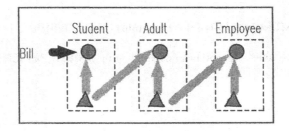

Figure 4.3: Rank of credible classes

### 4.1.4. Three types of information for starting a deduction

When a user wants to perform a deduction on an object which does not exist in the database, he would have to create it first. As we saw, we can only reason from the specification of its class. It may be convenient if we have only to perform deductions about the object (its description may be then useless). Our model allows three types of specification, as for the inheritance mechanism. For example, we can say:

- 'Tweety is a typical Bird' and then deduce that 'Tweety is a Flying Animal'.
- 'Tweety is a Bird' and then deduce that 'Tweety is credibly a Flying Animal'.
- 'Tweety is an atypical Bird'. The meaning of such a specification is obvious as soon as we suppose that the user has refused the two other specifications. It means obviously that 'Tweety is a Bird' and that 'it is not credible that Tweety is a typical Bird'. This prevents from deducing that 'Tweety is credibly a Flying Animal'.

These three types of information are obviously linked to the valuations of the 'is a' links from an instance to a class or a typical class. Thus

- the typical specification supposes that the valuation of the link 'x is a typical C' is positive;
- the two other specifications suppose that the valuation of the link 'x is a C' is positive and that the valuation of the link 'x is a typical C' is zero.

### 4.2. Reasoning from descriptions

We discussed how deducing conclusions from our database without using the objects descriptions. Now we are going to consider how using these descriptions in order to perform various kinds of reasoning. We have already seen that the descriptions justify all the links in the database. But they also allow to refine relationships between objects, by computing other indices (see Section 4.2.1.), they can be used for classification (see Section 4.2.2.), or for computing common features of objects (see Section 4.2.3.). Inheritance mechanisms (classical and bottom-up) are also kinds of reasoning but they have already been discussed in the model presentation (see Section 2.4).

### 4.2.1. Other indices

The relations between two objects can be refined by using degrees other than Dienes and Gödel inclusion indices. We can compute:

- $\Pi(R(a,C_1), R(a,C_2))$. This degree may allow us to foresee atypicality. Indeed $0 < \Pi(C_1,C_2) < 1$ means that no nonatypical instance of $C_1$ is a nonatypical instance of $C_2$ (and converselly) where $\Pi(C_1,C_2) = \min_a \Pi(R(a,C1), R(a,C2))$. Thus a subclass of $C_1$ and $C_2$ cannot have instances belonging completely to $C_1$ and $C_2$. An instance has to be atypical with respect to at least one of them. The following table presents the possible conclusions.

Table 1: Comparing two classes using $\Pi$ and $N_G$

| $\Pi(C_1,C_2)$ \ $N_G(C_1 \mid C_2)$ | 0 | $0<....<1$ | 1 |
|---|---|---|---|
| 0 | No $C_2$ is a $C_1$ (and conversely) | *impossible* | *impossible* |
| $0<....<1$ | Any common instance of $C_1$ and $C_2$ is atypical w.r.t. $C_1$ or $C_2$ | Any $C_2$ is a $C_1$ but no non-atypical $C_2$ is a non-atypical $C_1$ | *impossible* |
| 1 | $C_1$ and $C_2$ have non-atypical common elements and some typical $C_2$ are not in $C_1$ | Any $C_2$ is a $C_1$ and there is some non-atypical $C_1$ which are non-atypical $C_2$ | Any $C_2$ is a non-atypical $C_1$ |

- The possibility degree that an instance x belongs to a class C: $\Pi(C \mid x) = \min\{\Pi(R(\mathbf{a},C), P(\mathbf{a},x)) \mid \mathbf{a}$ is an attribute of C$\}$.

- The resemblance between two classes $C_1$ and $C_2$. It can be computed by symmetric indices of the form

  $$\min\{\min_{i=1,n} N(R(a_i,C_1) \circ T \mid R(a,C_2)), \min_{i=1,n} N(R(a_i,C_2) \circ T \mid R(a,C_1))\}$$

  where N defines a degree of inclusion in the sense of (3) and T is a tolerance (fuzzy) relation such that $A \circ T \supseteq A$. The composition $A \circ T$ being defined in terms of membership function by $\mu_{A \circ T}(u) = \sup_u \{\min(\mu_A(u'), \mu_T(u,u'))\}$.

- The 'negative' degrees. Such degrees, for example, express the non-membership or the non-inclusion. Such degrees could support the existence of negative links in the database. We have chosen that these negative links be not explicitly in the database and computed only if needed. These links can be defined by computing the membership or inclusion degrees of an instance or class in the complement of a class. 'Clyde is not an Elephant' is equivalent to 'Clyde is a non-Elephant'. If a class C is defined by its attributes $a_i$, $i = 1, ..., n$, and x is an instance of C defined by the fuzzy sets $\mu_{R(a_i,C)}$, the negation $\neg C$ of C, is defined as:

  $$\mu_{\neg C}(x) = \max_i \{1 - \mu_{R(a_i,C)}(u_i)\} = 1 - \min_i \{\mu_{R(a_i,C)}(u_i)\}.$$

This result is in accordance with intuition since non-C elements are elements which do not verify at least a property of C. $\neg C$ cannot be represented in the database because $\neg C$ is described as a disjunction of properties. However the use of negative degrees allows us to represent it, at least partially.

### 4.2.2. Classification

Classification consists in best locating a (possibly ill-described) instance or class in the hierarchy. The natural way is to look for the membership or inclusion in the most general classes first and then to go down along the branches of the hierarchy as far as possible. The great advantage of our representation with regard to the classification comes from the fact that it is useless to go on the classification process on subclasses of a class C if the classification process has already failed on C. This is a consequence of the transitivity relations (8) and (13) since given $N_G(C_1 \mid C_2) > 0$ and $N_G(C_1 \mid X) = 0$ (or $N(C \mid x) = 0$), (8) and (13) give

$$0 = N_G(C_1 \mid X) \geq \min (N_G(C_1 \mid C_2), N_G(C_2 \mid X)) \text{ and}$$
$$0 = N(C_1 \mid x) \geq \min(N_G(C_1 \mid C_2), N(C_2 \mid x))$$

which entails $N_G(C_2 \mid X) = 0$ and $N(C_2 \mid x) = 0$. The semantic network underlying our representation facilitates the classification process. In a general way, representations allowing such cuts in a classification process are not able to deal with exceptions, whereas representations dealing with exceptions have difficulties to perform classification because they have to examine all the objects of the base. Our formalism deals with both of them.

An object (even if its description is imprecise) may belong to several classes with various degrees of membership. The results of a classification process is given as a list of all the somewhat interesting classes.

In order to be quite close to the way human beings perform classification, we have to include the use of typical classes in the classification process. This can be done easily since the above formula is valid using typical class T(C) instead of class C.

Human beings use different kinds of reasoning. When the normal classification process fails, they may try to find other relations, for example what the unknown object cannot be. We can here use the 'negative' degrees introduced above. But note that the transitivity relation using $\neg C_1$ and $\neg C$ instead of $C_1$ and C:

$$N_G(\neg C_1 \mid C) \geq \min\{N_G(\neg C_1 \mid \neg C_2), N_G(\neg C_2 \mid C)\}$$

cannot be used in a powerful way. In most cases, $N_G(\neg C_1 \mid \neg C_2)$ is not available. $N_G(\neg C_1 \mid \neg C_2)$ cannot be computed neither from descriptions nor from $N_G(C_1 \mid C_2)$, except if $N_G(C_2 \mid C_1) = 1$ since then $N_G(\neg C_1 \mid \neg C_2) = 1$. So we can cut a negative classification process as soon as we have $N_G(\neg C_2 \mid C) = 1$ and $N_G(C_2 \mid C_1) = 1$, since then $N_G(\neg C_1 \mid C) = 1$ and thus any non-atypical subclass of $C_1$ cannot be a superclass of C. An immediate consequence is $N_G(\neg T(C_1) \mid C) = 1$. The negative classification process is similar for an instance x.

We are also able to perform a kind of "credible" classification. The main idea is then to refine the description of the unknown object by using the typical ranges of the classes for which the classification process succeeds. For example, if the process succeeds in comparing Tweety and Bird, we can continue the classification on Bird's subclasses, taking for granted that Tweety flies.

### 4.2.3. Search for a context

Rather than computing indices between two objects, we may prefer to know on which attributes these objects satisfy a given relation. The set of attribute satisfying the given relation is called context. For example, we can ask 'in which context a cetacean is a kind of fish' using then the inclusion degree, or 'in which context Tweety is a typical bird' then using membership degree, or 'in which context birds resembles bats' using here resemblance degree.

Other degrees such as the intersection degree or "negative" degrees may be also useful with respect to bounded context evaluations.

## 5. Conclusion

The proposed approach presents an object-centered representation completely based on possibility theory. We have focused here on the representation issue and on the inference process. Clearly, this work remains preliminary in various respects. Implementation in a database was out of the scope of this work. The main features of our model are:

- An intensionnal definition of classes via their description by (fuzzy) properties.
- A coherent treatment of general and prototypical instances.
- A justification of links by the descriptions of the objects in a class.
- A representation of the gradual notion of typicality by allowing the typical ranges to be fuzzy.

   Our model is based on the three following definitions:

- Definition of the possible and typical ranges of an attribute for a class.
- Definition of the inclusion degree of a subclass into a class.
- Definition of the membership degree of an instance in a class.

This minimal definitions set allows us to deal both with exceptions in inference processes and to perform classification easily. Moreover we handle three kinds of inheritance (typical, atypical and normal) when the defining new objects. Various degrees can also be used to refine our knowledge about the relationships that objects may satisfy.

Our model has not considered the estimation of membership grades in the various fuzzy classes. When domains are infinite and are intervals in the real line, membership grades are often obtained by interpolation between extreme membership values, as with trapezoidal fuzzy intervals. When domains are finite and without any a priori order, membership grades could be derived by means of data analysis methods applied to samples of objects in a given context.

The presented model could be improved in several ways. First, we may consider weighting the attributes describing a class, in order to distinguish between, for example, typical and less typical attributes as done by Torasso and Console[24]. Second, the presented object-centered representation may be used in association with (fuzzy) production rules expressing relations between attribute values; it may also include information about cardinalities of classes which may be of interest for supporting or discounting plausible inferences.

It would be also interesting to see how this model can handle plausible reasoning (generalization, specialization, analogy) as defined by Collins and Michalsky[6]. Lastly, we might also extend the underlying semantic network with negative links based on the "negative" degrees we have suggested.

## Acknowledgments

The work reported in this chapter was done when J.-P. Rossazza was at IRIT. He is presently with Alcatel-Alsthom Recherche (118 route de Nozay, 91460 Marcoussis, France)

## Appendix

In Table A1 we present six different inclusion degrees of the form $\text{Inf}_u \{\mu_A(u) * \rightarrow \mu_C(u)\}$, and their meaning when they take the values 0 or 1. Co(A) stands for the core of a fuzzy set A and Su(A) for its support. The inclusion relationships that appear are characteristic properties for extreme values of the inclusion indices. For continuous membership functions and Gödel implication, the condition $\text{Not}(\text{Su}(A) \supseteq \text{Su}(C))$ should be replaced by $\forall \alpha, \text{Not}(A_\alpha \supseteq C_\alpha)$ where $A_\alpha = \{u \mid \mu_A(u) \geq \alpha\}$.

Table A1: Characteristic properties of 6 indices of inclusion.

| | $\mu_A *\!\!\rightarrow \mu_C$ | $N_{\supseteq}(C \mid A) = 0$ | $N_{\supseteq}(C \mid A) = 1$ |
|---|---|---|---|
| Dienes | $Max(\mu_C(u), 1 - \mu_A(u))$ | $Co(A) \not\subset Su(C)$ | $Co(C) \supseteq Su(A)$ |
| Lukasiewicz | $Min(1, 1 - \mu_A(u) + \mu_C(u))$ | $Co(A) \not\subset Su(C)$ | $C \supseteq A$ |
| Gödel | $1 \qquad$ if $\mu_A(u) \leq \mu_C(u)$ <br><br> $\mu_C(u) \quad$ if $\mu_A(u) > \mu_C(u)$ | $Su(A) \not\subset Su(C)$ | $C \supseteq A$ |
| Gödel's reciprocal | $1 \qquad$ if $\mu_A(u) \leq \mu_C(u)$ <br><br> $1 - \mu_A(u)$ if $\mu_A(u) > \mu_C(u)$ | $Co(A) \not\subset Co(C)$ | $C \supseteq A$ |
| $N_1$ | $Max(\mu_C(u), 1 - \mu_A(u))$ <br> $\qquad$ if $\mu_A(u) \leq \mu_C(u)$ <br> $\mu_C(u) \quad$ if $\mu_A(u) > \mu_C(u)$ | $Su(A) \not\subset Su(C)$ | $Co(C) \supseteq Su(A)$ |
| $N_2$ | $Max(\mu_C(u), 1 - \mu_A(u))$ <br> if $\mu_A(u) \leq \mu_C(u)$ <br> $1 - \mu_A(u)$ if $\mu_A(u) > \mu_C(u)$ | $Co(A) \not\subset Su(C)$ | $Co(C) \supseteq Su(A)$ |

**Proof of the decomposability result —Eq (5)—:**

$N_G(C \times D \mid A \times B) = Min(N_G(C \mid A), N_G(D \mid B))$ when $\exists (s,t) / \mu_{A \times B}(s,t) = 1$

with $\qquad \mu_{A \times B}(s,t) = min(\mu_A(s), \mu_B(t)) \qquad \mu_{C \times D}(s,t) = min(\mu_C(s), \mu_D(t))$
$\qquad \quad N_G(C \mid A) = \inf_s (\mu_A(s) *\!\!\rightarrow \mu_C(s))$,

$\qquad$ and $a *\!\!\rightarrow c = \begin{cases} 1 & \text{if } c \geq a \\ c & \text{if } c < a \end{cases}$

Let $\Phi(s,t)$ and $\Psi(s,t)$ and $A - C$ be defined by

$\qquad \Phi(s,t) \quad = min (\mu_A(s), \mu_B(t)) *\!\!\rightarrow min(\mu_C(s), \mu_D(t))$
$\qquad \Psi(s,t) \quad = min (\mu_A(s) *\!\!\rightarrow \mu_C(s), \mu_B(t) *\!\!\rightarrow \mu_D(t))$
$\qquad A - C \quad = \{s / \mu_A(s) > \mu_C(s)\}$

Let us notice that

$$min(N_G(C \mid A), N_G(D \mid B)) = \inf_{s,t} \{Y(s,t)\}.$$

Moreover

$$\Phi(s,t) = \begin{cases} 1 & \text{if } (s,t) \notin (A \times B) - (C \times D) \\ \min(\mu_C(s), \mu_D(t)) & \text{if } (s,t) \in (A \times B) - (C \times D) \end{cases}$$

$$\Psi(s,t) = \begin{array}{ll} 1 & \text{if } s \notin A - C, t \notin B - D \\ \mu_C(s) & \text{if } s \in A - C, t \notin B - D \\ \mu_D(t) & \text{if } s \notin A - C, t \in B - D \\ \min(\mu_C(s), \mu_D(t)) & \text{if } s \in A - C, t \in B - D \end{array}$$

Clearly

$$\Phi(s,t) = \Psi(s,t) \qquad \begin{array}{l} \text{if } s \in A - C, t \in B - D \\ \text{if } s \notin A - C, t \notin B - D \end{array}$$

or

since $\mu_A(s) > \mu_C(s)$ and $\mu_B(t) > \mu_D(t)$ entails $\min(\mu_A(s), \mu_B(t)) > \min(\mu_C(s), \mu_D(t))$ and similarly changing '>' into '≤'.

It is then simple to check that $\Psi(s,t) \le \Phi(s,t)$ in the general case. Indeed if

$$\mu_A(s) > \mu_C(s), \mu_B(t) \le \mu_D(t) \qquad \text{and} \qquad \min(\mu_A(s), \mu_B(t)) > \min(\mu_C(s), \mu_D(t))$$

then $\quad \mu_C(s) \le \mu_D(t) \quad$ and so $\quad \Phi(s,t) = \Psi(s,t) = \mu_C(s)$.

The case when $\mu_A(s) \ge \mu_C(s)$ and $\mu_B(t) > \mu_D(t)$ is dealt with similarly. In other words

$$\Phi(s,t) = \Psi(s,t) \text{ or } \Phi(s,t) = 1 \text{ (since } (A \times B) - (C \times D) \in (A - C) \times (B - D)).$$

To prove the result, it is enough to check that the minimum of $\Psi$ is attained for at least one value where $\Phi = \Psi$.

The minimum of Y is attained on $(A - C) \times (B - D)$; indeed for instance

$$\inf_{s \in A-C, t \notin B-D} \Psi(s,t) = N_G(C \mid A) \ge \inf_{(s,t) \in (A-C) \times (B-D)} \Psi(s,t) \\ = \min(N_G(C \mid A), N_G(D \mid B))$$

The result is true of course if $(A - C) \times (B - D) \_ \emptyset$ i.e., neither $\mu_A \le \mu_C$ nor $\mu_B \ge \mu_D$ hold. In that case the decomposability result is obtained since $\Phi = \Psi$ on $(A - C) \times (B - D)$.

If $(A - C) \times (B - D) = \emptyset$ then $\mu_A \ge \mu_C$ or $\mu_B \ge \mu_D$. Let us assume $\mu_A \ge \mu_C$ only. The definition of $\Psi(s,t)$ simplifies since it is equal to $\mu_B(t) * \to \mu_D(t)$. The expression of $\Phi(s,t)$ boils down to

$$\Phi(s,t) = \begin{cases} 1 & \text{if } \min(\mu_A(s), \mu_B(t)) \geq \min(\mu_C(s), \mu_D(t)) \\ \mu_D(t) & \text{otherwise} \end{cases}$$

indeed $\min(\mu_A(s), \mu_B(t)) > \min(\mu_C(s), \mu_D(t))$ implies $\mu_B(t) > \mu_D(t)$ when $\mu_A(s) \geq \mu_C(s)$; moreover we also get

$$\mu_C(s) \geq \min(\mu_A(s), \mu_B(t)) > \min(\mu_C(s), \mu_D(t)) \text{ so that } \mu_C(s) > \mu_D(t).$$

To get the decomposability result, it is enough to find a minimum $(s,t)$ of $\Psi$ with $\Phi(s,t) = \Psi(s,t)$.

Let $t^*$ such that $\mu_B(t^*) * \to \mu_D(t^*) = \inf_t \{\mu_B(t) * \to \mu_D(t)\} = \mu_D(t^*)$.

Clearly $\mu_D(t^*) < 1$ since $\mu_B \leq \mu_D$ does not hold, and any $(s,t^*)$ is a minimum of Y. Hence we are left to find $(s,t^*)$ such that $\min(\mu_A(s), \mu_B(t^*)) > \mu_D(t^*)$ i.e., (due to $\mu_B(t^*) > \mu_D(t^*)$ find s such that $\mu_A(s) > \mu_D(t^*)$).

Now $\mu_D(t^*)$ can take any value smaller than 1. Hence only the normalization of A ensures that $\exists s^*$, $\mu_A(s^*) > \mu_D(t^*)$. In that case $\Phi(s^*,t^*) = \Psi(s^*,t^*) = \mu_D(t^*)$ and the decomposability holds.

Clearly if $\mu_B \geq \mu_D$ is assumed, we need the normalization of B.

The last case is when $\mu_B \geq \mu_D$ and $\mu_A \geq \mu_C$; then $\Phi = \Psi = 1$.

The requirement that A and B be normalized, needed for decomposability, is the extension of a non-emptiness condition in the non-fuzzy case, namely

$$C \times D \supseteq A \times B \Leftrightarrow C \supseteq A \text{ and } D \supseteq B$$

provided that $A \neq \emptyset$ and $B \neq \emptyset$ (or $A = B = \emptyset$).

**Proof of the transitivity result —Eq (8)—:**

$$N_G(C \mid A) \geq \min(N_G(C \mid B), N_G(B \mid A)).$$

Using the min associativity, we just have to prove the following property:

$$N_G(R(a,C) \mid R(a,A)) \geq \min \{N_G(R(a,C) \mid R(a,B)), N_G(R(a,C) \mid R(a,A))\}$$

Let **a** be an attribute of A, and $R_a = R(a,A)$, $R_c = R(a,C)$, $R_b = R(a,B)$.

If $N_G(R_c \mid R_a) = 1$, the property holds.

If $N_G(R_c \mid R_a) < 1$, then

$$
\begin{aligned}
N_G(R_c \mid R_a) &= \inf\{\mu_{R_c}(u) \,/\, \mu_{R_c}(u) < \mu_{R_a}(u)\} \\
&= \min\{\inf\{\mu_{R_c}(u) \,/\, \mu_{R_c}(u) < \mu_{R_b}(u) < \mu_{R_a}(u)\} \\
&\qquad\quad \inf\{\mu_{R_c}(u) \,/\, \mu_{R_c}(u) < \mu_{R_a}(u) < \mu_{R_b}(u)\} \\
&\qquad\quad \inf\{\mu_{R_c}(u) \,/\, \mu_{R_b}(u) \le \mu_{R_c}(u) \le \mu_{R_a}(u)\}\} \\
&= \min\{n_1, n_2, n_3\}
\end{aligned}
$$

We have

$$
\begin{aligned}
n_1 &\ge \inf\{\mu_{R_c}(u) \,/\, \mu_{R_c}(u) < \mu_{R_b}(u)\} \\
n_2 &\ge \inf\{\mu_{R_c}(u) \,/\, \mu_{R_c}(u) < \mu_{R_b}(u)\} \\
n_3 &\ge \inf\{\mu_{R_c}(u) \,/\, \mu_{R_b}(u) \le \mu_{R_c}(u) \le \mu_{R_a}(u)\} \\
&\ge \inf\{\mu_{R_c}(u) \,/\, \mu_{R_b}(u) < \mu_{R_a}(u)\}
\end{aligned}
$$

that is

$$
\begin{aligned}
n_1 &\ge N_G(R_c \mid R_b) \\
n_2 &\ge N_G(R_c \mid R_b) \\
n_3 &\ge N_G(R_b \mid R_a)
\end{aligned}
$$

hence

$$
N_G(C \mid A) \ge \min\{N_G(C \mid B), N_G(B \mid A)\}.
$$

## References

1.  W. Bandler, L. Kohout (1980) Fuzzy power sets and fuzzy implication operators. Fuzzy Sets and Systems, 4, 13-30.

2.  S. Benferhat, D. Dubois, H. Prade H. (1992) Representing default rules in possibilistic logic. Proc. of the 3rd Inter. Conf. on Principles of Knowledge Representation and Reasoning (KR'92), Cambridge, MA, Oct. 26-29, 673-684.

3.  G. Bordogna, D. Lucarella, G. Pasi (1994) A fuzzy object oriented data model. Proc. of the 3rd IEEE Inter. Conf. on Fuzzy Systems (FUZZ-IEEE'94), Orlando, FL, June 26-29, 313-318.

4.  M. Cayrol, H. Farreny, H. Prade (1982) Fuzzy pattern matching. Kybernetes, 11, 103-116, 1982.

5.  B. Cohen, G. Murphy (1984) Models of concepts. Cognitive Science, 8, 27-58.

6.  A. Collins, R. Michalski (1989) The logic of plausible reasoning: A core theory. Cognitive Science, 13, 1-49.

7.  P. Coupey (1989) Etude d'un réseau sémantique avec gestion des exceptions. Thèse 3ème Cycle, Université de Paris Nord, Villetaneuse.

8.  D. Dubois, H. Prade (1988) (with the collaboration of H. Farreny, R. Martin-Clouaire, C. Testemale) Possibility Theory — An Approach to the Computerized Processing of Information. Plenum Press, New-York.

9.  D. Dubois, H. Prade, J-P Rossazza (1991) Vagueness, typicality and uncertainty in class hierarchies. Int. J. of Intelligent Systems, 6, 167-183.

10. S.E. Fahlman (1979) NETL: A System for Representing and Using Real-World Knowledge. The MIT Press, Cambridge, MA.

11. R. George, B. Buckles, F. Petry (1993) Modeling class hierarchies in the fuzzy object-oriented data model. Fuzzy Sets and Systems, 60, 259-272.

12. A. Goldberg, D. Robson (1983) Smalltalk-80 the Language and its Implementation. Addison-Wesley.

13. M. Gonzalez-Gomez, C. Faucher, E. Chouraqui (1995) Classification approchée d'instances dans un langage de schémas: Etude de l'étape d'appariement. Actes des Rencontres Francophones sur la Logique Floue et ses Applications (LFA'95), Paris, 27-28 nov., 200-207.

14. I. Graham, P.L. Jones (1987) A theory of fuzzy frames. BUSEFAL (IRIT, Univ. P. Sabatier, Toulouse), Part 1: 31, 109-132; Part 2: 32, 120-135.

15. I. Graham, P.L. Jones (1988) Expert Systems: Knowledge, Uncertainty and Decision. Chapmann and Hall.

16. C. Granger (1988) An application of possibility theory to object recognition. Fuzzy Sets and Systems, 28(3), 351-362.

17. D. Kayser (1988) What kind of thing is a concept? Computational Intelligence, 4, 158-165.

18. M. Minsky (1975) A framework for representing Knowledge. In: The Psychology of Computer Vision (P.H. Winston, ed.), McGraw Hill, 211-277.

19. S. Na, S. Park (19) Management of fuzzy objects with fuzzy attribute values in a fuzzy object oriented data model. Proc. of the 1996 Workshop on Flexible Query-Answering Systems (FQAS'96) (H. Christiansen, H.L. Larsen, T. Andreasen, eds.), Roskilde, Denmark, May 22-24, 1996, 19-40.

20. L. Padgham (1988) A model and representation for type information and its use in reasoning with defaults. Proc. of National Conf. on Artificial Intelligence (AAAI'88), 409-414.

21. R. Reiter (1980) A logic for default reasoning. Artificial Intelligence, 13(1-2), 81-132.

22. J.-P. Rossazza (1990) Utilisation de hiérarchies de classes floues pour la représentation de connaissances inmprécises et sujettes à exceptions: Le système "SORCIER". Thèse 3ème Cycle, Université Paul Sabatier, Toulouse.

23. E.A. Rundensteiner, W. Bandler (1986) The equivalence of knowledge representation schemata: 'Semantic networks' and 'fuzzy relational products'. Proc. of the North-American Fuzzy Information Processing Society Conf. (NAFIPS'86), New Orleans, 477-501.

24. P. Torasso, L. Console (1989) Approximate reasoning and protypical knowledge. Int. J. of Approximate Reasoning, 3(2), 157-177.

25. N. Van Gyseghem, R. De Caluwe (1994) UFO, a fuzzy object-oriented database model. Actes des 4èmes Journées Nationales sur les Applications des Ensembles Flous, Lille, 1-2 déc., 265-273.

26. N. Van Gyseghem, R. De Caluwe, R. Vandenberghe (1993) UFO: Uncertainty and fuzziness in an object-oriented model. Proc. of the 2nd IEEE Inter. Conf. on Fuzzy Systems (FUZZ-IEEE'93), San Francisco, CA, March 28-April 1st, 773-7778.

27. P. Vignard (1985) Un mécanisme d'exploitation à base de filtrage flou pour une représentation des connaissances centrées objets. Thèse 3ème Cycle, Institut National Polytechnique de Grenoble.

28. P. H. Winston (1988) Artificial Intelligence. Addison-Wesley.

29. R.R. Yager (1984) Linguistic representations of default values in frames. IEEE Trans. on Systems, Man and Cybernetics, 14(4), 630-633.

30. R.R. Yager (1988) Nonmonotonic inheritance systems. IEEE Trans. on Systems, Man and Cybernetics, 18, 1028-1034.

31. L.A. Zadeh (1965) Fuzzy sets. Information and Control, 8, 338-353.

32. L.A. Zadeh (1975) The concept of a linguistic variable and its application to approximate reasoning. Information Sciences Part 1: 8, 199-249; Part 2: 8, 301-357; Part 3: 9, 43-80.

33. L.A. Zadeh (1982) A note on prototype theory. Cognition, 12, 291-297.

# MODELING IMPRECISENESS AND UNCERTAINTY IN THE OBJECT-ORIENTED DATA MODEL - A SIMILARITY-BASED APPROACH

R. GEORGE

*Department of Computer Science, Clark Atlanta University, Atlanta GA 30314, USA*

A. YAZICI

*Department of Computer Engineering, Middle East Technical University 06531 Ankara, Turkey*

F. E. PETRY, B. P. BUCKLES

*Department of Computer Science, Tulane University, New Orleans LA 70118, USA*

In this chapter, we extend the Object-Oriented Data Model to facilitate the enhanced representation of different types of imprecision. The modeling capability is derived by utilizing the similarity relation to generalize equality to similarity. Similarity permits the impreciseness in data to be represented. Imprecision in data results in uncertainty in classification. Both these mechanisms are explicitly accomodated in this model, which uses well defined semantics to differentiate between multi-valued objects with OR, XOR and AND connectives. It is shown that the addition of these semantics lead to a richer and more accurate representation of Object-Class relationships. A primitive op erator, the merge, that preserves nonredundancy in the data model is defined. An object algebra for the model is defined and implementation details are discussed. A typical next-generation application for the model is described.

## 1 Introduction

Object-Oriented Database Management Systems (OODBMS) have been developed to meet the challenge of complex data modeling requirements of large scale, data intensive applications. They are suitable for a variety of applications, including VLSI design, CAD/CAM, CASE, Geographic Information Systems, etc. [4]. This range of applicability can be attributed to the natural representation of the real world facilitated by the object-oriented paradigm. Despite this representational power, OODBMS are ill equipped in dealing with inherently vague, uncertain or imprecise data. However many applications do require the manipulation and reasoning based on incomplete and imprecise data. Traditionally, the solution has been to conform these types of data to precise values. This approach, detracts from the representational capability of the object-oriented paradigm and semantically overloads application programs. In this chapter we present a fuzzy logic based extension to the data model, permitting imprecise and uncertain data to be explicitly represented. Consequently, the ability to manipulate such data via semantically richer query languages is facilitated. The similarity relation, which replaces equality, is the basis of the extended data model. Any two values, **x** and **y** in a fuzzy attribute domain **D** obey the properties of symmetry, reflexivity, and transitivity.

$s(x,x) = 1$ **reflexivity**

$s(x,y) = s(y,x)$ **symmetry**

$s(x,y) \leq max_{z \in D}[min(s(x,z), s(z,y))]$ **transitivity**

This generalization of equality to similarity has important bearing on class structure as well as database operations. Traditionally, the view in databases (and artificial intelligence) has been that specialization (or alternately generalization) and instantiation produce classes and objects that are subsumed by their classes and superclasses respectively (in other words with a crisp membership)[4,6]. It has been shown that in an object-class and class- superclass hierarchical relationship, it is the prototypical object that is modelled [29]. Also, certain set operations, such as symmetric difference, can result in subclasses that inherit only some attributes and methods of its superclass [40]. We generalize subsumption of objects/classes in classes/superclasses so that the conventional view is a special case. The motivation for this extension is two fold. First, it permits more accurate knowledge representation of the Universe of Discourse. This has its advantages, for example in coupled Artificial Intelligence-Database System, where an outstanding bottleneck has been the mismatch between the two knowledge representation paradigms [20]. Another possible application area is in Object-Oriented Geographical Information Systems, where querying is not always on precise objects (i.e., those whose attributes are precisely known, apriori[23]). Secondly, a more powerful retrieval mechanism is facilitated by this extension. It becomes possible to retrieve fuzzy data, as well as typical and atypical members of a class via the query language. It should be noted that the retrieval of precise attributes and crisp members of a class is a special case of imprecise retrieval.

Previously Rudensteiner and Bandler [39] studied the problem of fuzzy semantic networks, proving equivalence with the binary relational representation models. Torrasso et al. [47], defined a frame based representation with three kinds of weighted attributes : necessary, sufficient, and supplementary. For object-oriented databases, Zicari [51] has considered issues of incompleteness, albeit without use of fuzzy concepts. In particular incomplete data in an object is handled by the introduction of explicit null values similarly to the relational and nested relational models. Dubois et al. [16], have utilized possibility theory to represent vagueness and uncertainty in class hierarchies. For single valued attributes they define the inclusion between classes to be the inclusion between the fuzzy ranges (which are possibility distributions). Van Gyseghem et al.[24] have proposed an object-oriented model that represents uncertainty and fuzzy information. These two concepts are distinguished by representing fuzzy information as (conjunctive) fuzzy sets and uncertainty by means of generalized fuzzy sets. Formally, a g eneralized fuzzy set (g-f-s) G on a universe U associates with each element x of U a fuzzy truth value p/true, n/false, where p = Possibility(x g) and n = Possibility(x g). Inoue et al.[27] proposed the "Fuzzy Set Object" (FzO) as a first-c lass object in the programming language, with the aim of developing a fuzzy computer system. Bordogna, Lucarella, and Pasi[5] have defined a graph based fuzzy object-oriented data model that permits attributes to take linguistic values. The associ ation between an object instance and instance properties are modeled through a fuzzy reference relation. The emphasis in our approach, is to define a data model that preserves the underlying features of its logical paradigm, while accommodating uncertainties in hierarchies. So, we account for non-singular object attribute values, that may be connected through logical operators such as the AND[43], the OR[9], etc. This is a reflection of the fact that in semantically expressive data models (for instance, the object-oriented, and semantic data models), there exists data with a variety of semantics, resulting from different database operations. Furthermore, we distinguish between uncertainty and impreciseness. Impreciseness is a property of data, which the similarity relationship tries to capture. Uncertainty arises out of the "aggregation" of the imprecision in object attribute values, and occurs at the class level. The "aggregation" is application dependent and so this model accounts for the relevance of the attributes to the fuzzy class and the conceptual (semantic) distance between the class and the objects (or subclasses).

In Section 2, we define the basic terminology and Section 3 discusses how impreciseness in object (or subclasses) attribute values result in membership values in classes. Fuzzy Class Schemas and a consistency preserving operation - the **Merge** are defined in Section 4. Section 5 describes an object algebra for the data model. Implementation details are discussed in Section 6, and a typical application for the model is described in Section 7. Section 8 concludes the chapter.

## 2 Objects and Classes

The object-oriented data model represents the universe of discourse as a collection of interacting objects. Identity and state characterize objects. Identity distinguishes one object from another. The state of an object consists of the values of its attributes. Similar objects are grouped together to form a class. The structure and the permitted behavior, define the class. The attributes of a given object may be basic or composite and a composite attribute may itself be composed of simple or composite attributes. This results in a directed, possibly cyclical graph, called the class-composition hierarchy [28]. A class may be derived from another resulting in class-subclass relationships (inheritance). The inheritance graph is a directed acyclic graph. Thus the object-oriented paradigm models real world situations through a class hierarchy and a class composition hierarchy (aggregation).

The domain of an attribute, $dom$, is the set of values the attribute may take, irrespective of the class it falls into. The range of an attribute, $rng$, is the set of allowed values that a member of a class, i.e., an object, may take for the attribute and in general, $rng \subseteq dom$. For instance, assume that age is an attribute and the domain of age is between 0 and 150. If there exists a class Employee, the range of age for the class may be 20 to 70. The range is clearly a subset of the domain of age, but is the subset that is most pertinent to the class definition of Employee.

A feature that distinguishes the fuzzy hierarchy from the classical one (crisp) is that the concepts which form the classes have "imprecise" boundaries. This uncertainty is a result of the imprecision in the values of the object attributes that form the class. For example, if we consider the class of Young-Students, the uncertainty in the class is directly a result of the fuzziness of the meaning of "young". Fuzzy logic, which explicitly premits the representation of "soft" thresholds is utilized to solve this problem. The presence of a soft threshold for the data suggests, that unlike the classical case (1,0 type approaches), it is possible to have objects which are members of a class with a degree of membership. There is another interesting aspect to this issue. A formal range is associated with each attribute value in a class. But it is possible that the actual attribute values within the class might be different from the formal value(s). Since the similarity relation links the attribute values in a domain (through transistivity), an object may be a member of a class though its attribute values might different from the elements of the formal range. The extent to which these values differ affects the membership of the object in the class and will be a part of the formulation of membership values. The relevance of the attribute to the concept modelled and the conceptual (or semantic) distance between a superclass and a class, or between a class and an object, have to be accounted in deriving membership values of the class/object in the superclass/class. In fuzzy hierarchies it is important to consider the conceptual (or semantic) distance between links. A class may not necessarily be contained in a superclass but may be only an approximate subclass. Thus there can exist situations in which the membership of a class in its superclasses increases as the inheritance hierarchy is ascended (strong ISA). Conversely, the membership could also decrease as the inheritance hierarchy is ascended (weak ISA).

### 2.1 Application : Oceanographic Modeling

The principal features of our modeling approach will be illustrated below through a running example based on a database schema (Figure 1) founded on the representations of oceanographic features. Associated similarity matrices for fuzzy attributes are shown in Tables 1-5. Oceanographic or geographical databases are ideal for illustration since classification of the various features can be very difficult and subjective due to cloud cover, lighting, seasonal variables,etc. The sample we give here is only a simplified part of a more complex database for such features. We will use it to illustrate the uncertain information in a similarity-based object-oriented model and to provide examples of the calculations of object-class and class-subclass relationships.

Satellite remote sensing is producing huge volumes of data that will require new approaches to data modelling and databases to effectively utilize the data. We have been involved in the design of approaches using fuzzy object-oriented databases for geographical information systems [23], and the development of a knowledge-based system to assist in interpretation of satellite imagery of the North Atlantic region [11].

The North Atlantic region has very dynamic oceanographic features, such as the Gulf Stream, which is a rapidly varying warm water current flow from the Gulf of Mexico. It flows north and north-eastward across the North Atlantic and in the area of interest it can be over 100 km. in width. Its boundaries may be detected as edges in remote sensed infrared images due to temperature gradients as the stream is much warmer than surrounding waters. The Gulf Stream has large meanders from its mean position. In a large southward meander, a loop may pinch off and surround a mass of cold water which then separates as a large eddy called a cold core ring. Similar northward meanders surround warm water and form warm core rings. These features range from 50-300 km. in diameter and persist for several weeks. Their motion and characteristics can impact fishing, ocean acoustics and many other diverse interests.

```
CLASS :  Seasonal_North_Atlantic_Features
PROPERTIES :
        Location
        Radius
        Season
END;


CLASS :  Cold_Core_Ring
INHERIT  :
        Seasonal_North_Atlantic_Features
PROPERTIES :
        Curvature
        Radius
        Temperature
END;
```

Figure 1: Schema of an Oceanographic Database

## 3 Modeling Uncertainty in Class Hierarchies

We assume the following notation

$Attr(C) = \{a_1, a_2, \ldots, a_n\}$, are the attributes of class C, and

$SClass(C) = \{C_1, C_2, \ldots, C_n\}$, are the superclasses of class C.

### 3.1 Object-Class Relationships

We first formulate the membership of an object $o_j$ in class C with attributes $Attr(C)$. Based on the considerations of relevance and ranges of attribute values outlined in the previous section, the membership of object $o_j$ in C is defined as

$$\mu_C(o_j) = \mathbf{g}[\mathbf{f}(RLV(a_i, C), INC(rng_C(a_i)/o_j(a_i)))] \tag{1}$$

where $RLV(a_i, C)$ indicates the relevance of the attribute $a_i$ to the concept C, and $INC(rng_C(a_i)/o_j(a_i))$ denotes the degree of inclusion of the attribute values of $o_j$ in the formal range of $a_i$ in the class C.

The degree of inclusion, determines the extent of similarity between a value (or a set of values) in the denominator with the value in the numerator (or a set of values). The function $\mathbf{f}$ represents the aggregation over the **n** attributes in the class and $\mathbf{g}$ reflects the nature of the semantic link existing between an instance(object) and a class/superclass. The value of $RLV(a_i, C)$ may be supplied by the user or computed in a manner similar to that in [17]. We consider several cases for the evaluation of $INC(rng(a_i)/o_j(a_i))$.

Example : For the class Cold_Core_Ring (abbreviated CCR) discussed previously, assume the following attribute ranges

$rng_{CCR}(curvature) = \{very\_high\}$

$rng_{CCR}(temperature) = \{frigid, very\_low, low\}$

$rng_{CCR}(radius) = 10 - 50$ miles

$rng_C CR(season) = \{winter\}$

$rng_C CR(rainfall) = \{heavy, very\_heavy\}$

$rng_C CR(location) = \{S\}$

**CASE I**

　　1.　　$o_j(a_i) \subseteq rng(a_i) : INC = 1$

If $o(temperature) = \{frigid, very\_low\}$.

Since $o(temperature) \subseteq rng_{CCR}(temperature)$

　　$INC(rng_{CCR}(temperature)/o(temperature)) = 1$

　　2.　　trivial case where $o_j(a_i) = \phi : INC = 0$

If $o(temperature) = \{\}$, i.e., a null value, (perhaps indicating unknown)

　　$INC(rng_{CCR}(temperature)/o(temperature)) = 0$

**CASE II**

If the cardinality of the attribute value, $card(o_j(a_i)) = 1$ and $o_j(a_i) \notin rng_C(a_i)$ then we base the value on the most similar element in the range of $a_i$ for this class:

$INC = Max(s(x,y))$ where $x \in o_j(a_i)$ and $y \in rng_C(a_i)$

If $o(temperature) = \{arctic\}$, i.e., a singleton value

$INC(rng_{CCR}(temperature)/o(temperature)) = Max[s(x,' arctic')] = 0.81$

where$x \in rng_C CR(temperature)$

**CASE III**

If $card(o_j(a_i)) > 1$ and $o_j(a_i) \not\subseteq rng_C(a_i)$, then three different interpretations are possible on $o_j(a_i)$. This is consonant with the different semantics that arise in databases when an object attribute takes more than one value. The attribute values may be connected through AND, XOR or inclusive OR semantics [9], [43]. The value for inclusion, INC, is now dependent on the attribute semantics.

TYPE I (AND semantics)

Under AND semantics, an attribute takes more than one value and all values exist simultaneously (are true). The Nest operation results in data with AND semantics.

Cohesion (**Coh**) indicates the minimum level of similarity between the elements of the object attribute value,

$INC(rng_C(a_i)/o_j(a_i)) = Min[Max(s(x,y)), Coh(o_j(a_i))]$,

where $x, z \in o_j(a_i)$, and $y \in rng_C(a_i)$.

**Coh($o_j(a_i)$)**, i.e., $Min(s(x,z))$, puts an upper bound on the inclusion of $o_j(a_i)$ in $rng_C(a_i)$. In other words, whatever the similarity between the elements of the attribute value and the range, the degree of inclusion cannot exceed the degree of cohesion or similarity existing between the elements of the object attribute value itself.

TYPE II (OR semantics)

With OR semantics an attribute takes more than one value, all or some of which may exist simultaneously (are true). When attribute values are linked through OR semantics there is less certainty about the data values in comparison with AND semantics. OR semantics may be exclusive OR inclusive OR, with different interpretations.

    1.    Type IIa (Exclusive OR semantics)

Exclusive OR semantics dictate that exactly one of the object attribute values is true.

$INC(rng_C(a_i)/o_j(a_i)) = Max(s(x,z))$ where $x \in o_j(a_i)$, $z \in rng_C(a_i)$

In this case we take an optimistic view of the inclusion of the individual attribute values in the range and assign the value to be the maximum of the similarities that exist between the elements of the range.

2.     Type IIb (Inclusive OR Semantics)

Assume an object attribute has two values say, a and b. Under inclusive OR interpretation the possible situations for this attribute's value may be $\{a\}, \{b\}$ or $\{a, b\}$. So here we find the value of INC to be

$INC(rng_C(a_i)/o_j(a_i)) = Max[Max(s(x,y)), Min[Max(s(x,y)), Thresh(o_j(a_i))]]$,

where $x \in o_j(a_i)$ and $y \in rng_C(a_i)$

Note, however that the inclusion of object value attributes with XOR or inclusive OR are nonetheless identical when evaluated in this approach.

Assume $o(temperature) = \{moderate, low\}, x \in o(temperature)$ and $y \in rng_{CCR}(temperature)$

1.     OR Semantics(XOR or Inclusive OR)

$INC(rng_{CCR}(temperature)/o(temperature)) = Max[s(x,y)]$

$= Max[0.75, 0.75, 1.0, 0.75, 0.75, 0.75] = 1.0$

2.     AND Semantics

$Threshold(o(temperature)) = 0.75$.

Therefore, $INC(rng_{CCR}(temperature)/o(temperature))$

$= Min[0.75, Max[0.75, 0.75, 1.0, 0.75, 0.75, 0.75]] = 0.75$


We can now compute the membership of an object in the class Cold_Core_Ring. Assume the following object attribute instantiations

    o(curvature) = {high}
    o(temperature) = {moderate, low}
    o(radius) = {25}
    o(season) = {winter}
    o(rainfall) = {heavy}
    o(location) = {SSW, SSE}

and the following relevance rules hold

    RLV(curvature,CCR) = 2.5
    RLV(temperature,CCR) = 0.25
    RLV(radius,CCR) = 0
    RLV(season,CCR) = 0.5
    RLV(rainfall,CCR) = 0.5
    RLV(location,CCR) = 2.0

$RLV_{Max}$ in this case is 2.5. Note that we follow the convention that if X very much determines Y, then RLV(X,Y) = 2.0 and if X more-or-less determines Y, RLV(X,Y) = 0.5 and so on. We use the max function for **g** and assume $f(a,b) = b * (a/RLV_{Max})$ i.e., normalizing the relevances[17]. Hence computing the membership of $o$ in the class Cold_Core_Ring,

$\mu_{CCR}(o) = Max(0.85 * 1, 0.75 * .1, 1 * 0, 1 * .2, 1 * .2, .9 * .8) = 0.85$

As previously, the membership of a class in its superclass has to account for the semantics of the attributes contributing to the class concept, the degree of inclusion of the attribute ranges of the class in the superclass and the conceptual distance between a class and its superclass.

## B. Class-Subclass Relationships

The membership of a class in its superclass has to account for the semantics of the attributes contributing to the class concept and the degree of inclusion of the attribute ranges of the class in the superclass. Also, the conceptual distance- a measure of the semantic distance between the two classes being modeled, between a class and its superclass, has to be considered.

Assume a class, $C$ and its superclass $C_i$ with $Attr(C_i) = \{a_1, a_2, \ldots, a_n\}$, and $Attr(C) = \{a_1, a_2, \ldots, a_n, a_{n+1}, \ldots, a_m\}$ where the first $n$ attributes are inherited from the superclass and the rest are local to the class C. So we have a membership relationship similar to (1) :

$$\mu_{C_i}(C) = \mathbf{g}[\mathbf{f}(RLV(a_j, C_i), INC(rng_{C_i}(a_j)/rng_C(a_j)))] \qquad (2)$$

where $j = 1, 2, \ldots, n$.

It is important to note that the range in (2) refers to the formal ranges of the attribute $a_j$ in the classes $C$ and $C_i$. The membership value, then derived for the classes $C$ and $C_i$, is an ideal value which relates the two concepts embodied in these classes. The actual attribute values (of object instances) that exist in these classes might be different. For the application area intended, i.e., object-oriented databases, this dichotomy is acceptable, since it is possible for both classes and metaclasses to co-exist. The question of membership between two classes arises only when we query the class definitions themselves. We have three different cases for $INC(rng_{C_i}(a_j)/rng_C(a_j))$, the inclusion of the range values of the subclass in the range values of the class/superclass.

**CASE I**

1. $rng_C(a_j) \subseteq rng_{C_i}(a_j) : INC(rng_{C_i}(a_j)/rng_C(a_j)) = 1$
2. Trivial case where, $rng_C(a_j) = \phi : INC(rng_{C_i}(a_j)/rng_C(a_j)) = 0$

**CASE II**

If $card[rng_C(a_j)] = 1$ and $rng_C(a_j) \not\subseteq rng_{C_i}(a_j)$ then
$\qquad INC(rng_{C_i}(a_j)/rng_C(a_j)) = Max[s(x, y)]$
where $x \in rng_C(a_j)$ and $y \in rng_{C_i}(a_j)$

**CASE III**

If $card[rng_C(a_j)] > 1$ and $rng_C(a_j) \not\subseteq (rng_{C_i}(a_j))$ then
$\qquad INC(rng_{C_i}(a_j)/rng_C(a_j)) = Max[s(x, y)],$
where $x \in rng_C(a_j)$ and $y \in rng_{C_i}(a_j)$

## 4 A Fuzzy Class Schema

The generalization of equality to similarity has important consequences for the data model and its permitted operations. In this section we formally define the data model and describe the effects of this generalization on database operations. A primitive operation of the model, the **merge** is defined, and it is shown that merge preserves the desired database property of non-redundancy. The results from Section 4 will be utilized in describing Fuzzy Class Schema, and the assumption made is that all membership values are thus derived.

We assume the following notation

$D_1, D_2, \ldots, D_n$ are a finite set of domains.

$dom(a_i)$ is the domain of attribute $a_i$.

$val(a_i)$ is the value of attribute $a_i$.

**Definition**:[Domains]

1. $a_i$ is a simple (atomic) attribute if $dom(a_i) = D_i$, $val(a_i) \in D_i$, and $card(val(a_i)) = 1$.

2. $a_i$ is a simple set attribute if $dom(a_i) = 2^{D_i}$ where $2^{D_i}$ represents the power set of $D_i$ excluding the null set, and $val(a_i) \in 2^{D_i}$.

3. $a_i$ is a composite tuple attribute if $a_i = \{a_{i+1}, a_{i+2}, \ldots, a_j, \ldots, a_n\}$, where $a_j$ is a composite tuple or a simple attribute and $dom(a_i) = dom(a_{i+1}) \times dom(a_{i+2}) \times \ldots \times dom(a_j) \times \ldots \times dom(a_n)$

4. $a_i$ is a composite set attribute if $dom(a_i) = 2^{dom(a_j)}$ where $a_j$ is a composite tuple
   attribute.

**Definition**:[Class]

A class, $C_i$, is defined as a set of attributes, $\{a_1, a_2, \ldots, a_j, \ldots, a_n\}$ where $a_j$ may be a simple atomic, simple set, composite tuple or composite set attribute. A composite tuple attribute is identical with the root of a class-composition hierarchy. The extension of $C_i$, $ext(C_i)$ is the set of objects that populate the class, i.e., the data, and $o(a_i)$ represents the value of attribute $a_i$ of object, $o$, where $o \in ext(C)$.

**Definition**:[Range Similar]

If $o(a_i) \not\subseteq rng_{C_i}(a_i)$, where $a_i$ is an attribute of $C_i$ (or $o$). $o(a_i)$ can be said to be range similar to $rng(a_i)$, denoted by $o(a_i) \sim_s rng_{C_i}(a_i)$. At the limit, when $INC(rng_{C_i}(a_i)/o(a_i)) = 1$, range similarity is the subset relation. For composite tuple and composite set valued objects range similarity is a vector.

**Definition:[Imprecise Object]**

$o$ is a fuzzy object in $C_i$ if $(\forall j)o(a_j) \sim_s rng_{C_i}(a_j)$ and $\mu_{C_i}(o)$ takes values in the range [0,1].

By this definition, only objects that have the same structure as its class may be imprecise objects, i.e., in other words an object in the hierarchical tree is permitted to be an imprecise object only in its classes and superclasses (thus disallowing arbitrary objects from being imprecise members of arbitrary classes). Structure thus is the defining character of the imprecise object.

**Definition:[Similarity Threshold]**

Assume $a_j$ is a non-composite attribute of the class, $C_i$. By definition of the fuzzy object $o(a_j) \sim_s rng_{C_i}(a_j)$. The threshold of $a_j$ is defined to be

$$Thresh(a_j) = min_{(\forall o)}(Coh(o(a_j)))$$

The threshold denotes the minimum similarity between the values of a class attribute. If the attribute domain is crisp, or values are atomic, then threshold = 1. As the threshold value approaches zero, larger chunks of information group together and the information conveyed about that attribute of the class decreases.

The threshold value of a composite attribute is undefined. A composite domain is constituted (at some level) by simple domains each of which has a threshold, i.e., the threshold for a composite object is a vector composed of the thresholds of simple domains.

We now define the merge, which is a primitive operator. A level value, for an attribute given a priori, $L_j$, determines which objects may be combined through the set union of the respective values. Note that the level value may be specified via the query language with the constraint that it never exceed the threshold value.

**Definition:[Merge]**

Assume objects, $o$, and $o'$, belonging to a class, $C_i$ with degrees of membership, $\mu_{C_i}(o)$ and $\mu_{C_i}(o')$ respectively (since the discussion is at object level, identities are used for object attribute values). The objects may be represented most generally as :

$o = (i, < a_k : i_k, a_{k+1} : i_{k+1}, \ldots, a_j : i_j, \ldots, a_m : i_m >, \mu_{C_i}(o))$, and

$o' = (i', < a_k : i'_k, a_{k+1} : i'_{k+1}, \ldots, a_j : i'_j, \ldots, a_m : i'_m >, \mu_{C_i}(o'))$

where $i$ and $i'$ are the identities of $o$ and $o'$, $i_j$ and $i'_j$, the identity of $o_j$ and $o'_j$, etc. (i.e., each attribute value is an object itself). If $\forall j : j = 1, 2, \ldots, m; a_j$ is non-composite, $L_j$ is the level value for the attribute $a_j$ and $x \in o(a_j)$ and $y \in o'(a_j)$ so that $min_{\forall x, \forall y}[s(x, y)] \geq L_j$ and $L_j \leq Thresh(a_j)$, then

**Merge**$(o, o') = o''$

$$= (i'', < a_k : i''_k, a_{k+1} : i''_{k+1}, \ldots, a_j : i''_j, \ldots, a_m : i''_m >, \mu_{C_i}(o'')),$$

where $o''_j = (i''_j, \{i_j, i'_j\})$ (i.e., two existing objects are used to create a new object, with a new identity) $\mu_{C_i}(o'')$ is the membership of $o''$ in class, $C_i$. Note that the membership of the new object $o''$ in class, $C_i$ is computed in as described in the previous section. The semantics of this operation is OR. Merge combines two objects provided the similarity between every attribute value in each of the objects is greater than some arbitrary level value set by the user. As in the case for threshold, the definition can be extended to composite objects.

A sample query would be of the form indicated below:

**Query** : Retrieve the co-ordinates of "Cold_Core_Rings" in the "North_Atlantic_ Basic" characterized by "frigid" temperatures and "moderate" rainfall. Translated to SQL-like code

> **SELECT** CCR_Latitude, CCR_Longitude
> **FROM** CCR: $\mu_{CCR} \geq 0.8$
> **WHERE** CCR.Temperature = "Frigid" and CCR.Rainfall = "Moderate":
> **LEVEL** CCR.Temperature $\geq 0.9$ and CCR.Rainfall $\geq 0.85$

Note that the retrieval involves membership values of the objects in the class and the fuzzy attribute values. This query would ensure for instance that all the objects retrieved are members of the class, Cold_Core_Ring, and have temperatures that were "frigid" to the level of 0.9, i.e., they could be any temperature in the set {arctic, frigid, very_low} and with rainfall in the set {torrential, very_heavy, heavy, moderate}.

## 5   A Fuzzy Object Algebra

In this section we define an identity independent algebra, which is an extension of relational algebra. Note that we take a purely structural view of the data model - methods are not a part of the query language. The five classic relational operators (Difference, Union, Product, Project, and Select) are extended to the fuzzy object-oriented data model. Two operators that have been defined as an extension to relational algebra CNest (Conjunctive Nest) and its corollary Unnest [43], are re-iterated for completeness. DNest (Disjunctive Nest) is a new operation that Merges objects at the schema level.

Assume a class $C_i$ with attributes $\{a_1, a_2, \ldots, a_i, a_{i+1}, \ldots, a_n\}$. If **op** $\in \{=, \neq, \leq, \geq\}$, and $L_j$ and $F_j$ are the set level that is utilized to merge objects and a condition on attribute $a_j$ of Class $C_i$ respectively, and $\mu$ is a value in [0,1]. For a class $C_i$ if attribute $a_j$ is defined, it is indicated notationally as,

$a_j(C_i) = true.$

**CNest:**

Let $C_i$ represent a fuzzy class schema. Let $S_1$ and $S_2$, be disjoint partitions of the schema such that $attr(S_1) \cup attr(S_2) = attr(C_i)$ and $S_1$ and $S_2$ are immediate descendants of $C_i$,

$$CN_{S'=S_1}[C_i] = \{o, \mu_{C_i}(o)|(\exists o' \in ext(C_i))o[S_2] = o'[S_2] \wedge$$
$$o[S_1] = \{o''[S_1]|o'' \in ext(C_i) \wedge o''[S_2] = o[S_2]\}\}$$

The CNest creates a new structure where the $o[S_2]$ part is the same (shared) for a number of objects which have different $o[S_1]$ values.

**Unnest:**

Let $C_i$ represents a fuzzy class schema. Let $S_1$ and $S_2$ be immediate descendent of $C_i$, such that $attr(S_1) \cup attr(S_2) = attr(C_i)$ then

$$CU_{S_i}[C_i] = \{o, \mu_C(o)|(\exists o' \in ext(C_i))o[S_2] = o'[S_2] \wedge o[S_1] \in (o'[S_1])\}$$

The Unnest operation reverses the CNest. For each value of $o'[S_2]$ we pick a value for the $S_i$ part and put these two values together to form the new object. Note that both CNest and Unnest cause membership values to change. Without further explanation, we state that CNest causes membership values to be non-increasing and Unnest vice-versa.


For the following discussion $C_i$ is assumed to be completely unnested, i.e., the attributes of $C_i : a_1, a_2, \ldots, a_n$ are simple.

**DNest:**

The Disjunctive Nest is a unary operator, similar to Merge, but operating at schema level. It permits groups of objects to be merged, depending on level values set by the user. $D\nu(C_i, L_j) =$

$$\{(o, \mu_{C_i}(o)|\exists o', o'' \in ext(C_i) \wedge \forall j([s(o'(a_j), o''(a_j))]$$
$$\geq L_j) \rightarrow (o = Merge(o', o''))\}$$

The DNest creates partitions in the schema, using the Merge as its primitive operator. By setting level values, everything within a partition can be considered synonymous, with respect to the level value set.

**FSelect:**

$$\sigma_{(<F_j, L_j>, \mu)}(C_i) =$$
$$= \{o, \mu_{C_i}(o)|o \in ext(C_i) \wedge (\forall x \in o(a_j))s(x, e_j) \geq L_j \wedge \mu_{C_i}(o)\mathbf{op}\mu\}$$

The level value $L_j$ specified determines which of the selected objects are then merged to form new objects and $e_j$ indicates value of the attribute, $a_j$ specified by the condition $F_j$.

**FProject:**

$$\Pi_{(a_j, \mu)}(C_i) = C_i'$$
$$= \{o|o \in ext(C_i) \wedge (a_j(C_i) = true) \rightarrow (a_j(C_i)' = true) \wedge \mu_{C_i}(o)\mathbf{op}\mu\}$$

FProject is a type-creating operation, which creates a new class $C_i'$. The membership of an object in the new class is undefined (these two conditions in fact accompany each other, since memberships are defined only on known types).

**FDifference**

The Fdifference operator computes the difference between two classes. The two classes have to be union compatible, i.e., $C_i - C_k'$ is defined only if $C_k'$ is a subclass of $C_i$ or vice versa.

Assume $\exists C_k$ such that $C_k$ is a subclass of $C_i$, and $C_k'$ and $C_k$ are of the equivalent type[40]. An additional constraint has to be met in the case of the difference between fuzzy classes. The classes have to be fuzzy schema compatible, i.e., the relevance values of all the attributes in their respective classes, $((RLV(a_j, C_k)$ and $RLV(a_j, C_k'))$ are equal, and the functions **f** and **g** are identical.

$$C_i - C_j =$$
$$\{o, \mu_{C_i}(o) | o \in ext(D\nu[C_k, Thresh_{min}]) \wedge o' \in ext(D\nu[C_k', Thresh_{min}]) \wedge$$
$$((\forall j)(x \in o(a_j) \rightarrow (\not\exists y) \in o'(a_j) \wedge x = y))\}$$

where $Thresh_{min}$ is a vector (since it is derived over all attributes $a_j$ and is equal to the $min(Thresh(C_k'(a_j)), Thresh(C_k(a_j))$

The FDifference operation is defined after the thresholds of each attribute in the class has been set to the minimum of the two classes. The DNest operation forces similar partitions to be created in both the schema taking part in difference operation. We eliminate from the resultant any objects that share values (i.e., since the partitions force similar elements to be grouped together).

**FUnion**

As in the case of the FDifference operator, FUnion is defined only on classes that are union compatible, fuzzy schema compatible, and have equal values for threshold. In a similar manner we assume classes $C_k$ and $C_k'$ with the properties described previously.

$$C_i \cup C_k = \{o, \mu_{C_i}(o) | o \in ext(D\nu[C_k', Thresh_{min}]) \vee o \in ext(D\nu[C_k, Thresh_{min}])\}$$

where $Thresh_{min}$ is a vector derived as in FDifference.

**FProduct**

The FProduct of two classes $C_i$ and $C_j$ is a new class $C_i'$ composed with the attributes of $C_i$ and $C_j$. In the same fashion the objects that populate $C_i'$ are created by the composition of objects from $C_i$ and $C_j$. FProduct is a type creating operation, and so also has membership values that are undefined. $\otimes$ denotes the composition operation.

$$C_i \times C_j = (< C_i, \mu_{C_i} > \times < C_j, \mu_{C_j} >$$
$$= \{o | \forall i(o_i \in C_i) \wedge \forall j(o_j \in C_j) \wedge \mu_{C_i}(o_i)\mathbf{op}\mu_{C_i} \wedge \mu_{C_j}(o_j)\mathbf{op}\mu_{C_j} \wedge o = o_i \otimes o_j\}$$

## 6 Implementation

The implementation language chosen is C++. This choice is dependent on its compatibility with EXODUS storage manager. The EXODUS Storage Manager (ESM) is a multi-user object storage system supporting versions, indexes, single-site transactions, distributed transactions, concurrency control, and recovery. The ESM client module is a library which is linked with an application program. An application begins by performing initialization and then a transaction. After starting a transaction, an application can begin accessing objects, files and indexes. When an ap plication requests an object that is not found in the clients buffer pool, the client requests the page(s) containing the object from the server. The request also contains the desired lock mode for the object. When an application attempts to change the st ate of an object, a request for an exclusive lock on the object will be sent to the server. ESM Server Module is a multi-thread process providing I/O, file, transaction, concurrency control and recovery services to clients. Wh! ! en a request arrives, the server assigns a thread from the inactive pool to handle the request and begins executing the thread. The thread runs until it has to wait for a resource, or voluntarily gives up the CPU, or completes the request.

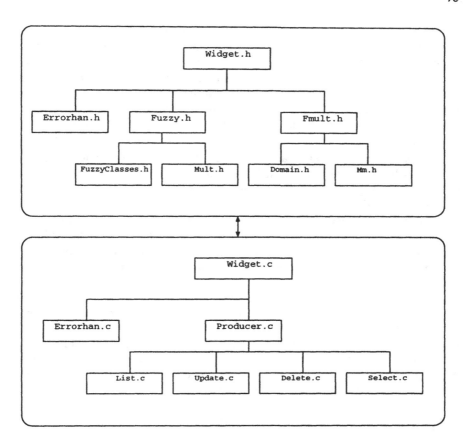

Figure 2: Software Architecture of the Fuzzy OODB

The software architecture (Figure 2) is designed so that a fuzzy class that can contain fuzzy and non-fuzzy attributes simultaneously. Fuzzy objects belonging to this class with a membership degree can be stored, retrieved, and accessed. Declarations and various definitions including all of the fuzzy definitions are kept in several header files (extension **.h**). Operations such as c reating new objects of a specified class, listing the instances of a class and making fuzzy queries on them are stored in the files with extension **.c**.

The system is a collection of various header files and we shall discuss them more specifically. **Domain.h** contains the similarity matrices of a fuzzy attibute whose structure is defined in **fmult.h**. This permits multivalued attributes with AND, OR, XOR semantics. The **mult.h** is an abtract class definition to provide a smooth interface among the fuzzy mutlivalued attribute. The fuzzy multivalued attributes are "type cast" to this class definition and inclusion calculations are performed. The database operations are defined in **widget.c** and can be called from other C programs such as **producer.c**, **list.c**, **select.c**, etc. The header file **widget.h** contains the external declarations of these procedu res to allow program linkage.

**Command Lines:** Basic operations such as creating new objects (of a specified class), listing the instances of a class and permitting fuzzy queries on them, are implemented as command lines in the Unix environment. The commands are implemented as ma in functions which call the procedures of the file **widget.c** containing no main part, but only the procedures. The object file **widget.o** is linked to all of the others. The header file **widget.h** contains the global declarations and procedur e signatures:

produce(FID* widgetfid, int widgetNum,
char className [MAX_CLASS]);
select(FID* widgetfid, char className [MAX_CLASS], float alpha);

**Fuzzy Object Structure:** The top level header file **domains.h** contains the possible domains for fuzzy attributes and their similarity matrices. The descriptions are kept in a seperate header file so as to let the new domains be introdu ced easily. The file is read-only to avoid nonprivilidged user modifications. Only specified groups can do updates on this file. When an addition is to be made, the structure shown below is followed:

typedef enum {fall, winter, spring} seasonDomain;
float seasonMatrix[3][3] = { {1.0, 0.8, 0.6}, {0.8, 1.0, 0.6}, {0.6, 0.6, 1.0} };

The similarity matrices are symmetric, and storing the upper triangle will suffice. However in that case, the search procedures have to be updated accordingly and the understandability of the code is harder. The system implemented currently does not have a large number of similarity matrices and the storage is lar ge enough to handle a significantly larger set. The new domain is added to the system definition and the global variable ATTRIBNUM should be incremented, and the new type should be added to system similarity matrix list with its domain size:

#define newType newDomain, I      /* where I is the next integer */

This header file only contains the similarity matrix definitions and domains. The actual fuzzy attribute class definition is in the header file **mm.h**. In the following section of code a template class is defined, which takes one of these domains as a parameter.

typedef enum {AND, OR, XOR} semanticsType;

/* T is the tag name of the parameter type which serves as a place holder for a particular type instances provided by the user */

```
template <class T, int TypeId> class Multivalued{
private:
int typeCode;
semanticsType semantics;
int elementNum;
void* owner;
void (*pf)(...);
T values[MAX_ATTRIB];
public:
Multivalued(semanticsType semant=OR);
void init(void* own, void(*ff));
Multivalued& operator<< (T element);
Multivalued& operator>>(T element);
void getValues();
void reset();
void showElements();
int subsetOf(Multivalued* superset);
int isEmpty();}
```

This template class enables any fuzzy class contain a fuzzy attribute with the same interface as if it has a nonfuzzy attribute. The operators $\ll$ and $\gg$ are overloaded so that the insertion and deletion operations can be appended one after the other.

Ex: object1.season$\ll$fall$\ll$winter$\ll$spring;

A key point in this template class is the attribute owner which refers to the owner of the attribute, so that automatic update of membership values are possible. In object-oriented programming with C++, the part does not know the whole.

Fuzzy.h contains an abstract "fuzzy class" definition to be inherited by fuzzy classes. It is abstract in the sense that there is actually no instance of this class. The attributes are the membership entries for class-object and class-superclass relations . The class-superclass membership is declared as a static variable, so that all of the instances of a fuzzy class will refer to the same class-superclass relation. The choice of static member will conserve storage and limit the chance of error. However ea ch object will have a different value for class-object membership.

class Fuzzy
float memship;
float CSCmemship;
....

The main contribution of this class is to define the methods that will enable automatic calculation of membership values. The procedures to be followed to find inclusion values are

float inc(void* , void*);
float CSCinc(void*, void*);

The first one deals with class-object level and the second one deals with class-superclass level.

**Range Definitions** Defining a range for a class attribute which does not have strict rules is not a straight forward operation. This is some point where fuzziness introduces a new aspect in the data structure. Consider a classical programming language where you can define a range for an attribute, say in Pascal you can define

var day_of_month: 1...31;

This is not a range definition in the sense discussed in our model. This is actually the domain of the attribute day_of_month. Such a declaration will not allow an assignment,

day_of_month = 32 /* Error */

With this model we permit let the attribute to have values beyond the boundaries defined. Such flexibility results in the need to keep range definitions as a class template. Two copies of declarations are needed, one class definition with attribute domains and one with range definitions representing the ideal object of the class which will be referred to by all of the instances of the class in order to determine the degree of their ideality in a sense . As an implementation decision, a pointer can be used to the range definitions in the template class Multivalued, such that any attribute will refer to its range definition. However if we treat range definitions at the attribute level, we will have an exc ess number of attribute type objects in the system, and the logical interpretation does not fit the design well. The point is that the range definition of an attribute is not meaningful outside the class definition. The range definition is meaningful at c lass level. We believe that the structure we use is the best in matching the logical interpretation of the range definitions. The instances of the class refer to the static object member Ranges which is a copy of the object itself and keeping the range definitions. The object itself however is free to use any value from the domain regardless of the range definitions. The class definitions in the header file **fuzzy.h** is as below:

```
class Cold_Core_Ring{
private:
Multivalued<curvatureType> curvature;
Multivalued<seasonType> season;
/* non fuzzy attributes are also possible here */
static Cold_Core_Ring Ranges;
public:
void setRanges();
void calcMship();
void calcCSCMemship();
. . .
}
void Cold_Core_Ring::SetRanges{
Ranges.curvatue()<<medium;
Ranges.season()<<fall<<winter;
}
```

The methods calcMship() and calcCSCmemship() make use of the inc() and CSCinc() methods defined in **fuzzy.h.**

```
void Cold_Core_Ring::calcMship(){
float result;
result = RLVcurvature*inc((void*)&curvature, (void*)&Ranges.curvature)
+ RLVseason*inc((void*)&season, (void*)&Ranges.season);
result = result/(RLVseason+RLVcurvature);
```

```
memhip = result;
}
```

Note that weighted average is chosen instead on MIN and MAX. The reason is thatthis will be more appropriate if we are considering the overall class definition where one attribute may have a RLV value of 2.1, but the number of all other attributes with RLV<<1 may be 15, for instance. The behaviour of the fuzzy classes are such that at the moment of creation, (in constructors) the class/subclass membership value is calculated and this value is shared by all of the instances of the class. The range definitions as well, are made availab le to all instances by the creation of object *Ranges* and the call to method *setRanges()*. The class/object membership is calculated on any addition, deletion or update of the attributes automatically. When an object is stored on disk the range definitions are of no importance since we already have the class/object membership values together with object. The range definition is recalled when an object is retrieved from the disk.

### 6.1   Operations on Fuzzy Objects

**New Object Creation**

The program **producer.c** has two parameters. The command
    producer class-name count
will create a new object of the specified class. The name of the class is first checked to see if the definition exist in the header file **fuzzyclasses.h.** This is an explicit search of class names. A class type is returned for each class, or -1 indi cating the definition is not known. If the class is present in the system, the file in which the objects are stored is found. The range definition appears on screen just to inform the user. The user is free to store any value on the object. They then init ialize the fuzzy object attributes and the system automatically determines the membership value of the object in the defined class and stores this information together with the object. In the case that the class was subclass of a fuzzy class, the inherited attributes are compared on the r ange definitions and a clas/subclass membership is calculated. This is a value that will be automatically updated with the command update coming next.

**Object Listing**

The program **list.c** has one parameter. The command
    list class-name
will list the objects of the specified class. The name of the class is first checked

to see if the definition exist in the header file **fuzzyclasses.h**. If the class is present in the system the file in which the objects are stored is found. The objec ts are listed then one after the other with their membership values.

## Object Update

The program update.c has two parameters. The command template is as below:
    update class-name
The name of the class is first checked to see if the definition exist. If the class is present in the system the file in which the objects are stored is found. That object is found in the class and the user adds/deletes attributes. As the user updates the fuzzy object attributes and the system automatically determines the membership value of the object in the defined class. The object is written back on the disk together with this updated information.

## Object Selection

The program **select.c** has two parameters. The command
    select class-name
will look for the objects satisfying the search criteria. The name of the class is first checked to see if the definition exist. If the class is present in the system the file in which the objects are stored is found. Search criteria to be applied is to be indicated. An object called searchObj is created and the criteria is entered on this object and the level values are asked for. These level values define the precision or similarity level to the objects the user is looking for. The objects are then examined one by o ne to see if their attribute values return an INC value greater or equal to the specified level. For example if the searchObj attribute season was given as
    searchObj.season= { fall, winter }
the object o1 is checked if its similarity is greater than the specified level
    o1.season={spring}
    if (inc((void*)&searchObj.season, (void*)&obj.season) >= level)
    obj.print();
In the case that the class was a superclass of a fuzzy class, that class is also searched. Here in this section we have summarized the implementation details of the prootype fuzzy object-oriented database model. Detailed description of the implementation can be found in [2].

## 7 Next Generation Applications

### 7.1 Hypertext-Based Systems

The term hypertext refers to documents that contain non-sequential directed links between its components. These links permit a reader to peruse the document in a non-linear fashion, moving between text components that capture his interest. The text components may be considered as nodes in a graph. A node may have several links. These links are associated with some smaller part of the text (anchors). Anchors are activated to navigate through the hypertext network, via the links. The data is not necessarily textual, it may consist of images, animation, sound or numbers. In this case a more general term- hypermedia is used to describe such systems. This discussion will use the term hypertext synonymously with hypermedia. The technology has found use in a variety of applications, including computer based training tools, on-line help systems, software engineering environments, etc. In its representational aspects hypertext can be considered to be a flexible knowledge representation environment, with strong similarity with semantic networks[35]. The structuring mechanisms provided are nodes and links (and anchors).

### 7.2 Hypertext and Database Systems

Browsing is the primary tool of search in hypertext. It permits an associative type of search in which the user follows a line of inquiry which is not necessarily unique. In contrast information retrieval or database systems use cued retrieval which always returns a unique answer. In cued retrieval the system is given a query and asked to complete the information. In short, associative recall retrieves information similar to the starting information rather than an explicit answer to a question or a query[35]. The ability of associative recall together with representational flexibility makes hypertext a natural front end to large database and information retrieval systems. With recent advances in object repositories and large scientific databases there is a need for new browsing tools and user friendly interfaces in place of the conventional reliance on data manipulation languages such as SQL, and hypertext provides a answer to this need.

The idea of combining hypertext with database technology has been examined in a variety of contexts[46]. The applications of database technology in hypertext include querying capabilities in large hypertext environments, management of links, automatic creation of links from documents, etc[46]. Delisle and Schwartz[15] proposed the use of hypertext as a software engineering environment for CAD. Coupling between the hypertext and a relational database was proposed as a technique for representing and manipulating granularity in information. For instance, it might be desirable to check all occurrences of a variable not only in the code but also in the documentation. The Node Query Language has been developed as a query language for large hypertext databases [18]. A similar proposal is the use of relational databases to provide a cued search mechanism for hypertext systems [19]. This retrieval capability would complement the associative search facility provided by the hypertext mechanism. Additional power is provided by a semi-automatic update facility for the hypertext via the data manipulation language (SQL) updating the relational tables. Bruza, et al. [8] propose a logic-based framework for a hypermedia system that incorporates structural information about the documents in the database, thus permitting both associative and keyword (cued) recall. Link management has been implemented the use of a relational DBMS in Intermedia [32], and via an object-oriented database system in InterSect [48]. In the following section we propose the use of the fuzzy object-oriented data model and its data manipulation language as a tool for the semi-automatic generation of hypertext, with the objective of representing enterprise information.

## 8 The Fuzzy Object-Oriented Data Model and the Generation of Hypertext

In a number of information systems applications it is not merely enough to be able to store data and retrieve data. It becomes necessary to point associations between data and the various documents which together comprise enterprise information. For example, the first step in environmental remediation consists of collecting all sources of information about the site. Other similar situations exist in Computer Aided Software Engineering repositories, environmental and geographical information systems, etc. Traditional database systems are not geared towards such representational flexibility. To meet such challenges we require systems with traditional data and text management facilities enhanced with the browsing functionality provided by hypertext, i.e., integrated database and information retrieval systems, with hypertext as the integrating (and retrieval) mechanism. Hypertext permits easy browsing of the data/text/graphics collection, allowing the user to navigate from a topic area to a related area, but by itself is unable to support large amounts of data. At the same time the hypertext interface should also permit the retrieval of text/data from the underlying collection. The challenge now posed is on how to generate hypertext using the data management and information retrieval facilities as the software backplane supporting the storage of multi-media objects.

Automatic generation of hypertext links is a hard task and is often left to human experts[41]. We propose fuzzy logic as a basis for the semi-automatic generation of such links through the use of the fuzzy object-oriented data model. The model permits the representation of uncertainty in objects and impreciseness in object data values to be explicitly modeled. Consequently, querying on uncertainty in objects and impreciseness in their data values is permitted. This facility is similar to an associative recall of objects that are similar to the starting object. One significant point of departure is that the querying is always deterministic and user prelidictions have little role in determining the objects that are retrieved. The query retrieval systems would ease the paradigm mismatch that exists between traditional data management systems and information retrieval systems and consequently ease their integration. This is achieved in two ways- first, the use of relevance values and similarity relations are typical of IR (information retrieval) type of operations; and second, the result of a query on the data model is a ranked set of data objects as members of a class. This ability for ranked retrieval could be used as an authoring too by the hypertext designer, where the keywords could be the anchors and links be constructed to the appropriate set of retrieved objects.

## 8.1 Application

Environmental remediation is an complex legal and scientific problem. Information technology can play a very useful role in supporting such activity. Information sources are not limited to the surveillance and measurement data from the site, but also includes hearsay, climatic data, land usage information, agricultural and wildlife data, environmental regulations, toxicology studies, legal documents, grant information, geophysical reports, etc. As mentioned previously, the first step in the process is collection of data from and about the site. These data could be numeric, linguistic, video, graphics or sound, with all the flexibility and the representational complexity it brings to the solution. They have to be integrated in a manner that is relevant to the decision maker. Hypertext is an obvious solution, but there exist the known problem of generating automatic links. Database and information retrieval support is crucial to the success of this approach. An obvious requirement are data models with higher representational power and flexible querying paradigms. The fuzzy object oriented data model can be utilized as the database backbone. Two advantages accrue- first, the representational power of the models, and second the flexibility in querying makes suitable for the semi-automation of hypertext generation. The assumption is that all relevant data and text information is arranged in object-oriented hierarchies. The key components of the query would constitute anchors within the hypertext. The database would provide the storage layer. Hypertext can be considered (as in the Dexter model) to be the software layer that surrounds the underlying database and information retrieval technology.

## 9  Conclusion

Uncertainty arises in a variety of ways – from the data values themselves, the semantics of the data and the type of hierarchy being modelled. At the data level, fuzziness arises from multi- valued attributes, which may be connected through boolean functions such as AND, OR and XOR. Attribute semantics, and fuzzy data combine to produce uncertainty at object level. All these aspects were accommodated in the data model defined. Fuzziness in data values have an effect on redundancy in databases and it was shown that no two objects in the data model have the same interpretation. A software architecture for the fuzzy OODB was described and implementation details provided. A new generation application was discussed.

A powerful knowledge representation methodology is facilitated in databases through this approach. Using classic knowledge representation considerations such normality, typicality, atypicality, etc., it is possible to constrain the attribute value ranges between the two classes, with correspondingly different class-subclass memberships. A point also needs to be made about implementation issues. Changes in similarity or relevance values can be considered to be schema changes, to be executed with care. Insertion and modification can be constrained to invoke methods that compute object membership. Since, only queries that query fuzzy attributes or objects need utilize these values, the average cost of evaluation would then be only slightly higher than a non-fuzzy database.

## Acknowledgements

This work is supported in part by the Army Center for Information Sciences, Clark Atlanta University under ARO Grant DAAL03-G-0377.

**Appendix**

## Similarity Relations of Fuzzy Attributes

| Curvature | | | |
|---|---|---|---|
| VeryHigh | 1.0 | 0.85 | 0.55 |
| High | 0.85 | 1.0 | 0.55 |
| Medium | 0.55 | 0.55 | 1.0 |

Table 1: Curvature = {VeryHigh, High, Medium}

| Season | | | |
|---|---|---|---|
| Fall | 1.0 | 0.8 | 0.6 |
| Winter | 0.8 | 1.0 | 0..6 |
| Spring | 0.6 | 0.6 | 1.0 |

Table 2: Season = {Fall, Winter, Spring}

| Location | | | | | | | |
|---|---|---|---|---|---|---|---|
| W | 1.0 | 0.8 | 0.4 | 0 | 0 | 0 | 0 |
| WSW | 0.8 | 1.0 | 0.4 | 0 | 0 | 0 | 0 |
| WNW | 0.4 | 0.4 | 1.0 | 0 | 0 | 0 | 0 |
| SW | 0 | 0 | 0 | 1.0 | 0.5 | 0.5 | 0.5 |
| SSW | 0 | 0 | 0 | 0.5 | 1.0 | 1.0 | 0.9 |
| S | 0 | 0 | 0 | 0.5 | 1.0 | 1.0 | 0.9 |
| SSE | 0 | 0 | 0 | 0.5 | 0.9 | 0.9 | 1.0 |

Table 3: Location = {W, WSW, WNW, SW, SSW, S, SSE}

| Rainfall | | | | | | | |
|---|---|---|---|---|---|---|---|
| Torrential | 1.0 | 0.9 | 0.9 | 0.85 | 0.75 | 0.75 | 0.75 | 0 |
| VeryHeavy | 0.9 | 1.0 | 0.95 | 0.85 | 0.75 | 0.75 | 0.75 | 0 |
| Heavy | 0.9 | 0.95 | 1.0 | 0.85 | 0.75 | 0.75 | 0.75 | 0 |
| Moderate | 0.85 | 0.85 | 0.85 | 1.0 | 0.75 | 0.75 | 0.75 | 0 |
| Normal | 0.75 | 0.75 | 0.75 | 0.75 | 1.0 | 0.8 | 0.8 | 0 |
| Medium | 0.75 | 0.75 | 0.75 | 0.75 | 0.8 | 1.0 | 0.85 | 0 |
| Low | 0.75 | 0.75 | 0.75 | 0.75 | 0.8 | 0.85 | 1.0 | 0 |
| VeryLow | 0 | 0 | 0 | 0 | 0 | 0 | 0 | 1.0 |

Table 4: Rainfall = {Torrential, VeryHeavy, Heavy, Moderate, Normal, Medium, Very-Low}

| Temperature | | | | | | |
|---|---|---|---|---|---|---|
| Arctic | 1.0 | 0.81 | 0.81 | 0.75 | 0.75 | 0.75 | 0.25 |
| Frigid | 0.81 | 1.0 | 0.9 | 0.75 | 0.75 | 0.75 | 0.25 |
| VeryLow | 0.81 | 1.0 | 1.0 | 0.75 | 0.75 | 0.75 | 0.25 |
| Low | 0.75 | 0.75 | 0.75 | 1.0 | 0.75 | 0.75 | 0.25 |
| Moderate | 0.75 | 0.75 | 0.75 | 0.75 | 1.0 | 0.75 | 0.25 |
| Normal | 0.75 | 0.75 | 0.75 | 0.75 | 0.75 | 1.0 | 0.25 |
| Mild | 0.25 | 0.25 | 0.25 | 0.25 | 0.25 | 0.25 | 1.0 |

Table 5: Temperature = {Arctic, Frigid, VeryLow, Low, Moderate, Normal, Mild}

## References

1. C. Ankebrandt, B. Buckles, F.Petry, "Scene Recognition Using Genetic Algorithms with Semantic Nets," *Pattern Recognition Letters*, 11, pp. 285-293, **April** 1990.
2. Demet Aksoy, "Implementing the Fuzzy Object-Oriented Database Model," M. S. Thesis, Middle East Technical University, Ankara, Turkey, 1994.
3. H O. Banks, "Conceptual System Design for an Environmental Information Base for the Management of Water and Related Information by States," *Report to the Office of Water Resources Research*, Contract No. 14-31-0001-3414, **Belmont, CA**, 1973.
4. E. Bertino, and L. Martino, "Object-Oriented Database Management Systems: Concepts and Issues," *IEEE Computer*,pp. 65-81, **March** 1991.

5. G. Bordogna, D. Lucarella, G. Pasi, "A Fuzzy Object-Oriented Data Model," *Proceedings of the IEEE 3rd International Conference on Fuzzy Systems,*, **Vol. 1**, pp. 313-318,**Orlando, FL, June** 1994.

6. R. J.Brachman, "What IS-A Is and Isn't: An Analysis of Taxonomic Links in Semantic Networks," *IEEE Computer*, 16, pp. 30-37, **October** 1983.

7. P. J. Brown, "Turning Ideas into Products : The Guide System," *Hypertext'87*, University of North Carolina, Chapel Hill, North Carolina, pp. 33-40, 1987.

8. P. D. Bruza, and T. P. van der Weide, "Stratified Hypermedia Structures for Information Disclosure," *The Computer Journal*, Vol. 35, No. 3, pp. 208-220, **March** 1992.

9. B. P. Buckles, and F. E. Petry, "A Fuzzy Representation of Data for Relational Databases," *Fuzzy Sets and Systems*, 7, pp. 213-226, **May** 1982.

10. B. P. Buckles, F. E. Petry, "Uncertainty Models in Information and Database Systems," *Journal of Information Science:Principles and Practice* 11, pp. 77-8, **September** 1985.

11. B. P. Buckles, F. E. Petry and M. Lybanon, "Ocean Feature Recognition using Genetic Algorithms with Fuzzy Fitness Functions(GA/F3)," *Proc. NAFIPS 90*, pp. 394-397, **Washington D. C., March** 1990.

12. P. A. Burrough, "Fuzzy Mathematical Methods for Soil Survey and Land Evaluation," *Journal of Soil Science*, pp. 477-492, **September** 1989.

13. R. G. G. Cattell, *Object Data Management*, Addison Wesley, 1991.

14. W. B. Croft, and H. Turtle, "A Retrieval Model for Incorporating Hypertext Links," *Hypertext'89*, pp. 213-223, **Pittsburg** 1989.

15. N. Delisle, and M. Schwarts, "Neptune-A Hypertext System for CAD Applications," *Proceedings of ACM SIGMOD'86*, pp. 132-143, **Washington D. C.** 1986.

16. D. Dubois, H. Prade, and J.-P. Rossazza, "Vagueness, Typicality and Uncertainty in Class Hierarchies," *International Journal of Intelligent Systems*, 6, pp. 167-183, **July** 1991.

17. Soumitra Dutta, "Approximate Reasoning by Analogy to Answer Null Queries," *International Journal of Approximate Reasoning*, 5, pp. 373-398, **June** 1991.

18. **M. Fuller**, "Querying in a Large Hyperbase," *Proc. of the International Conf. on Database and Expert System Applications (DEXA91)*, Springer Verlag, pp. 455-458, **Berlin, Germany, September** 1991.

19. L. Gallagher, R. Furuta, and P. D. Stotts, "Increasing the Power of Hypertext Search with Relational Queries," *Hypermedia*, Vol. 2, No. 1,

pp. 1-14, **January** 1990.

20. R. George, B.. P. Buckles and F. E. Petry, "Integrating Artificial Intelligence and Databases– Where Do We Manage Uncertainty," *Proceedings of the IJCAI'91 Workshop on Integrating Artificial Intelligence and Database Systems*, **Vol. 1**, pp. 77-84, **Melbourne, Australia, August** 1991.

21. R. George, B. P. Buckles, and F. E. Petry, "Behavioral Characterization of the Fuzzy Object-Oriented Data Model," *Proceedings of the IEEE International Conference on Systems, Man, and Cybernetics*, pp. 1303-1307, **Chicago, IL, October** 1992.

22. R. George, B. P. Buckles and F. E. Petry, "Modeling Class Hierarchies in the Fuzzy Object-Oriented Data Model," *International Journal of Fuzzy Sets and Systems*, 60, pp. 259-272, **December** 1993.

23. R. George, A. Yazici, B. P. Buckles, F. E. Petry "Uncertainty Modeling in Object-Oriented Geographical Information Systems," *Proceedings of the Conf. on Database and Expert System Applications (DEXA)*, **Valencia, Spain, September** 1992.

24. N. Van Gyseghem, R. De Caluwe, R. Vandenberghe, "UFO : Uncertainty and Fuzziness in an Object-Oriented Model," *Proceedings of the IEEE 2nd. International Conference on Fuzzy Systems*, pp. 773-778, **Vol. 2, San Fransisco, CA, March** 1993.

25. M. Guo, S. Y. W. Su, and H. Lam, "An Association Algebra for Processing Object-Oriented Databases," *7th International Conference on Data Engineering*, pp. 23-32, **Vol. 1, Kobe, Japan, April** 1991.

26. F. Halasz, and M. Schwartz, "The Dexter Hypertext Reference Model," *Communications of the ACM*, Vol. 37, No. 2, pp. 95-133, **February** 1994.

27. Y. Inoue, S. Yamamoto, and S. Yasunobu, "The Fuzzy Set Object: Fuzzy Set as a First Class Object," *Proceedings of IFSA'91*, Brussels, 1991.

28. W. Kim, "A Model of Queries for Object-Oriented Database Systems," *Proc. of the International Conf. on Very Large Databases (VLDB)*, pp. 423-432, **Vol. 1, Amsterdam, Holland, August** 1989.

29. G. Lakoff, *Women, Fire, and Dangerous Things*, University of Chicago Press, Chicago, IL, 1987.

30. N. A. Lorentzos and V. J. Killias, "The Handling of Depth and Time Intervals in Soil-Information Systems," *Computers & Geosciences*, 15, 3, pp.395-401, **March** 1989.

31. C. Medeiros, and F. Pires, "Databases for GIS," *SIGMOD RECORD*, 23, 1, pp. 107-116, **January** 1994.

32. N. Meyerowitz, "Intermedia:The Architecture and Construction of an Object-Oriented Hypermedia System and Applications Framework," *Proc. OOPSLA'86*, pp. 186-201, **Portland, Oregon, September** 1986.

33. A. Motro, "Accommodating Imprecision in Database Systems: Issues and Solutions," *SIGMOD RECORD*, 19, 4, pp. 15-23, **December** 1990.

34. J. A. Orenstein, and F. A. Manola, "PROBE - Spatial Data Modeling and Query Processing in Image Database Applications," *IEEE Transactions on Software Engineering*, Vol. 14, 5, pp. 611-629, **May 1988**.

35. K. Parsaye, M. Chignell, S. Khoshafian, and H. Wong, *Intelligent Databases- Object-Oriented, Deductive Hypermedia Technologies*, Wiley, 1989.

36. A. F. Pitty, *Geography and Soil Properties*, Methuen and Co., London, 1978.

37. R. Rada, *Hypertext: From Text to Expertext*, McGrawHill, NY, 1992.

38. V. B. Robinson, "Some Implications of Fuzzy Set Theory Applied to Geographic Databases," *Computers, Environment, and Urban Systems*, 12, pp. 89-97, **April** 1988.

39. E. Rundensteiner, and W. Bandler, "The Equivalence of Knowledge Representation Schemata: Semantic Networks and Fuzzy Relational Products," *Proceedings of the NAFIPS Conference*, pp. 477-501, **Austin, TX, March** 1986.

40. E. Rundensteiner, and Lubomir Bic, "Set Operations in Object-Based Data Models," *IEEE Trans. on Knowledge and Data Engineering*, **Vol. 4, No. 4, pp. 382-398, August** 1992.

41. G. Salton, J. Allan, and C. Buckley, "Automatic Structuring and Retrieval of Large Text Files," *Communications of the ACM*, Vol. 37, No. 2, pp. 1-17, **February** 1994.

42. G. M. Shaw, and S. B. Zdonik, "An Object- Oriented Query Algebra," *Bulletin of the IEEE Technical Committee on Data Engineering*, 12, 3, pp. 29-36, **March** 1989.

43. H.Schek, and M. H. Scholl, "The Relational Model with Relation-Valued Attributes," *Information Systems*, **Vol. 11, No. 2, pp. 382-398, February** 1986.

44. D. D. Straube, "Queries and Query Processing in Object-Oriented Database Systems,", *Ph. D. Thesis*, Department of Computer Science, University of Alberta, 1991.

45. N. Streitz, J. Hannemann, and M. Thuring, "From Ideas and Arguments to Hyperdocuments:Traveling through Activity Spaces," *Hypertext'89*, **Vol. 1**,pp. 343-372, **Pittsburg, PA, November** 1989.

46. K. Tanaka, and Qing Qian, "Two-Level Schemata and Generalized Links for Hypertext Database Models," *Proc. of the 2nd Far East Workship on Future Database Systems,*, Kyoto, Japan, **April** 1992.

47. P. Torasso, and L. Console, "Approximate Reasoning and Prototypical Knowledge," *International Journal of Approximate Reasoning*, 3, pp. 157-77, **March** 1989.

48. B. Wang, and P. Hitchhock, "Intersect: A General Purpose Hypertext System Based on an Object-Oriented Database," *Proc. of the International Conference on Database and Expert System Applications* (DEXA 91), Springer Verlag, **Vol. 1**, pp. 458-464, **Berlin, Germany, September** 1991.

49. **Alan Wild**, *Soils and the Environment: An Introduction*, Cambridge University Press, Cambridge, 1993.

50. M. Zemenkova, and A. Kandel, "Implementing Imprecision in Information Systems," *Information Sciences*, 37, pp. 107-141, **December** 1985.

51. R. Zicari, "Incomplete Information in Object-Oriented Databases," *SIGMOD RECORD*, 19, pp. 33-40, **September** 1990. iWWidWteeeeeTEXT

# EXTENDING A GRAPH-BASED DATA MODEL TO MANAGE FUZZY AND UNCERTAIN INFORMATION

G.BORDOGNA and G.PASI

*ITIM-CNR via Ampere 56, 20131 Milano, Italy*

D.LUCARELLA

*CRA-ENEL, via Volta 1, Cologno Monzese, Milano, Italy*

*In this contribution a fuzzy object oriented data model is defined to manage crisp and imperfect information. This model is based on a visual paradigm that supports the representation of the data semantics and the direct browsing of the information. The model is defined as an extension of a graph-based object model, in which both the database schema and instances are represented as directed labelled graphs. This model allows to deal the requisites of many current applications involving data of different nature and with complex interrelationships.*

## 1    Introduction

Object Oriented Data Models (OODM) support a semantic modelling of data with abstraction mechanisms, such as the intensional definition of classes, more powerful than traditional database models and, at the same time, they offer tools to manage hierarchies of structured objects in an efficient way through the inheritance relationship. These characteristics make the OODMs suitable to deal with applications in both consolidated and emerging fields such as Computer Aided Design, office automation, Geographic Information Systems, cultural heritage, involving large amounts of highly interrelated information.[1,2,3,4,5] Among the OODMs, those based on graphs, named Graph-based Object Models (GOM), are particularly appealing: the main reason is that, since both the database schema and instances are represented as directed labelled graphs,[6,7] users can manipulate and retrieve information by simply performing actions on the graph structure visualised on the screen, without the need to formulate complex queries.[8,9]

On the other side, the increasing complexity of real applications in several fields has raised the need for enhancing the capabilities of current database management systems in order to deal also with imperfect information. By imperfect information in databases we mean here imprecise, vague, inconsistent and uncertain information, which may characterise either the data themselves, or the user queries or both. To manage imperfect information different levels of extension of Object Oriented Database Management Systems can be conceived, which serve different purposes: either to enrich the variety of data that can be represented and stored, or to soften the interaction with the user by introducing browsing capabilities and by defining flexible query languages. As a consequence of these extensions, the query evaluation mechanism is no more designed based on an exact matching, but on a partial matching producing discriminated answers according to their pertinence to the user's request.

In the literature several generalisations of the relational database model have been defined within the framework of fuzzy set theory, which either support flexible queries or manage fuzzy information.10 More recently, fuzzy generalisations of the OODM have been proposed, related to the management of imprecise or vague data.11,13,14,20,22,24 Some approaches focus on particular aspects, such as the definition of fuzzy classes10,11 or fuzzy inheritance,11,12,13 some of them also take care of implementation aspects. 11,14

In this contribution, a Fuzzy Object Oriented Data Model, named FOOD, is presented, which is defined starting from an existing graph-based object model supporting a visual representation based on graphs.7,8,24 In the FOOD model precise and vague or imprecise information, and certainty and uncertainty on precise and vague or imprecise information are modelled separately; graphical elements are defined to represent and identify vague and uncertain information. On this basis, a visual browser of imperfect data can be easily designed.

Vagueness and imprecision are directly related to the data values and they are represented by defining vague attribute values as possibility distributions over the attribute domain; uncertainty is modelled in the association of a value with an attribute, and is represented by introducing in the database schema uncertain property relationships; the uncertain relationship linking an object to its attribute value is defined then as a fuzzy relation. Another aspect taken into account in the FOOD model is the association of a different strength with the property relationship; in order to avoid ambiguities between uncertainty and strength, the former is expressed by a numeric degree, whereas the latter is expressed by a linguistic qualifier such as *high, low, medium.*

A strength can be also associated with both the instance relationship associating an object with a class, and the inheritance relationship linking two classes in a class hierarchy. These two situations are modelled through the definition of fuzzy classes and fuzzy hierarchies of classes.

In FOOD imperfect information is then dealt with at the following levels:

- Definition of vague attribute values;
- Definition of uncertain property relationships;
- Definition of strengthened property relationships;
- Definition of fuzzy classes;
- Definition of fuzzy class hierarchies.

The contribution is organised as follows: in section 2 the way in which imperfect information is meant in this contribution is defined; in section 3 the crisp object oriented database model is introduced; in section 4 the FOOD model is introduced with reference to a real application; in section 5 the model is formally defined.

## 2   Imperfect information

In daily life, one has to deal with information which is characterised to some extent by some kind of *imperfection*. By the word imperfection it is meant one of the following faults of information: imprecision, vagueness, uncertainty, and inconsistency, which are briefly discussed in the following. Imprecision and vagueness are related to the information contents of a proposition; more precisely they deal with the granularity of the value of some attribute involved in a proposition with respect to the universe of discourse. If, for example, one is evaluating the speed of a moving car, and is not able to select the exact numeric value of speed, only an imprecise or vague judgement can be assessed, such as "between 70 and 100mph" or "about 80mph" respectively. In this example the attribute considered is the speed of a car, and the values of speed are usually expressed in a numeric form; however since in this case a numeric value can not be assessed, only values with a lower granularity can be employed, corresponding to a set of supposed values. It is important to notice that the imprecision and vagueness are related to the reference set of values of an attribute.

Uncertainty is related to the truth of a proposition, intended as the conformity of the information carried by the proposition with the considered reality. Linguistic expressions such as "probably", and "it is possible that", are commonly used to declare the ignorance about the truth of the information stated in a proposition. Of course there are situations in which information is affected by both uncertainty and vagueness (imprecision); e.g. in a proposition such as "probably John is very young".

Inconsistency comes from the simultaneous presence of contradictory information about the same reality: "John's age is under 40" and "John's age is over 45".

To manage imperfect information in a unique formal context, the linguistic variables and the theory of possibility have been defined.15,16

In a DBMS, the information related to a given application area is managed at two distinct levels:
- in the representation of the information;
- in the formulation of user's information needs formally expressed through queries to select stored data of interest.

At both levels the information can be affected by imperfection; when structuring and storing the information in a database one may not be able to select a precise value for a datum. The extreme case of imperfection in databases is given by null values which have been extensively studied in the relational database model.10,17 Different causes of null values may exist: for example, when the value of an object's attribute is unknown, or when no value in the domain is applicable due to inconsistencies.

In the literature a unifying approach to represent incomplete data has been proposed and widely adopted, which represents data through fuzzy set interpreted as possibility distributions.17 As previously outlined, the imperfection related to a datum observed in a real application is mainly due either to the inability to select one single value from the domain of possible values of the datum or to the uncertainty in associating a value with the attribute. An imprecise or vague value can be specified as a fuzzy set defined on the domain of the data values, which is interpreted as a possibility distribution; in this case the degree of membership of each value in the domain expresses the degree of possibility that this value is the actual value. Within possibility theory a fuzzy set has then a disjunctive interpretation.15 In Figure 1 and in Figure 2 the representation of an imprecise and of a vague datum respectively are shown.

In Figure 1 an imprecise value for the attribute Age of the person John is selected: Age(John) = *between 20 and 25*; this imprecise value is represented through a possibility distribution $\mu_{Age(John)}(d)=1$  $\forall d \in [20,25]$ and $\mu_{Age(John)}(d')=0$, $\forall d' \in [20,25]$.

In Figure 2 the function $\mu_{young}(d)$ is interpreted as the possibility distribution associated with the event Age(John) = *young*, and it corresponds to the restriction imposed by the fuzzy set young on the numeric age of John.

Since imprecision can be considered as a particular case of vagueness, from now on in this contribution the term vagueness will be used to indicate both concepts.

Within possibility theory, the uncertainty in associating a value with an attribute can also be modelled. In Figure 3 the possibility distribution of a vague and uncertain attribute value is represented. No value of the domain is impossible; all the domain values have a degree of possibility different from 0. The value ε represents to some extent the degree of uncertainty of the truth of the proposition "John is *young*".

In query formulation, vagueness plays a role at two main levels: expression of simple conditions through predicates and expression of complex conditions through the aggregation of conditions by quantifiers. When formulating a request the use of vague predicates is more natural than the selection of a binary predicate; as previously outlined, a vague predicate is represented by a fuzzy set. Vagueness can be also modelled in the aggregation of selection conditions; in query languages of traditional databases one can ask for the satisfaction of *all* or *at least one* selection predicates (universal and existential quantifiers respectively). Fuzzy linguistic quantifiers have been introduced in DBMSs to allow for softer aggregations of a set of criteria;18,19 examples of linguistic quantifiers are: *at least n, most of, at least half of* etc.

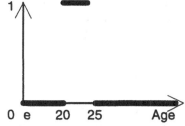

Figure 1 Representation of the datum
Age(John) = between 20 and 25  (imprecise value)

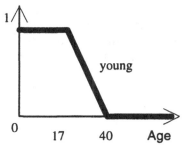

Figure 2 representation of the datum
Age(John) = young (vague value)

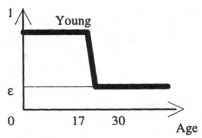

Figure 3 representation of the uncertain datum

Age(John) = *young*

Depending on the presence of imperfect information in either one of the two levels (representation of data and query language), or in both of them, the following three situations could be faced by a query evaluation mechanism: 17

1. precise data and vague queries (with vague predicates);
2. incomplete data and crisp queries (with Boolean predicates);
3. incomplete data and vague queries (with vague predicates).

The so-called fuzzy pattern matching formalised within possibility theory constitutes a general framework in which to define the query evaluation mechanism.15

## 3    The Graph-based Object Model

Graph-based data models provide a natural way of handling data appearing in applications such as hypertext or multimedia information systems.

In a graph based object model both the database schema and instances can be seen as graphs with the data manipulation language expressed in terms of graph transformations.6 Lucarella and Zanzi7 have proposed a graph-based object model which has been used for both conceptual modelling and direct manipulation (browsing, querying and viewing) of the stored objects.

In the following we summarise the formal definition of this model.

The conceptual schema $\Sigma$ is defined as a quintuple:

$$\{ C, T, A, H, P \}$$

In which:

- C is a finite set of class names; at the intensional level each class $c \in C$ denotes a structure, i.e., a set of attributes (properties); at the extensional level it identifies the collection of objects having that structure.
- T is a finite set of types; each $t \in T$ denotes a type collecting primitive objects, with $V(t)$ denoting the set of associated values.
- A is a set of attribute names; attributes can be either simple or complex depending on the kind of their domain: the domain of a simple attribute is a type $t \in T$, the domain of a complex attribute is a class $c \in C$. Moreover, it can be made a distinction between single-valued attributes As and multi-valued attributes Am according to the characteristics of the value they take, with $A = As \cup Am$.
- $P \subseteq C \times A \times (C \cup T)$ is the property relation. If $(c_i, a, c_j) \in P$, then class $c_i$ has the attribute named a, whose domain is the class $c_j$.
- $H \subseteq C \times C$ is the inheritance partial ordering relation; if $(c_i, c_j) \in H$, class $c_i$ is a subclass of class $c_j$; this means that $c_i$ inherits the attributes of $c_j$.

The conceptual schema can be represented as a directed labelled graph $G(\Sigma) = (N, E)$ in which:

- $N = (C \cup T)$ is the set of nodes; each class $c \in C$ is represented by a rectangular-shaped node labelled c. Each primitive class $t \in T$ is represented by an oval-shaped node labelled t.
- $E = (H \cup P)$ is the set of edges. For each $(c_i, c_j) \in H$ there is associated a bold edge labelled "is a" directed from $c_i$ to $c_j$. For each $(c_i, a, c_j) \in P$ there is an associated edge labelled a, directed from $c_i$ to $c_j$. In particular, if $a \in As$ the edge has a single arrow, while if $a \in Am$ the edge has a double arrow.

In Figure 4 an example is shown of a graph representing a part of the conceptual schema $\Sigma$ of a database storing the projects carried out by a given laboratory. The set of class names is C={project, person, laboratory, realisation, product, publication}; the set of types is T={string, integer, real, date, picture, movie, text}; the set of single-valued attribute names is As={name, expertise, photo, age, affiliation, demo, objective, funds, price, content, title, date, deadline} and the set of multi-valued attribute names is Am={staff, team, results, keywords}; moreover there are two hierarchical class-superclass relationships:

H= {(product, realisation), (publication, realisation)}.

For example, a research project has a name, it is described by a demo and by a text specifying its objective, it has a given amount of funds and a deadline; moreover it is led by a person (identified by name, expertise, photo, age and affiliation laboratory), it is carried out by one or more laboratories having a given staff of involved persons. Finally a project yields as a result a certain number of realisations, which can be either products (such as a software or hardware component, which can be sold at a given price), or publications (described by a title, a set of keywords, and a content).

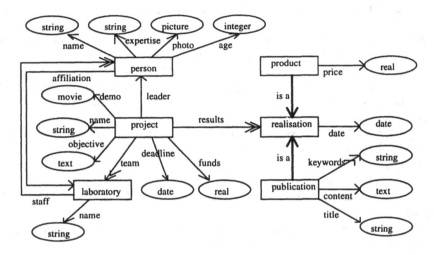

Figure 4: Conceptual schema graph

The database system is defined by the four-tuple $S = (\Sigma, O, I, L)$ in which:

- $\Sigma$ is the conceptual scheme defined previously;
- O is the set of actual objects stored into the system; $V(T)$ is the set of all primitive objects (values): $V(T) = \bigcup_i V(t_i)$;
- $I \subseteq (O \cup C) \times (V(T) \cup T)$ is the instance relation; each object $o \in O$ is an instance of a class $c \in C$, and each value $v \in V(t)$ is an instance of a class $t \in T$;
- $L \subseteq O \times A \times (O \cup V(T))$ is the link relation. $(oi, a, oj) \in L$ iff $(ci, a, cj) \in P$.

Given the schema graph $G(\Sigma)$, the instance graphs can be generated through the application of the instance relationship; in an instance graph the nodes correspond to actual objects and values stored into the system.

In Figure 5, an instance graph over the conceptual schema graph reported in Figure 4 is depicted. It describes a research project named QFLY funded with an amount of 80.000ecu with the deadline on June, the 16th, 1996, and the project leader M.Rossi, director of the IMLAB laboratory. It involves the two team-partners IMLAB, and TEXLAB which supply some human resources (staff). The project has produced as a result some publications. Some of the data are missing, e.g. the photo of the project leader M.Rossi.

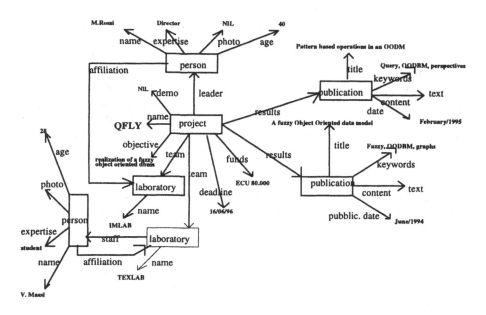

Figure 5: An instance graph over the schema in Figure 4

## 4  A fuzzy extension of the graph-based object model: the FOOD model

The graph-based object model described in section 3. has been designed to handle only crisp information, that is to say:

1. precise data values;
2. crisp properties of objects;
3. precise classification of objects;
4. crisp hierarchies of classes,

and to handle only precise queries, i.e.:

1. crisp selection conditions on data values
2. Boolean aggregation of selection conditions.

This model is unable to handle imperfect information, which is often the only available information. In an object oriented database, imperfect information about a considered reality can be modelled at different levels (e.g., at the level of attribute values, properties, association of objects to classes or definition of class hierarchies), depending on the imperfection of the information, and, sometimes on a subjective choice of the database designer. Moreover, it is important to distinguish the type of imperfection in order to represent it in a suitable formal context. For example, let us consider the subgraph of Figure 5, representing the object M.Rossi with its attribute age; let us suppose that we have to store the age of M.Rossi known only by sight. One possible choice is to store a precise value for M.Rossi's age (for example 40) and to express the subjective uncertainty that 40 is the actual age of M.Rossi. This can be done by associating either a numeric uncertainty degree or a qualifier (such as *not completely sure*) with the property linking M.Rossi to the value of its attribute age.

Another possibility is to select a vague or imprecise value for the age of M.Rossi, for example *young* or *between 25 and 45*, thus assuming a set of possible values; in this case being more confident on our guess, we can maintain crisp, i.e. certain, the property link *age* of the object M.Rossi.

A more general case occurs when modelling both vagueness and uncertainty at the same time: this case can be dealt with by storing a vague value for the attribute age of M.Rossi, which becomes a fuzzy attribute, as well as by associating an uncertainty degree to the property linking M.Rossi to his age. In this case the uncertainty degree expresses that the actual value of the attribute can be different from those assumed. From this example it is clear that, even when the information fault may be coped by introducing either imprecision in data values or uncertainty in associating a value to data, in general both vagueness in data values and uncertainty in associating the value to data can coexist.

It is then necessary to be able to model separately:
1.  precise and vague information;
2.  certainty and uncertainty on precise and vague information;

Since our model is based on a graphical representation of the database in which each kind of information (i.e. objects, attribute values, relations, is-a relation) has its own representation (rectangular shape, oval shape, arrow etc.),7 it gives us the chance of graphically representing the presence of vagueness and uncertainty.

Vagueness can be directly incorporated in the data values, by defining them as possibility distributions over the attribute domain; uncertainty can be modelled in the property relations.

Another feature that we have introduced is the chance of associating a different strength with the property relationships. For example, the link referring to "staff " in

Figure 4 can be defined so as to associate with each triple (oi, a, oj) a linguistic degree indicating the strength of involvement of each person of the staff in the project. In this case the degree does not express the uncertainty on the information, but the strength of the relationship. In order to avoid ambiguities we decided to express uncertainty by a numeric degree, whereas the strength by a linguistic qualifier such as *high, low, medium*.

A strength can be associated also with both the instance relationship and the inheritance relationship. These two situations can be modelled through the definition of fuzzy classes and fuzzy hierarchies of classes; these two concepts are interrelated; in fact, as it will be shown by an example, when a fuzzy hierarchy of fuzzy classes is defined, the membership of an object to a subclass is affected by the fuzzy "is a" relationship with the superclass. In this approach, fuzzy class hierarchies are defined for classification purposes. The partial inheritance of attributes is not dealt with in this framework.

For example, let us assume that we want to classify the publications in the schema graph in Figure 4 as applicative or theoretical. This classification does not define a clear-cut partition, but a fuzzy partition; in fact, in this context a paper may deal with both theoretical aspects and applicative issues, and then it may belong with different degrees to both the subclasses applicative publication (mainly), and theoretical publications (marginally). These membership degrees to the subclasses do not depend on the *is-a* relation, but depend on the satisfaction of a vague or fuzzy constraint imposed on the actual attribute values of the paper. For example, to classify a paper as applicative, we can ask an expert to do it: in this case he/she will associate a label such as *high, low, etc.*, with the instance relationship between a paper and a class. In case of automatic classification, the strength of the instance relationship may depend, for example, on the evaluation of the number of the terms in the applicative thesaurus which are found as values of some attributes of the paper: for example, the membership of a paper to the class of the applicative publications is evaluated as *high* if *most of* the paper keywords and terms in the title and content are drawn from an applicative thesaurus.

Another case of strength of the association of an object with a class occurs when we want to define a fuzzy class-subclass hierarchy. Fuzzy hierarchies are here intended as means to organise (classify) objects in fuzzy subclasses which specialise or generalise to a different level (strength) the concept of the fuzzy superclass. In case of specialisation the extensions of these fuzzy subclasses are included in the extensions of the fuzzy superclasses: this means that the instance of an object to a superclass is always higher than its instance to any subclass. The contrary occurs in case of generalisation.

The strength of the *is-a* relation, which is expressed by a modifier such as *"very"* or *"more or less"* (specialisation and generalisation respectively), is used to compute the instance strength of an object to the subclass from the instance strength of the object to the superclass. For example, let us assume that we want to introduce in the schema graph in Figure 4 the fuzzy superclass *"important project"* whose instances are the projects with a membership value expressing the satisfaction of the vague constraint *"important"* depending on the amount of funds and number of partners in the team involved. A subclass *"very important project"* can be defined which specialises or better restricts the constraint *important*. The fuzzy *is-a* relation has the strength *"very"*, so that a project whose membership to *"important project"* is *high* will have a membership to *"very important project"* decreased to , say, *medium*, assuming that the modifier *very* applied to the linguistic value *medium* produces the linguistic value *high*.

These considerations lead to different levels of extensions of our model:

1. *Definition of vague attribute value;*
2. *Definition of uncertain property and link relationships;*
3. *Definition of strengthened property and link relationships;*
4. *Definition of fuzzy classes;*
5. *Definition of fuzzy class hierarchies.*

In the following the five aforementioned topics are analysed separately and then formalised in FOOD.

## 4.1   Vague attribute values

Vague attribute values are represented by means of possibility distributions $\pi$ on the attribute domain. These values allow to model situations in which the precise value of a given attribute is unknown. The set of type names in FOOD is extended to include vague types.

Tv is the set of names of vague types: vague types are characterised by vague or imprecise values, which are represented by possibility distributions. In order to identify the vague types in the extended schema graph $G(\Sigma e)$ each $t \in Tv$ is represented by a cloud-shaped node labelled t. Te is then defined as $Te = T \cup Tv$ a finite set of type names. Each $t \in Te$ denotes a type collecting primitive objects whose values are identified by V(t).

For example, the schema graph in Figure 4 has been extended with vague types as shown in Figure 6. The vague type names *String, Integer, Real, Date* $\in Tv$ have been introduced which denote the names of the domains of the properties expertise, age, price and date respectively. Their values are expressed as possibility distributions on the domains string, integer, reals and dates respectively. In the case of attributes with numeric domains such as age, price and date, the possible vague values can be expressed by means of linguistic terms belonging to the term set of the linguistic variables *Age, Price* and *Date* respectively: T(*Age*) = {*very young, young, medium aged, old, very old*}, T(*Price*) = {*very low, low, high, very high*}, T(*Date*) = {*very recent, recent, not very recent, not recent*}. When the domain of an attribute is non-numeric, as in the case of "expertise" in Figure 4, vagueness is still represented through a possibility distribution, but in this case it cannot be synthesised by a linguistic value. If one wants to represent that Mr. M.Rossi has either a *good-level* or a *not-very-good-level* expertise, the vague value can be represented as the possibility distribution {1/*good-level*, 1/*not-very-good-level*}. If it is more credible that Mr. M.Rossi's experience is *good-level*, then a possibility distribution such as {1/*good-level*, 0.7/*not-very-good-level*} can be defined.

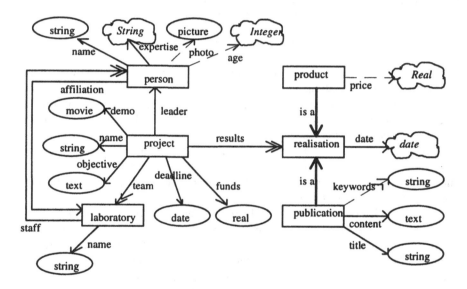

Figure 6: fuzzy conceptual schema describing
a research project carried out in a laboratory.

## 4.2   Uncertain properties of objects

The uncertainty in associating a value with the attribute of an object can be formally represented through the definition of an uncertain property Pu in the FOOD scheme. In the extended schema graph $G(\Sigma e)$, for each $(c_i, a, c_j) \in Pu$, there is a dashed edge labelled au, directed from $c_i$ to $c_j$. In particular if $a \in As$, i.e. is a single valued attribute, the edge has a single arrow head, while if $a \in Am$, i.e. is a multi valued attribute, the edge has a double arrow head. For each uncertain property relation $Pu \subseteq Cex Ax(Ce \cup Te)$ $(Pu = \{(c_i, a, c_j)\})$ in the schema, there exists an uncertain link relation Lu in the corresponding information system; in the case of a single valued attribute $a \in As$ the relation Lu associates with an object $o_k$ of $c_i$ the value $o_h$ of $c_j$ with an uncertainty degree $\mu \in [0,1]$. In case of multi-valued attributes $a \in Am$ the relation Lu associates with an object $o_k$ of $c_i$ m values $o_1 \dots o_m$ of $c_j$ with an uncertainty degree $\mu \in [0,1]$.

The uncertain link relation can then be defined as:

$$Lu: Oex Ax(P(Oe) \cup P(V(Te))) \to [0,1]$$

in which $P(.)$ denote the power set. The uncertain link relation is then formalised as a fuzzy relation.

In the correspondent instance graph, for each $(o_k, a, \{o_1, \dots, o_m\}, \mu) \in Lu$ there exist m dashed edges from $o_k$ directed to $o_1, \dots, o_m$ respectively; they have a common origin in a circle (if m>1) labelled $<a, \mu>$.

In the schema graph in Figure 6 four uncertain properties have been defined, (person, photo, picture), (person, age, *Integer*), (product, price, *Real*) and (publication, keywords, string); it can be noticed that the domains can be either precise (string) or vague (*Integer*, *Real*).

The semantics of the uncertainty degree is that of specifying that there can be other possible value(s) of the attribute besides those specified in the correspondent link relation. In $(o_k, a, \{o_1, \dots, o_m\}, \mu) \in Lu$ the value $\mu = 0$ means that there is no doubt on the fact that the only possible values of the attribute a for $o_k$ of $c_i$ are $\{o_1, \dots, o_m\}$ of $c_j$; in other words there is no uncertainty. When $\mu = 1$, as in the case of (M.Rossi, photo, NIL) it means that any value of the domain is completely possible, then there is complete uncertainty; this is the case in which the actual value is completely unknown, i.e. we have an unknown value. The uncertainty degree is then an indication of the completeness of the stored information.

In Figure 7 an instance graph of the schema graph in Figure 6 is shown. Mr.M.Rossi is known to be *middle-aged* with an uncertainty degree of 0.3 (it is almost certain, but it cannot be excluded that his age might be different), while Mr.V.Massi is certainly *young*.

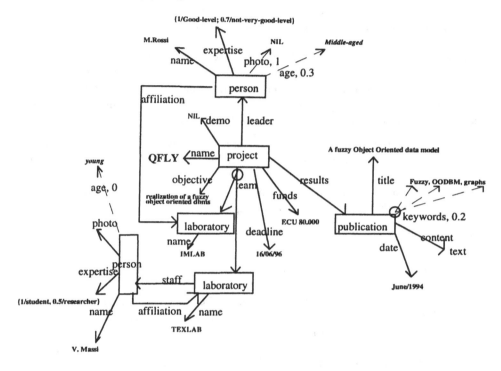

Figure 7: An instance Graph over the fuzzy conceptual graph in Figure 6.

The multi valued attribute keywords of the publication titled "A fuzzy Object Oriented data model" takes the values "Fuzzy", "OODM", "Graphs", with an uncertainty degree of 0.2; this means that the set of keywords used to synthesise the paper content is not exhaustive, but other keywords might be used and added to these.

At this point one could ask the way in which the uncertainty degree of the link relationship and the vagueness of the attribute values affect the evaluation of queries. For instance, when evaluating a query asking for the persons whose age is greater than thirty five years old, age(person)>35, besides considering the vague values of the persons'ages stored in the database, ex. age(M.Rossi)="*middle aged*", against the precise condition, >35, it is necessary to take into account the uncertainty of the link relation (M.Rossi,age, *middle-aged*)=0.3. To this aim the uncertainty degree can be incorporated into the inner representation of the attribute values. In fact, as seen in section 2. and shown in Figure 3., the uncertainty of the association of a value with an attribute can be incorporated within the possibility distribution representing the value itself. In case the attribute value is precise, the possibility distribution representing it consists of a single value whose membership degree=1. When the precise value is associated with an object with an uncertainty degree $\mu$, the membership degrees of the complement domain values are set to $\mu$; in the case the value of the attribute is vague, the possibility distribution representing it is modified to obtain a new possibility distribution $\pi$modified = max ($\mu$, $\pi$actual).

The evaluation of the query reduces then to the fuzzy pattern matching between the modified possibility distribution representing the stored information, $\pi$stored information = max (0.3,$\pi$middle-aged), and the fuzzy set representing the desired attribute values specified by the query condition, fdesired values = $\sum_{i=1}^{35} 0/i + \sum_{j=36}^{110} 1/j$. Notice that this approach can be used even in case the query contains vague conditions, such as "*young*".

## 4.3    Strengthened properties of objects

In the definition of the property relationship another useful modelling feature is the expression of the strength of the property relationship. It can be formally represented through the definition of a strengthened property Ps in the FOOD scheme. Also an uncertain property can be enriched with strength; correspondingly a set of properties Psu are defined in the FOOD scheme. In the extended schema graph G($\Sigma$e), for each (ci,a,cj)∈Ps, there is a bold edge labelled a, directed from ci to cj;  for each (ci,a,cj)∈Psu, with there is a bold dashed edge labelled a, directed from ci to cj.

For each strengthened property relation Ps $\subseteq$ Ce x As x (Ce∪Te) (Ps = {(ci,a,cj)}) in the schema, there exists a strengthened link relation Ls in the corresponding information system, denoting that the attribute a of an object ok of ci has the value oh of cj (or the m values ol ,..., om of cj) with a degree (m degrees) of strength expressed in the form of a linguistic label (m linguistic labels) belonging to the term set *T* of the linguistic variable *Strength*:

$$T(\ Strength)=\{none,\ very\ low,\ low,\ high,\ very\ high,\ full\}.$$

An ascending order is defined between the values of the term set $T(Strength)$ so that a value in it corresponds to a higher (lower) strength than its preceding (following) value; *none* corresponds to no strength, *full* corresponds to maximum strength.

The strengthened link relation Ls is then defined as:

$$\text{Ls} \subseteq \text{Oe x A x } [\text{P}(\text{Oe x } T(Strength)) \cup [\text{P (V(Te) x } T(Strength))$$

in which P (.) denotes the power set. In the correspondent instance graph, for each (ok, a, {(o1,s1) ... ,(om, sm)}) ∈ Ls there exist m bold edges from ok directed to o1,...,om and labelled s1,...,sm respectively; they have a common origin in a circle (if m>1) labelled a.

For each uncertain strengthened property relation Psu $\subseteq$ Ce x A x (Ce$\cup$Te)) (Psu={(ci,a,cj)}) there exists an uncertain strengthened link relation Lsu defined as:

$$\text{Lsu: Oe x A x } [\text{P}(\text{Oe x } T(Strength)) \cup \text{P}(\text{V(Te) x } T(Strength)] \rightarrow [0,1]$$

in which P(.) denotes the power set.

In the correspondent instance graph, for each (ok, a, {(o1,s1),...,(om,sm)}, μ) ∈ Lsu there exist m bold dashed edges from ok directed to o1,...,om and labelled s1,...,sm respectively; they have a common origin in a circle (if m>1) labelled a.

In the schema graph in Figure 8 three strengthened property relations are introduced "staff involved" "deadline" and "keywords"; this last relation is also uncertain. In the corresponding instance graph in Figure 9 the strengthened link relations are shown: Mr.V.Massi is the only one in the staff of the laboratory TEXLAB which is involved in the QFLY project; his involvement in the project is *high*; the project deadline is the 16/6/96 and there is no possibility of postponing it since it is associated with a *very high* strength; the paper titled "A fuzzy Object Oriented Data Model" deals with a different strength (importance) with the concepts represented by each of the keywords: it deals *low* with fuzzy, *very high* with OODM and *high* with graphs.

### 4.4. Fuzzy classes

In the crisp OODM an object is forced either to belong or not to a class. However, there are real situations in which it is useful to be able to represent the partial membership of an object to a class. These cases often occur when the concepts defining the class are vaguely formulated, and the membership of an object to the class is dependent on the satisfaction of a fuzzy constraint imposed on some attribute

114

values of the object. Let us recall the case of classifying a paper as an applicative one discussed previously.

The handling of fuzzy classification of objects is achieved in FOOD by defining fuzzy classes Cf, characterised by objects whose membership to the class is gradual. Since this graduality expresses the strength of the instance relationship, it is represented in FOOD by a linguistic qualifier such as those already defined for the strength of the link relationship Lf. A fuzzy class is then characterised by a fuzzy *instance of* relation If $\subseteq$ O x Cf x *T(Strength)* (i.e. If: Of x Cf $\rightarrow$*T(Strength)*). A fuzzy instance (ok, ci, s)$\in$ If associates the object ok with the fuzzy class ci, with a membership expressed by s$\in$ *T(Strength)*. The *instance of* relation is then formalised as a fuzzy relation of the second order, i.e. it takes as values fuzzy sets interpreted as possibility distributions on the set [0,1]. The schema graph of Figure 6 has been modified in Figure 8 with the introduction of two fuzzy subclasses of the class publication: *applicative* and *theoretical publications*.

The fuzzy classes are represented in the extended schema by shadowed rectangular-shaped boxes. The paper titled "A fuzzy Object Oriented data model" in the instance graph in Figure 5 is an instance of the fuzzy classes *theoretical publications* with a strength equal to *high*, as well as *applicative publications* with a strength equal to *low*. Since the fuzzy classes are defined as subclasses of *publication*, the paper inherits the attribute date of the superclass.

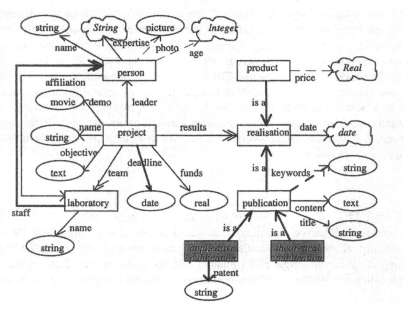

Figure 8: fuzzy conceptual schema graph with fuzzy classes.

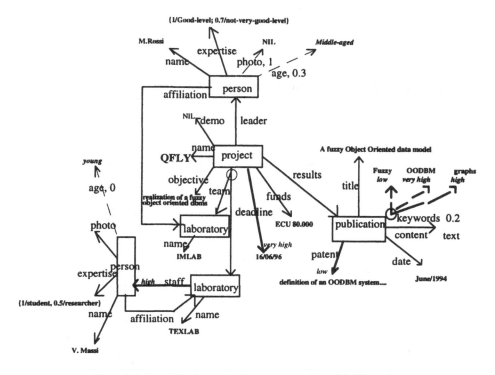

Figure 9: Instance Graph over the fuzzy conceptual graph in Figure 8.

## 4.5. Definition of fuzzy class hierarchies.

In this context, the definition of fuzzy class hierarchies are considered as a useful means to represent the vagueness in a hierarchy defined for classification purposes.12,13,23 This situation occurs when both the superclass and the subclass are fuzzy: in fact, due to this fact the vague concepts represented in the superclass can be specialised/generalised by the vague concepts represented in the subclass to a vague extent, which can be specified by a linguistic modifier such as "*very*" for specialisation and "*more or less*" for generalisation.

To this aim, the fuzzy inheritance partial ordering relation Hf is defined as: Hf ⊆ (Cf x Cf x *Modifiers*), in which *Modifiers* is a set of names of operators applying modifications of the strength of an object to a fuzzy class. Notice that in this context, the notion of modifier does not have the usual meaning of linguistic modifiers. ($c_i$ , $c_j$ , *very* ) $\in$ Hf indicates that the fuzzy class $c_i$ specialises the concepts in the fuzzy superclass $c_j$ to the extent *very*.

Let us recall the example previously described which introduced in the schema graph in Figure 4 the fuzzy superclass "*important project*" and the fuzzy subclass "*very important project*". As already mentioned, the extent of the fuzzy inheritance relation affects the computation of the membership strength of an object to the fuzzy class in the hierarchy. This occurs when querying the database for the members of a fuzzy class in a fuzzy hierarchy. For example, let us assume that the "QFLY" project is a member of the fuzzy class "*important project*" with the strength "*high*", i.e., If$\in$ ("QFLY", "*important project*") = *high* and that one submit a query asking for the *very important project*. In order to supply discriminated answers to the query reflecting the degree of membership of the objects to the requested fuzzy class "*very important project*", it is necessary to compute the membership of "QFLY" to the fuzzy subclass "*very important project*": since the "*very important project*" class is a fuzzy specialisation of the superclass, it is direct that If("QFLY","*very important project*") = $m \in$ T(*Strength*) such that $m \leq$ If("QFLY",*important project*")= *high*. A simple way to achieve this behaviour is to define the modifiers as operators working on values drawn from an ordinal scale. For this reason the values of T(*Strength*) are ordered so that the ith label corresponds to a higher strength than the preceding label i-1 and to a lower strength than the following one i+1. In this case the specialisation modifiers, such as "*very*", can be defined as operators applying a left shift to the label index so as to select a new label $S_j$ with j<i. In the same way, the fuzzy subclasses which generalise the concepts of the fuzzy superclass have a fuzzy *is a* relation labelled by a "weakening" modifier such as "*more or less*", "*not very*", which can be defined by operators applying a right shift.

## 5. Formal definition of the FOOD model

In this section the formal definition of the FOOD model is summarised.

A *conceptual schema* of a graph-based data model is defined by a quintuple $\Sigma e$=(Ce,Te,Ae,He,Pe) where:

- Ce is a finite set of class names; each class $c \in$ Ce denotes a structure, i.e. it is constituted by attributes (properties), and it identifies the collection of abstract objects having this structure; in the extensional sense a class can be either a crisp or a fuzzy collection of objects; then Ce=C$\cup$Cf in which C is the set of crisp class identifiers and Cf is the set of fuzzy class identifiers. The membership degree of an object to a fuzzy class is determined by the instance-of relation;

- Te is a finite set of type names (primitive class names such as integer, text, string) built-in into the system. Each $t \in Te$ denotes a type collecting primitive objects whose values are identified by $V(t)$. $Te=T \cup TV$ in which TV is the set of names of vague types: vague types are characterised by vague values, i.e. linguistic labels such as *high, low* etc. which are represented by possibility distributions.

- $Ae \equiv A$ is a finite set of attribute names (or property names); attributes can be either simple or complex depending on the kind of their domain: the domain of a simple attribute is a type $t \in Te$, the domain of a complex attribute is a class $c \in Ce$. Moreover, it can be made a distinction between single-valued attributes and multi-valued attributes according to the fact that they take as value a single object or more than one object of the domain class; then $A=As \cup Am$.

- $He \subseteq H \cup Hf$ is the inheritance partial ordering relation, in which $H \subseteq CexCe$ and $Hf \subseteq CfxCfxModifiers$, in which *Modifiers* is a set of linguistic modifiers such as *very, more or less* etc. If $(ci,cj) \in H$ class ci is a sub-class of class cj; this means that ci inherits the attributes of cj. If $(ci,cj) \in Hf$ the superclass and the subclass are fuzzy classes; in thid case the linguistic modifier specified in the Hf relation acts as a modifier of the membership of an object to its immediate fuzzy class (the class to which it is defined as part of the extension); more precisely it operates on the indexes of the labels expressing the fuzzy instance relationship strength of the object to its immediate class in order to produce the label expressing the strength to the requested fuzzy class in the hierarchy. This extension is applied to model class hierarchies. However at the current stage the partial inheritance of attributes is not investigated further.

- $Pe \subseteq Ce \times A \times (Ce \cup Te)$ is the property relation, where $Pe=P \cup Pu \cup Ps \cup Psu$. A property can either be a crisp, or an uncertain, or a strengthened, or an uncertain/strengthened relation.

The conceptual scheme $\Sigma$ is represented by a *directed labelled graph* $G(\Sigma)=(N,E)$ where:

- $N=Ce \cup Te$ is the set of nodes of $G(\Sigma)$, where $Ce=C \cup Cf$ and $Te=T \cup TV$. Each class $c \in C$ is represented by a rectangular-shaped node labelled c; each class $c \in Cf$ is represented by a dashed rectangular shaped node labelled c. Each type $t \in T$ is represented by an oval-shaped node labelled t, each type $t \in TV$ is represented by a cloud-shaped node labelled t.

- $E=He \cup Pe$ is the set of edges in $G(\Sigma e)$, where $He=H \cup Hf$ and $Pe=P \cup Pu \cup Ps \cup Psu$. For each $(ci,cj) \in H$ there is a bold edge labelled "is-a" directed from the sub-class ci to the superclass cj. For each $(ci,cj,m) \in Hf$ there is a dashed bold edge labelled "is-a m" directed from the sub-class ci to the superclass cj.

For each $(ci,a,cj) \in P$, with $a \in A$, there is an edge labelled a, directed from ci to cj. For each $(ci,a,cj) \in Pu$, there is a dashed edge labelled a, directed from ci to cj. For each $(ci,a,cj) \in Ps$, there is a bold edge labelled a, directed from ci to cj. For each $(ci,a,cj) \in Psu$, there is a bold dashed edge labelled a, directed from ci to cj. In particular if $a \in As$ the edge has a single arrow head, while if $a \in Am$ the edge has a double arrow head.

A Fuzzy Object Oriented Multimedia System is defined by the four-tuple $M = (\Sigma e, O, Ie, Le)$ where:

- $\Sigma e$ is the conceptual scheme defined above;
- O is the set of all the objects stored into the system, belonging either to crisp or fuzzy classes, and $V(Te) = V(T) \cup V(Tv)$ is the set of all the primitive objects (values), being either crisp values ($V(T)$) or vague values (possibility distributions) ($V(Tv)$);
- $Ie = I \cup If$ in which $I \subseteq (O \times C) \cup (V(Te) \times Te)$ is the crisp instance relation and $If \subseteq (O \times Cf \times T(Strength))$ is the fuzzy instance relation, in which $T(Strength)$ is a set of linguistic values denoting the strength of membership of an object to a class.
- $Le = L \cup Lu \cup Ls \cup Lsu$, where:

$L \subseteq O \times A \times (P(O) \cup P(V(Te))$ is the crisp link relation.

$Lu \subseteq O \times A \times (P(O) \cup P(V(Te))) \times [0,1]$ is the uncertain link relation. $(oi,a,oj,\mu) \in Lu$ denotes that the attribute a of object oi has the value oj with an uncertainty degree equal to $\mu$.

$Ls \subseteq O \times A \times [P(O \times T(Strength)) \cup P(V(Te) \times T(Strength))]$ is the strengthened link relation.

$Lsu \subseteq O \times A \times [P(O \times T(Strength)) \cup P(V(Te) \times T(Strength))] \times [0,1]$ is the uncertain strengthened link relation.

Also an instance of the conceptual scheme can be represented as a directed labelled graph, which we call object graph; it is generated from the scheme graph $G(\Sigma)$ with the actual objects and values into the nodes.


## 6. Conclusion

In this contribution a Fuzzy Object Oriented Data model has been defined to manage both precise, vague and uncertain information. The model has been designed as an extension of a Graph-based object model7 so as to explicitly represent in a graphical form the different levels at which vague and uncertain information occurs in the database.

At present, the FOOD model is being implemented in a prototypal system. The commercial Object Oriented Database Management System O2 25 is used as the kernel system on which to implement the extensions.

The first objective of the implementation is to supply the system with the facility to represent and store vague and uncertain information at the different levels described in this contribution. A graphic user interface is also being designed based on the paradigm of graphic utilities such as DRAW. The main idea is to enable the database manager to define the database schema graph simply by selecting graphic elements representing the type of the data to be stored among a set of predefined ones, (oval and rectangular shaped boxes, arrows, clouds, etc.) and combine them on a virtual sheet.

As far as the query language is concerned, Graph-based object models offer the facility to navigate in the database by indicating the paths directly on the schema graphs visualised on the screen. This avoid the user from the burden step of formulating a query in the system query language and makes it possible to design a visual query language. This query language which is under definition is defined based on the concept of perspective, and graph transformation.26

## Acknowledgements

This research activity has been carried out within a research contract between ITIM-CNR and CRA-ENEL that has provided funds for the acquisition of the hardware and software necessary for the implementation of the FOOD model. Moreover we would like to thank Patrick Bosc for the useful discussion on the subject of this contribution.

# References

1. J.L. Schnase, J.J. Legget, D.L. Hicks, R.L. Szabo, Semantic data modeling of hypermedia associations. *ACM Transactions on Information Systems* **11(1)**, 27 (1993).

2. C. Beeri, A Formal Approach to Object-Oriented Databaes, *Data and Knowledge Engineering* **5(4)**, 353 (1990).

3. E. Bertino, L. Martino, Object-Oriented Database Management Systems: Concepts and Issues. *IEEE Computer* **4**, 33 (1991).

4. K.Lieberherr, C. Xiao, Formal Foundations for Object-Oriented Data Modeling. *IEEE Transactions on Knowledge and Data Engineering* **5(3)**, 462 (1993).

5. K.R. Dittrich, A. Dogac, M.B. Ozsu, A. Biliris, Object-Oriented Data Model Concepts, 29. in *Advances in Object-Oriented Database Systems* ed. T. Sellis, (Springer Verlag, Berlin, 1994).

6. M.Gyssens,J.Paradaens and D.Van Gucht, A Graph Oriented Object Database model, *Proc ACM Symposium on Principle of Database Systems,* 417 (Nashville, USA, 1990).

7. D.Lucarella, A.Zanzi, A Visual Retrieval Environment for hypermedia information systems. *ACM Transactions on Information Systems* **14(1)**, 3 (1996).

8. D.Lucarella, S.Parisotto, A.Zanzi, MORE: Multimedia Object Retrieval Environment, *Proc. ACM Conference on Hypertext*, 39 (Seattle, USA, 1993).

9. R.P.Epstein, Graphical query languages for object oriented data models, *Proc. IEEE Workshop on Visual Languages*, 36 (Rome, Italy, 1990).

10. F. E. Petry, *Fuzzy Databases Principles and Applications*, (Kluwer Academic Publishers, 1996).

11. N.Van Gyseghem, R. De Caluwe, R. Vandenberghe, UFO: Uncertainty and Fuzziness in an Object-Oriented model, *II IEEE Int. Conf. on Fuzzy Systems*, **1,** 489 (San Francisco, USA, 1993).

12. D. Dubois, H. Prade, J-P. Rossazza, Vagueness, Typicality and Uncertainty in Class Hierarchies, *Int. Journal of Intelligent Systems*, **6**, 167 (1991).

13. R.George, B.P. Buckles, F.E. Petry, Modelling Class Hierarchies in the Fuzzy Object-Oriented Data Model, *Fuzzy Sets and Systems* **60(3)**, (1993).

14. K.Tanaka, S.Kobayashi, T. Sakanoue, Uncertainty Management in Object-Oriented Database Systems, *DEXA*, 251 (1991).

15. D. Dubois, H. Prade, *Theorie des possibilites, Applications a la representation des connaissances en informatique, Method + programmes*, (Masson, Paris, 1988).

16. L.A.Zadeh, Fuzzy sets as a basis for a theory of possibility. *Fuzzy sets and Systems* **1**, 3 (1978).

17. P.Bosc, H. Prade, An introduction to fuzzy set and possibility theory-based treatment of soft queries and uncertain or imprecise databases. *Report IRIT/93-57-R*, (1993).

18. P.Bosc, O.Pivert, Some approaches for relational databases flexible querying, *International Journal of Intelligent Systems* **1**, 323-354 (1992).

19. P.Bosc, M.Galibourg, G.Hamon, Fuzzy querying with SQL: extensions and implementation aspects. *Fuzzy sets and Systems*, **28**, 333-349 (1988).

20. V. Cross, Fuzzy extensions to the Object Model, *IEEE Conf. on SMC*, 3630-3635 (Vancouver, Canada, 1995).

21. R. Zicari, Incomplete Information in Object-Oriented Databases, *SIGMOD RECORD*, **19,** 33-40 (1990).

22. N. Van Gyseghem, R, De Caluwe, Fuzzy Behaviour and Relationships in a Fuzzy OODB-Model, *Proc. of the 10th Annual ACM Symposium on Applied Computing, ACM-SAC'95*, 503-507 (Nashville, USA 1995).

23. K.S.Leung, M.H. Wong, Fuzzy Concepts in an Object Oriented Expert System Shell. *International Journal of Intelligent Systems, 7,* 171-192 (1992).

24. G.Bordogna, D. Lucarella, G.Pasi, A Fuzzy Object Oriented Data Model, *Proc. of the 3th IEEE Conference on Fuzzy Systems,* (Orlando, USA, 1994).

25. The O2 System manuals, (1995).

26. D. Lucarella, G. Bordogna, G. Pasi, Pattern-based Retrieval in a Fuzzy Object Oriented Data Base, *Proc. of the ACM Computing week, SAC '95,* (Nashville, USA, 1995).

# THE UFO DATABASE MODEL :
# DEALING WITH IMPERFECT INFORMATION

N. VAN GYSEGHEM, R. DE CALUWE

*Computer Science Laboratory, University of Ghent,*
*Sint-Pietersnieuwstraat 41, B-9000 Ghent, Belgium*

The ultimate goal of the research discussed in this paper, is the design of a database model with a true flavour of reality. Because the real world is not always perfect and, moreover, because the world of the application model is not an ideal reflection of the real world, the "ideal" database model should be able to process imperfect information about the database application in a convenient and flexible way. This paper describes an effort to reach this goal with the UFO database model. UFO extends an object-oriented database model, which defines flexible modelling concepts, with capabilities to handle major forms of imperfection in information. The extended concepts cover all layers of the model and are explained here in detail. A practical implementation via an interface to an extended relational database model is also outlined.

## 1   Introduction

Dealing with imperfect information within the formal and crisp environment of computers has lately been encouraged by the success of two different research topics: the fuzzy set theory and the object-oriented paradigm.

The fuzzy set theory, and the related possibility theory, have already been successfully applied to model imperfect (i.e. fuzzy, uncertain, imprecise) information within crisp environments, such as a control systems or, to a lesser extend, (extended) relational database systems. Also, the rigidness of the traditional database models, such as the relational database model, has already been relaxed in the object-oriented database model (OODBM), which uses the powerful, but crisp, modelling capabilities of the object-oriented paradigm. It therefore seems worthwhile to investigate a "fuzzy" extension of an OODBM, in our case, resulting in the UFO database model ("Uncertainty and Fuzziness in an Object-oriented database model").

Unlike other proposals, which usually view the "fuzzy" extension in a limited framework, the UFO database model aims at being an extension of a full-fledged OODBM, as completely as possible : it models imperfect information at all layers of the model (i.e. the data level as well as the metalevel), considers the interaction with other key notions from the OODBM, and treats both the static and the dynamic aspect. For practical reasons, the underlying OODBM adheres to the ODMG-93 standard proposal for OODBM's as close as possible. [Cattell, 1996]

## 1.1 Notations and Concepts from the Underlying OODBM

The basic concepts concerning object-orientation, and the notations used in this paper, are explained here :

- *Objects* are the key elements in an OODBM, and are used to model any real-world concept or entity. They have an unique *object identity* (OID), an encapsulated *structure* (defined by their attributes) and show *behaviour* (defined by their methods). Attributes and methods are also called *properties* of the objects. The *internal state* of an object consists of all of its attributes values. Methods are invoked by sending a *message* to the object. An *accessor method* returns (part of) the internal state of the object, a *transformation method* performs changes to the internal state. A *primitive* or *literal* object does not have any transformation methods, and therefore cannot change the value of its attributes; the OID of a literal object usually equals its internal state.

- *Classes* define and group objects with similar structure and behaviour. The definition of the similar objects of a class is called the *intention* of the class (or the *type*); the set of the objects is called the *extent* of the class; and the objects are called *instances* of this class.

- A subtype or *inheritance* relationship between classes is expressed by means of the subclass-superclass hierarchy, making reuse of class definitions possible : subclasses *inherit* the properties defined by the superclasses, may *specialize* the inherited properties and may define *specific* properties of their own. The subclasses define a *specialization* of the superclass. An instance of a subclass is called a *member* of a superclass; the set of all instances and members of a class is called the *maximal extent* of the class.

- $o, fs, John, Jane, pdo, pdx, \ldots$ : denote objects.

    P, A, M, AGE, SPOUSE, DEFUZ, CHANGE-PI, ... : denote properties (i.e. attributes and methods, defining the structure and the behaviour of objects).

    C, CL, CLX, FUZZYSET, PERSON, POSS, ROLE, ... : denote classes.

    SPCL : superclass of CL, denoted as : CL $\prec$ SPCL.

SBCL : subclass of CL.

- *o*.A : denotes the value of the attribute A, which is an attribute defined for the CL-object *o*. The set of allowed values, i.e. the domain, is usually defined as the maximal extent of a class. A constraint property, defined by CL, can restrict attribute values to a subset of its domain; such a constraint property is inherited by and may be further refined in subclasses of CL.

- signature of a method : M ( *x*:CLX, ... ) → *y*:CLY
defines a method (i.e. its name M, the names *x* and classes CLX of its parameters, the name *y* and class CLY of the result).

 *o*.M ( *x*, ... ) : a message that invokes the method M on the object *o*, with parameter(s) *x*, ...

- instance vs. member : *o* is an instance only of its immediate class (i.e. the most specialized class, in the subclass-superclass hierarchy, that defines *o*), and a member of its immediate class and all of its superclasses. [Bertino & Martino, 1991]

- CL-object : instance or member of CL.

- generic class GCL (CLASS C) , also called parameterized class : is used in an OODBM to generate classes. For each class CL, given as an argument to this generic class, a class instantiation GCL ( CL ) is generated.

 SET-object : instance or member of a class instantiation of the generic class SET, i.e. by supplying a class CL as an argument, a new class SET ( CL ) is generated, of which this object is an instance or a member, modelling a set of CL-objects.

- iterator : a construct, defined by each generic class instantiation that defines "collection objects" (which gather objects from the parameter class CL, e.g. SET ( CL )-objects), to access the contained CL-objects through a "collection object".

- multivalued attribute : an attribute of which the value is a "collection object".

- abstract class : a class which does not define instances. It is solely intended to provide a superclass for several other classes, which share a common part in their intentions. The definition of the structure and behaviour in the abstract class is incomplete, and is to be completed in the subclasses. An abstract class defines a *total specialization*.

## 1.2 The UFO Database Model

Fuzziness and uncertainty (imprecision) define two types of imperfect information, discussed in this paper. Because of their different treatment within the UFO database model, this extension of the OODBM can be considered to consist of two parts : its "fuzziness part" and its "uncertainty part".

In the "fuzziness part", the fuzziness stands for the impossibility to define sharp or precise borders for some information, and therefore represents an inherent gradation. Fuzzy information is modelled here by means of fuzzy sets or fuzzy (i.e. partial) degrees. The fuzziness part of the UFO database model enhances the modelling capabilities of database applications, by allowing the flexible modelling, within the database scheme, of approximations of reality.

As opposed to a similar extension of the relational database model, the considered extension here is completely performed within the OODBM itself. This is possible because every class and every metaclass (i.e. a class that defines classes) in themselves are considered as objects, allowing modifications to the structure and to the behaviour of both objects and classes, and therefore allowing modifications at the metalevel of the model.

The UFO database model discusses both static and dynamic fuzzy extensions, i.e. extensions to both structure and behaviour. The general procedure followed, consists of replacing the concept of a (crisp) "set" with that of a "fuzzy set", wherever the concept of a set is used in an OODBM and whenever it is possible and meaningful. Special attention has been paid to the meaning of a fuzzification of the concepts. The proposed extension is not a mere computing "exercise" to introduce numbers between 0 and 1 as much as possible in an object-oriented database model - a fuzzification of a database model is only useful when it adds an extra, meaningful value to it.

The "uncertainty part" of the UFO database model handles uncertain and imprecise information; it also allows the modelling of hypothetical information. Uncertainty and imprecision dilutes information which actually should have been crisply described if more knowledge would have been available. In the absence of such extra knowledge, the information can already be given by means of possibility distributions, not forcing a choice between the different alternatives.

Most database models and their "fuzzy" extensions, including the UFO database model, adopt the closed world assumption, and thus require, in the case of imprecise and uncertain information, that all alternatives are entered into the database. Therefore, imprecision is modelled here using normalized possibility distributions; uncertainty is modelled by introducing a non-zero plinth to a possibility distribution.

This part of the UFO database model shows how uncertainty and imprecision in both the data and information can be modelled by means of possibility distributions, and processed in a, to the user, implicit and transparent way. The major concept here is the concept of "role object", which models uncertain roles of an object, i.e. its uncertain or imprecise relationships to other objects or classes of objects.

### 1.3 Notations and Concepts from the UFO Database Model

The notations used in the UFO database model, and some of its basic concepts, are explained here :

- FuzzySet-object : object representing a fuzzy set; it is a member of a class instantiation of the generic class FuzzySet.
- { m / o, ... } : representation of a fuzzy set, in which m is the membership degree associated with the object (or the element of the considered universe) o, ...
- fs.MU ( o ) : a message that invokes a method which returns the membership degree associated with the object o by the FuzzySet-object fs.

- { p / o, ... }$_\pi$ : representation of a possibility distribution, in which p is the possibility degree associated with the object (or the element of the considered universe) o, ...
- fuzzy set vs. possibility distribution : it is very important here to understand the differences in the interpretation between the two concepts. A fuzzy set models gradations between elements, which together may constitute a vague concept. It intrinsically has a conjunctive, multivalued nature, with an imposed AND-semantics, such as in the fuzzy set *young*, which represents *all* ages that are considered "young" (to a certain degree). A possibility distribution models possible alternatives for a value. It represents disjunctive information, with an imposed XOR-semantics. In many cases, a possibility distribution can be derived from a normalized fuzzy set, such as in the imprecise description of a person's age as the possibility distribution derived from the fuzzy set *young* : only one of the alternatives given by this possibility distribution corresponds with the person's age, but it is not stated which one. [Yager, 1987] [OFTA, 1994]
- *o-r, o-1, o-2, ..., Jane-1, Jane-1-2, ...* : role objects associated with the regular objects *o*, resp. *Jane, ...*

The legend for all figures in this paper is shown in Figure 1.

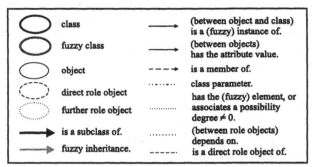

Figure 1: Graphical syntax used by UFO.

## 1.4 Outline of the Paper

The rest of the paper discusses the UFO database model in more detail. First, some preliminary extensions of the underlying OODBM are formulated in Sec. 2. The "fuzziness part" of the UFO database model is discussed in Sec. 3. It includes subsections on the fuzzifications of several object-oriented concepts, such as fuzzy attribute values, fuzzy properties and soft modelling, fuzzy instances and fuzzy classes, fuzzy specialization and fuzzy inheritance. This section concludes with a short summary of this part of the UFO database model. Sec. 4 discusses the "uncertainty part" of the UFO database model. It includes subsections on the handling of uncertainty and imprecision at the data level, i.e. the handling of uncertain and imprecise (crisp or fuzzy) attribute values, of uncertain applicability of (crisp or fuzzy) properties and of uncertain classifications of (crisp or fuzzy) objects. It also includes a subsection on the handling of uncertainty at the metalevel (also called the database scheme level), i.e. hypothetic modelling, and concludes with a short summary of this part of the UFO database model. Sec. 5 outlines a mapping of the UFO database model onto an extended relational database model, Sec. 6 discusses some further topics of research on the UFO database model, and the paper concludes in Sec. 7.

## 2 Preliminary Extensions

The following "crisp" concepts are also defined in the underlying OODBM, to prepare for the extension to the UFO database model :

- Extra system attributes are defined by each class CL and for each object $o$ :
    - CL.$\wp$ : "set" of properties defined by CL.
    CL.EXTENT : extent of the class CL, i.e. "set" of all its instances.
    CL.MAX-EXTENT : maximal extent of CL, i.e. "set" of all its members.
    CL.SUPER : "set" of immediate superclasses of CL.
    - $o.\tau$ : "set" of properties defined for $o$.
    $o$.IMM-CLASS : references the immediate class of $o$.
- Extra system methods are defined by every class CL and SBCL, and for every object $o$ :
    - CL.$\iota$ ( $o$ ) : returns the *instance degree* of $o$ in CL, which indicates whether or not $o$ is an instance of CL :
        $$CL.\iota ( o ) = 1 : o \text{ is an instance of CL,}$$
        $$CL.\iota ( o ) = 0 : o \text{ is not an instance of CL.}$$
    - CL.$\mu$ ( $o$ ) : returns the *membership degree* of $o$ in CL, which indicates whether or not $o$ is a member of CL :
        $$CL.\mu ( o ) = 1 : o \text{ is a member of CL,}$$
        $$CL.\mu ( o ) = 0 : o \text{ is not a member of CL.}$$
    If : SBCL $\prec$ CL, then : SBCL.$\mu$ ( $o$ ) $\leq$ CL.$\mu$ ( $o$ )
    - SBCL.$\iota$ ( CL ) : returns the *inheritance degree* associated by SBCL with CL, which indicates whether or not SBCL is a subclass of CL :
        $$SBCL.\iota ( CL ) = 1 : SBCL \text{ is a subclass of CL,}$$
        $$SBCL.\iota ( CL ) = 0 : SBCL \text{ is not a subclass of CL.}$$

- As a fuzzy set is defined by means of a mapping onto the unit interval [ 0, 1 ], a literal class UNITINTERVAL is defined as a standard built-in subclass of the literal class REAL.
- The iterator, defined by the generic class SET, is extended to allow an "element by element" execution of methods invoked on a SET-object : when receiving a message, the iterator will iterate over all elements of the SET-object, passing the message to each of the elements :
    - methods that are defined for CL-objects, automatically are also defined for SET ( CL )-objects.

- when such a method is invoked on a SET ( CL )-object $s$, the iterator invokes the method on each of the elements of s, and groups each of the resulting objects in a resulting set. Formally, a message sent to $s$ to invoke the method M, which is defined by CL with the signature M ( $x$:CLX, ... )→ $y$:CLY, results in a SET ( CLY)-object $sy$ that represents the set :

$$\{ y \mid \forall \text{ CLY-object } y, \forall \text{ CL-object } o, o \in s : o.M ( x, ... ) = y \},$$

i.e. a CLY-object $y$ is an element of $sy$ if $y$ is returned as a result of an invocation of M on a CL-object $o$, which is an element of the set $s$.

For example, the method NAME ( ) returns the value of the NAME attribute of a PERSON-object; invoking this method on the SET ( PERSON )-object *Univ*.STUDENTS results in the set of names of the students at this university.                                    ∎

## 3   The "Fuzziness Part" of the UFO Database Model

In this section, the underlying OODBM is further extended, so that it allows the processing and recording of fuzzy information. Note that no uncertainty whatsoever is assumed in this section, neither about the data in the database, nor within the database scheme itself. Some of the information to be modelled, however, is intrinsically vague (gradual), for which the vagueness cannot be reduced, neither by a better understanding of the application, nor by a more profound knowledge of the data concerning the application. The UFO database model uses the fuzzy set theory to model such fuzzy information.

Introducing a fuzzy set semantics at all layers of the OODBM is obtained by replacing the concept of a "set" with that of a "fuzzy set", wherever the concept of a set is used in an OODBM and whenever it is meaningful. By doing so, some object-oriented concepts are fuzzified and fuzzy degrees are introduced. The fuzzification process in the UFO database model attempts to adhere, as closely as possible, to the original principles of the object-oriented paradigm.

The "fuzzy" extensions are summarized in Table 1, and discussed in detail in the next subsections :

Table 1: The "fuzziness part" of the UFO database model.

| 1. fuzzy values for multivalued attributes | 2. a. soft modelling<br>b. fuzzy properties |
|---|---|
| 3. a. fuzzy instances, members, classes<br>b. fuzzy specialization | 4. fuzzy inheritance |

### 3.1 Fuzzy Values for Multivalued Attributes

This section explains how fuzzy, or gradual, data about objects is modelled in the UFO database model. "Crisp" data about an object is modelled in an OODBM (and thus also in the UFO database model) by the "crisp" values of the attributes defined for the object. "Fuzzy" data about an object is modelled in the UFO database model by "fuzzy" values of the attributes defined for the object.

In general, an attribute defined for an object in an OODBM is not necessarily atomic or single-valued, but may be multivalued. A multivalued attribute models a 1-N or M-N relationship between (literal or non-literal) objects. Its domain is defined, for instance, by the generic class SET as the maximal extent of a class instantiation SET ( CL ).

A fuzzy, or gradual, 1-N or M-N relationship between (literal or non-literal) objects, such as someone's friends, or the languages someone speaks, is also modelled by a multivalued attribute, however, the value of which is a "fuzzy set" of objects. The "fuzzy" value of a multivalued attribute is modelled here by introducing the generic class FUZZYSET : by supplying a class CL as an argument, a new class FUZZYSET ( CL ) is instantiated, which models fuzzy sets of CL-objects.

For example, Univ.GOOD-STUDENTS is a FUZZYSET ( PERSON )-object, representing the fuzzy set : { 1 / John, 1 / Jane, 0.8 / Susan, 0.6 / Peter, 0.2 / Alice, ... }; it gradually lists the good students of the university Univ : the membership degrees express the degree with which the PERSON-objects, which are students at Univ, conform with the relative notion of "good student". Similarly, John.LANGUAGES is a FUZZYSET ( LANGUAGES )-object, representing the fuzzy set { 1/ English, 0.2 / Dutch }; it models the languages that John masters : the membership degrees express how well John masters these languages (usually, a membership degree 1 is associated with the native language).     ∎

FUZZYSET is defined as a subclass of the generic class COLLECTION, and as superclass of the generic class SET, because every set is a special fuzzy set, of which the membership function only takes values from the set { 0, 1 }, instead of from the entire interval [ 0, 1].

The methods, defined by the generic class FUZZYSET (CLASS C), to handle FUZZYSET-objects (i.e. to model their behaviour), are, to mention a few :
* methods inherited from the superclass COLLECTION, e.g. :
  * CREATE-ITERATOR ( *stable*:BOOLEAN ) → y:ITERATOR
    Defines an iterator over the FUZZYSET-object.
* methods inherited from the superclass COLLECTION, and further specialized, e.g. :
  * UNION ( *fs'*:FUZZYSET ( C ) ) → *fsy*:FUZZYSET ( C )
    Returns the Zadeh-union of the FUZZYSET-object and *fs'*.
* specific methods, e.g. :
  * MU ( *o*:C ) → m:UNITINTERVAL
    Returns the membership degree of the object *o* in the FUZZYSET-object.
  * CUT ( $\alpha$:UNITINTERVAL ) → *sy*:SET ( C )
    Returns the $\alpha$-cut of the FUZZYSET-object.
  * THRESHOLD> ( m:UNITINTERVAL ) → *fsy*:FUZZYSET ( C )
    When invoked on a FUZZYSET-object *fs*, it returns a "threshold" fuzzy set, i.e. the fuzzy set *fsy* which, for every C-object *o*, associates the following membership degree :
    $$\text{if}: fs.\text{MU} ( o ) \leq m, \qquad \text{then}: fsy.\text{MU} ( o ) = 0,$$
    $$\text{if}: fs.\text{MU} ( o ) > m, \qquad \text{then}: fsy.\text{MU} ( o ) = fs.\text{MU} ( o ).$$
* specific methods defined only for parameter classes of non-literal objects, e.g. :
  * CHANGE-MU ( *o*:C, m:UNITINTERVAL )
    Replaces the membership degree of the object *o* in the FUZZYSET-object by the new membership degree m.

An extended iterator, similar to the one described in Sec. 2, is defined by the generic class FUZZYSET, to allow a gradual "element by element" execution of methods invoked on a FUZZYSET-object : when receiving a message, the iterator iterates over all objects that have a non-zero membership degree in the FUZZYSET-object, forwards the message to each of these objects, and groups the resulting objects in a new fuzzy set.

Formally, a message *fs*.M ( *x*, ... ), sent to a FUZZYSET ( CL )-object *fs* to invoke the method M, which is defined by CL with the signature M ( *x*:CLX, ... ) → *y*:CLY, is forwarded to the CL-objects $o$ that have a non-zero membership degree in $fs$, and results in a FUZZYSET ( CLY )-object $fsy$ which associates the following membership degree with each CLY-object $y$ :

$$fsy.\text{MU} ( y ) = \max \{ fs.\text{MU} ( o ) \mid \forall \text{CL-object } o, fs.\text{MU} ( o ) > 0 :$$
$$o.\text{M} ( x, \dots ) = y \}$$

i.e. a CLY-object $y$ has a non-zero membership degree in $fsy$ if $y$ is returned as a result of an invocation of M on a CL-object $o$, which has a non-zero membership degree in the fuzzy set $fs$. This is an immediate fuzzification of the "crisp" iterator for SET-objects.

The iterator is further fuzzified for non-literal FUZZYSET-objects, to allow queries and transformations with crisp or fuzzy (i.e. relative to the membership degree) side-effects: [Van Gyseghem & De Caluwe, 1995]

- The method is only to be invoked on the objects with the "highest" membership degrees in a FUZZYSET ( CL )-object $fs$.

  Formally, a message $fs.\text{M} ( x, \dots )$:THRESHOLD m, sent to $fs$, is equal to the message $fs.\text{THRESHOLD}> ( m ).\text{M} ( x, \dots )$. By means of the iterator, the message is forwarded to the CL-objects $o$ that have a non-zero membership degree in $fs.\text{THRESHOLD}> ( m )$, and thus that have a membership degree in $fs$ greater than the given threshold m. This results in a FUZZYSET ( CLY )-object $fsy$ which associates the following membership degree with each CLY-object $y$ :

$$fsy.\text{MU} ( y ) = \max \{ fs.\text{MU} ( o ) \mid \forall \text{CL-object } o,$$
$$fs.\text{THRESHOLD}> ( m ).\text{MU} ( o ) > 0 :$$
$$o.\text{M} ( x, \dots ) = y \}$$
$$= \max \{ fs.\text{MU} ( o ) \mid \forall \text{CL-object } o,$$
$$fs.\text{MU} ( o ) > m : o.\text{M} ( x, \dots ) = y \}$$

- The method is to be invoked "with fuzzy side-effects".

  The result of invoking a transformation method M on a FUZZYSET ( CL )-object $fs$ *"with fuzzy side-effect"*, where M is defined by CL with the signature M ( $x$:CLX, $\dots$ ) → $y$:CLY, is that the internal states of CL-objects $o$ are changed by M, with the changes being relative to the membership degrees of $o$ in $fs$. A change of internal state usually is determined by one or more of the parameters of the transformation method; for a fuzzy side-effect, the values of these parameters are therefore to be adjusted relative to the membership degrees. Formally, this is achieved by sending the message $fs.\text{M} ( x$ :MMU, $\dots$ ):MU. By means of the iterator, adjusted messages are then sent to the CL-objects $o$ that have non-zero membership degrees in *fs* : *o*.M ( *x*.MMU ( *fs*.MU ( *o* ) ), ... ). The values of the parameters are adjusted here, according to the membership degrees, by an *adjusting method* MMU, optionally given in the original message. MMU is a method, defined by CLX, statically specified either as the default adjusting method for CLX or as the default adjusting method associated with M, or dynamically specified in the message.

For example, LANGUAGES ( ) and NAME ( ) are methods, defined by the class PERSON, that return the value of the attributes LANGUAGES and NAME, also defined by PERSON. The message *Univ*.GOOD-STUDENTS.LANGUAGES ( ) returns a FUZZYSET ( FUZZYSET ( LANGUAGES ) )-object representing the fuzzy set of level 2 :

{   1   / { 1 / *English*, 0.2 / *Dutch* },   1   / { 1 / *English* },
    0.8 / { 1 / *English*, 1 / *Spanish* },   0.6 / { 1 / *English*, ... },
    0.8 / { 1 / *English*, 1 / *French* },   ... }.

The message *Univ*.GOOD-STUDENTS.NAME ( ) :THRESHOLD 0.5 returns the FUZZYSET ( STRING )-object *StudentNames* representing the fuzzy set (Figure 2) :

{   1 / "John Doe", 1 / "Jane Way", 0.8 / "Susan Cue", 0.6/ "Peter Picard" }

The message *Univ*.GOOD-STUDENTS.ADD-SCORE ( 10 ) :THRESHOLD 0.6 :MU has a fuzzy side-effect to add points to the general scores, relative to the membership degrees, with the default adjusting method for SCORES being * (i.e. multiplication) :

| | *John* : 20 | *Jane* : 15 | *Susan* : 15 | *Peter* : 10 |
|---|---|---|---|---|
| (before) | | | | |
| (after ADD-SCORE) | +10 : 30 | + 10 : 25 | + 8 : 23 | + 6 : 16 |

A so-called "fuzzy" value of a single-valued attribute should explicitly state the meaning of the involved "number", e.g. does it represent a gradation, or actually an uncertainty or imprecision ? Into which fuzzy set is it a membership degree ? What does a zero membership degree mean ? In this case, is the attribute defined for the object ? ... Therefore, the UFO database model does not allow for a "fuzzy" value of single-valued attributes. Instead, it offers fuzzy properties, which are defined at the level of the database scheme and which offer a clear semantics.

### 3.2 Soft Modelling and Fuzzy Properties

Unlike fuzziness about multivalued attributes, which is considered at the "data" level of the UFO database model, fuzziness about single-valued attributes and fuzziness about methods is considered only at the level of the database scheme. Fuzzy information about properties is interpreted here as a gradation in the applicability of the properties defined for objects, allowing the flexible modelling of an application.

Usually, only the classes which are really relevant for the application are defined within the database scheme. Even though completeness is aimed for, it can only be achieved within the boundaries defined by the application. Absolute completeness is not really a requirement and even if it were, it could only be modelled approximately within the database scheme (nevertheless, this approximation may result in a complex database scheme).

For example, consider a taxonomy of animals : among scientists, there exists a striving for a "complete" taxonomy of all animals living on earth. However, as new species are discovered every now and then, every taxonomy merely reflects the "complete" taxonomy at a certain moment, and consequently an approximation of the actual "complete" taxonomy.　　　　　　　　　　　　　　　　　　　　　　　■

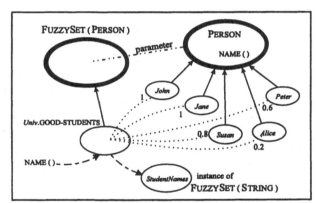

Figure 2: *Univ*.GOOD-STUDENTS.NAME ( ) :THRESHOLD 0.5

Therefore it should be possible to model approximations of reality in a flexible way within the database scheme. This is called *soft modelling*, similar to the notion of *soft computing*, a strategy which, by modelling a simplified version of the actual problem, very quickly leads to the desired good results. The UFO database model allows for soft modelling by giving classes the ability to define both required and optional properties. *Optional properties* correspond with specific properties of possible subclasses, which are not defined within the database scheme of the application. The optional properties are a surrogate for an incomplete specialization.

For example, although SWIM ( ) is a property of most PERSON-objects, it is not a required property, as some people cannot swim. However, it might be of interest to have this optional property defined and implemented by the class PERSON, without having to define subclasses for, respectively, people who can swim and people who cannot swim. ∎

Each object $o$ indicates at its creation time which of the optional properties are defined for $o$ (a dynamic allocation and change in applicability of optional properties is to be handled in the same way as a dynamic change of the immediate class of $o$ is to be handled; this feature is not yet defined in the UFO database model). $o.\tau$ is a subset of all properties defined by the immediate class of $o$. An optional property is not necessarily inherited by subclasses defined in the database scheme; if it is inherited, it may be inherited either as a required property for the subclass or as an optional property. [Van Gyseghem & De Caluwe, 1995]

The "crisp" concepts of required and optional properties are now fuzzified to the concept of fuzzy properties. A *fuzzy property* is a property which is not necessarily completely applicable for all members of a class, nor should it be applicable with the same degree. Each object $o$ associates a *degree of applicability* with each fuzzy property P, indicating the degree with which P is applicable for $o$. By doing so, the "crisp" set $o.\tau$ is fuzzified to a fuzzy set, for which $o.\tau.\text{MU} ( P )$ equals this degree of applicability :

$o.\tau.\text{MU} ( P ) = 1$ means that P is completely defined and fully applicable for $o$,

$o.\tau.\text{MU} ( P ) = 0$ means that P is not defined, and therefore not applicable for $o$,

$0 < o.\tau.\text{MU} ( P ) < 1$ means that P is defined for $o$, but that it is only partially applicable (i.e. to some degree) for $o$.

For example, PERSON-objects have different degrees in their ability to perform the method SWIM ( ), or have a full-time, part-time or no MAIN-JOB. Also fuzzy partial 1-1 or 1-N relationships between objects, such as the single-valued attribute BEST-FRIEND, are modelled by means of fuzzy properties. ■

Each class CL defines per fuzzy property P the possible degrees of applicability :

■₁ either by associating a lower limit (threshold) with the required or optional fuzzy property : $CL.\theta$ ( P ), which indicates the minimum degree of applicability of P for each CL-object. Therefore, if P is inherited by a subclass, the threshold may not be lowered by the subclass. This case is indicated by the mark ■₁.

■₂ or by explicitly listing all possible degrees of applicability in a non-empty set associated with the fuzzy property : $CL.\Theta$ ( P ), which restricts the degree of applicability of P for each CL-object $o$ by : $o.\tau.MU$ ( P ) $\in CL.\Theta$ ( P ). From this, it follows that :

■ P is an optional property if $0 \in CL.\Theta$ ( P ), otherwise it is a required property,

■ if P is inherited by a subclass SBCL, the set of possible degrees of applicability may not be expanded : $SBCL.\Theta$ ( P ) $\subseteq CL.\Theta$ ( P ).

For a crisp required property RP, the degree of applicability equals 1, so that $CL.\Theta$ ( RP ) = { 1 } and RP is inherited by every subclass of CL. A crisp optional property OP is either applicable or not applicable, so that $CL.\Theta$ ( OP ) = { 0, 1 }; a subclass SBCL of CL inherits the crisp optional property OP and associates one of the following sets of possible degrees of applicability with it :

$SBCL.\Theta$ ( P ) = { 0 } :   the property OP is not inherited by SBCL;

$SBCL.\Theta$ ( P ) = { 1 } :   the property OP is inherited as a crisp required property;

$SBCL.\Theta$ ( P ) = { 0, 1 } :   the property OP is inherited as a crisp optional property.

This case is indicated by the mark ■₂.

In each case, the "set" of properties, defined by $CL.\rho$, is a *"conditional"* set of properties, i.e. a "set" of which the elements are properties with which the possible degrees of applicability are associated as a "condition" :

■₁ $CL.\rho$ = { $CL.\theta$ ( P ) / P, ... }, resembling a fuzzy set of properties, in which the membership degree is the minimum degree of applicability,

■₂ $CL.\rho$ = { $CL.\Theta$ ( P )/ P, ... }.

### 3.3 Fuzzy Instances, Fuzzy Members , Fuzzy Classes and Fuzzy Specialization

As discussed in the previous sections, fuzzy information about objects may result in fuzzy values of multivalued attributes, or fuzzy properties defined for the object. Fuzzy information about an object or within the definition of a class may also result in a "fuzzy" classification of the object, which in turn results in fuzzy extents of classes.

Some classes are semantically fuzzy, which means that some objects $o$ are instances or members of this class CL only "to some degree". By fuzzifying the instance degree and membership degree of $o$ in CL, these degrees now indicate the extent to which $o$ is considered an instance or member of CL. Both CL.ι ( $o$ ) and CL.μ ( $o$ ) return a UNITINTERVAL-object, where :

   CL.ι ( $o$ ) = 1 : $o$ is a (full) instance of CL,
   CL.ι ( $o$ ) = 0 : $o$ is not an instance of CL,
   0 < CL.ι ( $o$ ) < 1 : $o$ is a partial or *fuzzy instance* of CL.
   CL.μ ( $o$ ) = 1 : $o$ is a (full) member of CL,
   CL.μ ( $o$ ) = 0 : $o$ is not a member of CL,
   0 < CL.μ ( $o$ ) < 1 : $o$ is a partial or *fuzzy member* of CL.

Such a class CL is called a *fuzzy class*, and both CL.EXTENT and CL.MAX-EXTENT are fuzzy sets of objects. For a fuzzy instance $o$, $o$.IMM-CLASS is a fuzzy set of classes, associating the instance degree of $o$ in each class. This fuzzy set is unimodal, which means that an instance degree 1 is associated with exactly one class; this class is the root-class SPCL of the (sub-)hierarchy of classes, in which $o$ has non-zero instance degrees : SPCL.ι ( $o$ ) = 1, and for each class CL and subclass SBCL in this (sub-)hierarchy, SBCL.ι ( $o$ ) ≤ CL.ι ( $o$ ).

For example, the PERSON-object *Jane* is a part-time student, and thus defined as a full instance of the class PERSON and a partial instance of the subclass STUDENT :

   PERSON.ι ( *Jane* ) = 1,         STUDENT.ι ( *Jane* ) = 0.5,
   *Jane*.IMM-CLASS   = { 1 / PERSON, 0.5 / STUDENT }.

Also, a subclass which is defined by imposing a fuzzy restriction upon a superclass, naturally emerges as a fuzzy class. For example, the fuzzy class YOUNGPERSON is defined as a subclass of PERSON, with a constraint property restricting the domain of the attribute AGE to the FUZZYSET ( AGES )-object *young* ( AGES ); assume that *young* ( AGES ).MU ( 33 ) = 0.8 and *John*.AGE = 33, then :

   YOUNGPERSON.ι ( *John* ) = 0.8,         PERSON.ι ( *John* ) = 1,
   *John*.IMM-CLASS = { 1 / PERSON, 0.8 / YOUNGPERSON }.         ∎

A subclass, defined by imposing a fuzzy constraint property upon a superclass, defines a *fuzzy specialization* of the superclass. A *total fuzzy specialization* is defined by a *fuzzy abstract class*, i.e. a class of which all instances are also fuzzy instances of at least one of the subclasses.

For example, the fuzzy classes YOUNGPEOPLE, MIDDLEAGEDPEOPLE and OLDPEOPLE, shown in Figure 3, define a total fuzzy specialization of the fuzzy abstract class LIVINGPEOPLE : all LIVINGPEOPLE-objects are also a member or fuzzy member of at least one of the subclasses. The domain of the attribute AGE in each of the subclasses is restricted to respectively *young* ( AGES ), *middle-age* ( AGES ) and *old* ( AGES ).  ▪

A fuzzy class may have both fuzzy and "crisp" classes as subclass.

For example, in Figure 3, the fuzzy class CHILD is a subclass of the fuzzy class YOUNGPEOPLE, and the crisp class FIRSTGRADER is a subclass of the fuzzy class CHILD.▪

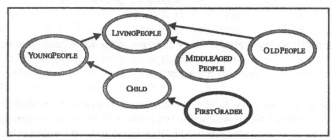

Figure 3: Fuzzy classes in a hierarchy.

Because a fuzzy member $o$ is only a member of a fuzzy class CL "to some degree", $o$ only partially complies with the definition of a "CL-object". Therefore, not all of the required properties, defined by CL, are necessarily defined for $o$ :
- only the properties that are considered as being "core" required properties of CL are necessarily defined,
- the other properties, defined by CL, are considered optional for $o$.

For a fuzzy member $o$, the "core" required properties, defined by a fuzzy class CL for which $0 < CL.\mu ( o ) < 1$, are the required (possibly fuzzy) properties P, defined by CL, for which :

$$\blacksquare_1 \qquad 1 - \text{CL}.\mu\,(\,o\,) < \text{CL}.\theta\,(\,\text{P}\,),$$
$$\blacksquare_2 \qquad 1 - \text{CL}.\mu\,(\,o\,) < \min\,\{\,a \mid a \in \text{CL}.\Theta\,(\,\text{P}\,)\,\}.$$

All "core" required properties are applicable for $o$. [Van Gyseghem & De Caluwe, 1995]

Note that it is possible that a property P, defined by the fuzzy class CL and inherited by SBCL with :

$$\blacksquare_1 \qquad \text{SBCL}.\theta\,(\,\text{P}\,) > \text{CL}.\theta\,(\,\text{P}\,),$$
$$\blacksquare_2 \qquad \min\,\{\,a \mid a \in \text{SBCL}.\Theta\,(\,\text{P}\,)\,\} > \min\,\{\,a \mid a \in \text{CL}.\Theta\,(\,\text{P}\,)\,\},$$

is not necessarily applicable for an object $o$, when $o$ is considered as a fuzzy member of SBCL, having $\text{SBCL}.\mu\,(\,o\,) < \text{CL}.\mu\,(\,o\,)$, if :

$$\blacksquare_1 \qquad 1 - \text{SBCL}.\mu\,(\,o\,) \nless \text{SBCL}.\theta\,(\,\text{P}\,),$$
$$\blacksquare_2 \qquad 1 - \text{SBCL}.\mu\,(\,o\,) \nless \min\,\{\,a \mid a \in \text{SBCL}.\Theta\,(\,\text{P}\,)\,\}.$$

However, when $o$ is considered as a (fuzzy) member of CL, P may necessarily be defined for $o$, if :

$$\blacksquare_1 \qquad 1 - \text{CL}.\mu\,(\,o\,) < \text{CL}.\theta\,(\,\text{P}\,),$$
$$\blacksquare_2 \qquad 1 - \text{CL}.\mu\,(\,o\,) < \min\,\{\,a \mid a \in \text{CL}.\Theta\,(\,\text{P}\,)\,\}.$$

The property P then is applicable for $o$, in a degree determined by :

$$\blacksquare_1 \qquad o.\tau.\text{MU}\,(\,\text{P}\,) \geq \text{CL}.\theta\,(\,\text{P}\,),$$
$$\blacksquare_2 \qquad o.\tau.\text{MU}\,(\,\text{P}\,) \in \text{CL}.\Theta\,(\,\text{P}\,).$$

The degree of applicability therefore is not determined by SBCL, so it may be that :

$$\blacksquare_1 \qquad o.\tau.\text{MU}\,(\,\text{P}\,) \ngeq \text{SBCL}.\theta\,(\,\text{P}\,),$$
$$\blacksquare_2 \qquad o.\tau.\text{MU}\,(\,\text{P}\,) \notin \text{SBCL}.\Theta\,(\,\text{P}\,).$$

For example, assume that faculty members (i.e. researchers, professors, ...) of the university *Univ*, modelled by a subclass FACMEMBER of PERSON, show a minimum ability to do research and write scientific papers (which is not necessarily required for all part-time faculty members) : $\text{FACMEMBER}.\theta\,(\,\text{WRITE-PAPER}\,(\,)\,) = 0.4$, and that a higher ability to do so is required for tenure, modelled by a subclass TENURE of FACMEMBER with $\text{TENURE}.\theta\,(\,\text{WRITE-PAPER}\,(\,)\,) = 0.6$. Suppose now that *John* is a part time faculty member, whose position is defined as 30% employee in industry, 40% researcher with a grant from the National Fund and 30% tenure :

$\text{FACMEMBER}.\mu\,(\,John\,) = 0.7$ and $\text{TENURE}.\mu\,(\,John\,) = 0.3$.

Then, by default, the method WRITE-PAPER ( ) would not necessarily be applicable for the fuzzy member *John* of TENURE, because :

$1 - \text{TENURE}.\mu\,(\,John\,) = 0.7$,

$\text{TENURE}.\theta\,(\,\text{WRITE-PAPER}\,(\,)\,) = 0.6 \qquad$ and $0.7 \nless 0.6$, but it is applicable, because *John* is a fuzzy member of FacMember in a sufficient degree:

$1$ - FacMember.$\mu$ ( *John* ) = 0.3,

FacMember.$\theta$ ( write-paper ( ) ) = 0.4     and 0.3 < 0.4.

The method write-paper ( ) therefore is applicable for *John*, with :

*John*.$\tau$.MU ( write-paper ( ) ) $\geq$ 0.4.     ■

If within a database scheme, the domain of an attribute is defined as the $\alpha$-cut of the maximal extent of a fuzzy class CL, i.e. the domain D equals CL.max-extent.cut ( $\alpha$ ), then only the "core" required properties for this $\alpha$-cut are necessarily defined for this domain, i.e. the required properties, defined by CL, for which :

■$_1$     $1 - \alpha$ < CL.$\theta$ ( P ),

■$_2$     $1 - \alpha$ < min { a | a $\in$ CL.$\Theta$ ( P ) }.

The other properties, defined by CL, are considered optional for the domain.

### 3.4  Fuzzy Inheritance

The way in which a fuzzy classification of objects is handled in the UFO database model, leads the way to define a fuzzy classification of the classes within the subclass-superclass hierarchy, i.e. to define a fuzzy inheritance relationship between classes. Multiple inheritance is assumed here, which means that a class may have several superclasses (i.e. for each class CL, CL.super is not restricted to be a singleton).

A fuzzy inheritance relationship between classes is defined to overcome the rigidness of the inheritance hierarchy in an OODBM, as a fuzzy inheritance hierarchy allows the flexible modelling of fuzzy extensions of both crisp and fuzzy notions. However, the principle that a subclass inherits and specializes the structure and the behaviour defined by the superclass, remains essential in the UFO database model : although this principle is fuzzified for a fuzzy inheritance relationship - such that only a "core" part of the structure and the behaviour defined by the superclass CL in the fuzzy inheritance relationship, is inherited by the subclass SbCL - care is taken that the proposed fuzzy inheritance relationship does not allow the definition of a "subclass" SbCL which, semantically, should be a superclass of CL.

A fuzzy inheritance relationship between a "subclass" SbCL and a "superclass" CL is denoted by : SbCL $\tilde{\prec}$ CL.

In the simplest case of fuzzy inheritance, a "subclass" SbCL defines an extended (possibly fuzzy) boundary of a crisp notion, which is modelled by a "crisp" class CL. The boundary is called "extended", because it is not necessarily included within the crisp notion. This is useful, for instance, when a legal concept is defined more strictly than its commonly accepted counterpart, and when the latter is generally treated the same as the former. The legal concept then is modelled by CL, its commonly accepted extended (fuzzy) boundary by SBCL.

The objects which belong to the extended boundary of CL, are defined by SBCL and are fuzzy members of CL. The method that returns the inheritance degree is fuzzified, so that for fuzzy inheritance : $0 < $ SBCL.í ( CL ) $ < 1$. A fuzzy inheritance degree defines an upper limit for the membership degree of every SBCL-object $o$ in CL :

$$\text{CL.}\mu\ (\ o\ ) = \min\ \{\ \text{SBCL.í} (\ \text{CL}\ ), \text{SBCL.}\mu\ (\ o\ )\ \},$$

prohibiting the "subclass" SBCL from creating full members of CL. All SBCL-objects only partially comply with the definition of "CL-objects"; this type of inheritance is therefore also called *partial inheritance*. Partial inheritance also means that only the "core" required properties, defined by CL, are inherited as required properties by SBCL. For the "subclass" SBCL, the "core" required properties, defined by CL with $0 < $ SBCL.í ( CL ) $ < 1$, are the required (possibly fuzzy) properties P, defined by CL, for which :

$$\blacksquare_1 \qquad 1 - \text{SBCL.í} (\ \text{CL}\ ) < \text{CL.}\theta\ (\ \text{P}\ ),$$

$$\blacksquare_2 \qquad 1 - \text{SBCL.í} (\ \text{CL}\ ) < \min\ \{\ a\ |\ a \in \text{CL.}\Theta(\ \text{P}\ )\ \}.$$

They are inherited by SBCL with the same restrictions on possible degrees of applicability as defined by CL. The other properties are inherited as optional properties by SBCL. However, if a property, defined by CL, is redefined or specialized by SBCL, it is considered in the same way as a specific property defined by SBCL; the fuzzy inheritance degree then is not taken into account when deciding whether or not the property is applicable for a SBCL-object.

Similar to the fact that not all of the required attributes and methods defined by CL are required by SBCL, not all of the constraint properties defined by CL are necessarily satisfied by SBCL-objects, because SBCL only defines fuzzy members of CL. However, since SBCL defines a fuzzy boundary for the notion modelled by CL, SBCL-objects satisfy constraints referring to boundary areas of relaxed constraint properties. [Van Gyseghem & De Caluwe, 1996].

The "set" of immediate superclasses of SBCL now is a *"conditional" set* of superclasses, i.e. a set of which the elements are classes with which the inheritance degrees are associated as a "condition" : SBCL.SUPER = { SBCL.í ( CL ) / CL, ... }, resembling a fuzzy set of classes, in which the membership degrees represent the inheritance degrees. If

SBCL is a fuzzy class, SBCL.SUPER should be normalized (i.e. at least one "crisp" or full inheritance is to be defined), in order for the fuzzy members of SBCL to have a unimodal fuzzy set of immediate classes.

Also, with partial inheritance, CL.EXTENT is a "crisp" set of objects, because CL is a crisp class, while CL.MAX-EXTENT is a fuzzy set of objects, because of the fuzzy inheritance.

For example, the concept "adult" may (in some countries) legally be defined as a person of over 21 years old. To model adults, a class ADULT is defined as a (crisp) subclass of PERSON with the additional constraint : "AGE $\geq$ 21". More commonly, however, people of "almost 21 years old", are also considered adults (to some degree). This is modelled by the class ALMOST21, which is a subclass of ADULT with inheritance degree ALMOST21.$\mathfrak{i}$ ( ADULT ) < 1, so that :

ALMOST21.SUPER = { 1 / PERSON, ALMOST21.$\mathfrak{i}$ ( ADULT ) / ADULT ) }.

Instead of inheriting the constraint property from the "superclass" ADULT, ALMOST21 defines a constraint property referring to its extended fuzzy boundary area :

"*almost21* ( AGES ).MU ( AGE ) > 0",

in which *almost21* ( AGES ) is a fuzzy set representing the ages that are considered as "almost 21 years". (Figure 4) An instance of ALMOST21 is a fuzzy member of ADULT with membership degree equal to : ALMOST21.$\mathfrak{i}$ ( ADULT ); a fuzzy instance $o$ of ALMOST21, with instance degree defined by :

ALMOST21.$\mathfrak{\iota}$ ( $o$ ) = *almost21* ( AGES ).MU ( $o$.AGE ),

is also a fuzzy member of ADULT, but with membership degree equal to :

min { ALMOST21.$\mathfrak{i}$ ( ADULT ), ALMOST21.$\mathfrak{\iota}$ ( $o$ ) }. ■

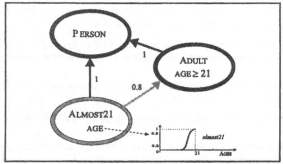

Figure 4: Fuzzy inheritance between ALMOST21 and ADULT.

The simplest case of fuzzy inheritance as explained here, only handles partial inheritance from a crisp superclass. When the superclass CL is a fuzzy class, or when determining the membership degree of SBCL-objects in CL is more complex, the method which defines the inheritance degree, is redefined to return, for each SBCL-object $o$, its membership degree in CL. The extended inheritance method is invoked by the message: SBCL.í ( CL, $o$ ), taking the SBCL-object $o$ into account, such that :

$$\text{CL.}\mu\,(\,o\,) = \text{SBCL.í}\,(\,\text{CL}, o\,).$$

The "subclass" SBCL models an extended (possibly fuzzy) boundary for the (possibly fuzzy) notion modelled by the (possibly fuzzy) class CL. Note that such fuzzy inheritance allows the creation of SBCL-objects that are full members of CL, and of SBCL-objects of which the membership degree in SBCL is greater than the membership degree in CL.

All required properties, defined by CL, are "conditionally" inherited by SBCL, which means that these properties are not necessarily applicable for all SBCL-objects; this type of inheritance therefore is also called *conditional inheritance*. The extended inheritance method determines for each SBCL-object $o$ which properties P of the "conditionally" inherited required properties, defined by CL, are "core" required properties for $o$, and thus are necessarily applicable for $o$ :

- if P is redefined or specialized by SBCL, P is considered in the same way as specific properties defined by SBCL, and thus is necessarily applicable if :
    - $\blacksquare_1$      $1 - \text{SBCL.}\mu\,(\,o\,) < \text{SBCL.}\theta\,(\,\text{P}\,)$,
    - $\blacksquare_2$      $1 - \text{SBCL.}\mu\,(\,o\,) < \min\,\{\,a \mid a \in \text{SBCL.}\Theta\,(\,\text{P}\,)\,\}$.

- otherwise, P is necessarily applicable if :
    - $\blacksquare_1$      $1 - \text{SBCL.í}\,(\,\text{CL}, o\,) < \text{CL.}\theta\,(\,\text{P}\,)$,
    - $\blacksquare_2$      $1 - \text{SBCL.í}\,(\,\text{CL}, o\,) < \min\,\{\,a \mid a \in \text{CL.}\Theta\,(\,\text{P}\,)\,\}$.

The other properties are considered optional for $o$.

Partial inheritance is a special case of conditional inheritance : both the inheritance method and the "core" required properties are then independent of the considered SBCL-object.

Since, with conditional inheritance, SBCL defines an extended fuzzy boundary for the (fuzzy) notion modelled by CL, SBCL-objects do not necessarily satisfy the (possibly fuzzy) constraints defined by CL, but satisfy constraints referring to boundary areas of relaxed constraint properties.

Also with conditional inheritance, CL.MAX-EXTENT is a fuzzy set of objects and SBCL.SUPER is a "conditional" set of classes, associating the extended inheritance method with the classes. When SBCL is a fuzzy class, at least one "crisp" inheritance is to be defined for it, in order for the fuzzy members of SBCL to have a unimodal fuzzy set of immediate classes; when CL is a fuzzy class, then CL.EXTENT is also a fuzzy set of objects.

For example, the crisp class 18TO24YEAROLD defines objects which either are full members of ADULT, or partially belong to an extended fuzzy boundary of ADULT (such as the fuzzy boundary defined by "*almost21* ( AGES ).MU ( AGE ) > 0"). The class 18TO24YEAROLD is a subclass of ADULT by conditional inheritance, with extended inheritance method 18TO24YEAROLD.í ( ADULT, $o$ ), which returns, for each 18TO24YEAROLD-object $o$, its membership degree in ADULT :

$$\text{ADULT.}\mu ( o ) = 18\text{TO24YEAROLD.í ( ADULT, } o )$$
$$= {\geq}almost21 ( \text{AGES} ).\text{MU} ( o.\text{AGE} ),$$

in which $\geq almost21$ ( AGES ) is a fuzzy set, representing the ages which are considered as "greater than or equal to almost 21 years".

Instead of inheriting the constraint property "AGE $\geq$ 21" from the "superclass" ADULT, 18TO24YEAROLDdefines a constraint property referring to its extended, but crisp boundary area : "18 $\leq$ AGE $\leq$ 24". Both ADULT.EXTENT and 18TO24YEAROLD.EXTENT are crisp sets of objects, but ADULT.MAX-EXTENT is a fuzzy set of objects.  ∎

### 3.5 Summary of the "Fuzziness Part" of the UFO Database Model

The previous sections gave a detailed overview of the fuzziness part of the UFO database model. They discussed fuzzifications of object-oriented concepts at several layers of the model :

- Properties : attributes (multivalued and single-valued) and methods
  The value of a "semantically fuzzy" multivalued attribute is a fuzzy set, i.e. an object of a class instantiation of the introduced generic class FUZZYSET. A fuzzy value of a multivalued attribute usually expresses a fuzzy relationship with a number of (literal or non-literal) objects. Messages sent to a fuzzy set of objects, instead of to a single object, are forwarded to the members of the fuzzy set with an associated non-zero membership degree; the invoked methods may show fuzzy side-effects, depending on the membership degree of each object addressed.
  The "semantically fuzzy" applicability of a property for an object is expressed by a degree of applicability, for which thresholds are defined in the class. The structure and

behaviour of an object therefore is described by a fuzzy set of properties. The degree of applicability leads to the definition of optional and required properties and to the soft modelling of database applications. A "fuzzy" single-valued attribute usually expresses a fuzzy relationship with another (literal or non-literal) object; a "fuzzy" method expresses a behaviour that is not a constant over all objects of the class.

- Objects :
  The classification of an object may be "fuzzy", which means that the object may be a fuzzy (partial) instance of several classes. Its "immediate class" is a unimodal fuzzy set of classes; the classes involved have fuzzy sets of objects as extent and/or maximal extent, and are called fuzzy classes. A fuzzy instance is partially defined by the involved fuzzy classes, and the applicability of a property, defined by such a class, for the fuzzy instance, depends on the membership degree of the fuzzy instance in the fuzzy class.

- Classes :
  The inheritance relationship between classes may be fuzzified, allowing partial or conditional inheritance, defined by an extended inheritance method. A class therefore may have a fuzzy set of immediate superclasses. Objects of a "subclass in a fuzzy inheritance relationship" belong to a (possibly fuzzy) extended boundary of the notion described by the "superclass in the fuzzy inheritance relationship", and therefore may be a member of the "superclass" in a lesser degree than of the "subclass".

## 4 The "Uncertainty Part" of the UFO Database Model

In this section, the UFO database model, as described thus far, is further extended to allow for the processing and recording of imprecise and uncertain information, whether or not this information is intrinsically vague. The UFO database model uses the possibility theory to model such information. At first, only crisp information is assumed, but later on, the introduced procedures for handling imprecision and uncertainty are also applied for vague information that can be represented in the UFO database model.

Imprecise and uncertain information may be found at all layers of the OODBM, when there exists a lack of full knowledge about the data or about the database application itself. It is described by a possibility distribution, which represents all possible alternatives corresponding with the information. The UFO database model aims at handling imprecision and uncertainty in a, to the user, implicit and transparent way, not requiring a special treatment at the database scheme level. To this end, additional role objects are introduced in the UFO database model to model uncertain roles and tentative behaviour caused by the imprecision and uncertainty.

The extensions necessary to handle imprecision and uncertainty, are summarized in Table 2, and discussed in detail in the next subsections :

Table 2: The "uncertainty part" of the UFO database model.

| 1. a. uncertain literal attribute values<br>b. uncertain non-literal attribute values | 3. a. hypothetic modelling<br>b. uncertain properties |
|---|---|
| 2. a. uncertain applicability of properties<br>b. uncertain instances | 4. uncertain inheritance |

### 4.1 Uncertain and Imprecise Attribute Values

This section discusses how imprecise or uncertain data about objects is modelled in the UFO database model. As "crisp" or "fuzzy" data about an object is modelled by the "crisp" or "fuzzy" values of the attributes defined for the object, imprecise or uncertain data about an object is modelled by imprecise or uncertain values of the attributes defined for the object, such as the imprecisely given age of "about 30", or the uncertain age "30 or 31" or the not exactly known spouse "probably *Jane*, but maybe *Susan* or *Lucy*".

Uncertain and imprecise values are modelled by the generic system class POSS : by supplying a class CL as an argument, a new class POSS ( CL ) is instantiated, which models possibility distributions of CL-objects.

For example, the imprecisely given age of the PERSON-object *Jane*, modelled by *Jane*.AGE, is a POSS ( AGES )-object, representing the possibility distribution "about 33 years old", which is named *about-33* and derived from the fuzzy set *about-33* ( AGES ); the possibility degrees express the degree with which the actual value *Jane*.AGE, if it were exactly known, equals the considered AGES-objects. Similarly, the value *John*.SPOUSE is not exactly known for the PERSON-object *John*; it is a POSS ( PERSON )-object *pd1*, representing the possibility distribution : (Figure 5)

$\{ 1 / Jane, 0.5 / Susan, 0.4 / Lucy \}_{\pi}$. ∎

If the domain of an attribute is defined as the maximal extent of a class CL, then its value is restricted to be a CL-object, even when this value is not yet exactly or certainly known. To keep transparency, if an uncertain or imprecise attribute value is given as a "possibility distribution of CL-objects", this value should also be a CL-object. Therefore, each class instantiation POSS ( CL ) is defined as a subclass of the parameter class CL (with "crisp" inheritance), and thus defines members of CL. This allows any attribute to take an imperfect value, without needing to change the original (crisp) database scheme of the application.

The special subclasses for possibility distributions also make modelling higher level possibility distributions (i.e. possibility distributions of possibility distributions) very easy : because instances of POSS ( CL ) are members of CL, a "possibility distribution of CL-objects" in turn is also a member of CL, and thus a CL-object.

For example, if *Jane*.AGE = *about-33*, *Susan*.AGE = *30or31*, and *Lucy*.AGE = *young*, where *about-33*, *30or31* and *young* are POSS ( AGES )-objects, then the value *John*.SPOUSE.AGE is also a POSS ( AGES )-object, representing the higher level possibility distribution :
{ 1 / *about-33*, 0.5 / *30or31*, 0.4 / *young* }$_\pi$.                                    ∎

The specific methods, defined by the generic class POSS (CLASS C), are, to mention a few :
■ methods defined for parameter classes of either literal or non-literal objects, e.g. :
    ■ CREATE-ITERATOR ( *stable*:BOOLEAN ) → *y*:ITERATOR

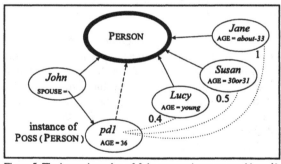

Figure 5: The imprecise value of *John*.SPOUSE is represented by *pd1*.

Defines an iterator over the POSS-object.

- PI ( $o$:C ) → p:UNITINTERVAL

  Returns the possibility degree of the object $o$ in the POSS-object.

- methods defined only for parameter classes of non-literal objects, e.g. :

  - CHANGE-PI ( $o$:C, p:UNITINTERVAL )

    Replaces the possibility degree of the object $o$ in the POSS-object by p.

  - DEFUZ ( $o$:C )

    Replaces all references within the database to the POSS-object by the (certain) object $o$, and removes the POSS-object from the database.

An extended iterator, similar to the one described in Sec. 2, is defined by the generic class POSS, to allow an "element by element" execution of methods invoked on a POSS-object, following the extension principle of Zadeh : when receiving a message, the iterator iterates over all objects that have a non-zero possibility degree in the POSS-object, forwards the message to each of these objects, and groups the resulting objects in a new possibility distribution. Formally, a message $pd$.M ( $x$, ... ), sent to a POSS ( CL )-object $pd$ to invoke the method M, which is defined by CL with the signature M ( $x$:CLX, ... ) → $y$:CLY, is forwarded to the CL-objects $o$ that have a non-zero possibility degree in $pd$, and results in a POSS ( CLY )-object $pdy$ which associates the following possibility degree with each CLY-object $y$ (which, in turn, may actually be a POSS ( CLY )-object ) :

$$pdy.\text{PI} \ ( y ) = \max \{ \ pd.\text{PI} \ ( o ) \ | \ \forall \ \text{CL-object} \ o, \ pd.\text{PI} \ ( o ) > 0 : o.\text{M} \ ( x, ... ) = y \ \}$$

i.e. a CLY-object $y$ has a non-zero possibility degree in $pdy$ if $y$ is returned as a result of an invocation of M on a CL-object $o$, which has a non-zero possibility degree in the possibility distribution $pd$.

When receiving a message in which the arguments of the method M are also POSS-objects, the iterator also iterates over all objects that have a non-zero possibility degree in the POSS-object, but forwards "crisp submessages" to each of these objects, and groups the resulting objects in a new possibility distribution, according to the extension principle of Zadeh. Formally, for a message $pd$.M ( $pdx$, ... ), sent to a POSS ( CL )-object $pd$ to invoke the method M, which is defined by CL with the signature M ( $x$:CLX, ... ) → $y$:CLY, several "submessages" $o$.M ( $x$, ... ) are sent to the CL-objects $o$ that have a non-zero possibility degree in $pd$, one message for each combination of CLX-objects $x$ that have a non-zero possibility degree in $pdx$, ... It results in a POSS ( CLY )-object $pdy$ which associates the following possibility degree with each CLY-object $y$ : [Van Gyseghem & De Caluwe, 1996b]

$$pdy.\text{PI} ( y ) = \max \{ \min \{ pd.\text{PI} ( o ), pdx.\text{PI} ( x ), \dots \} \mid$$
$$\forall \text{ CL-object } o, \forall \text{ CLX-object } x,$$
$$pd.\text{PI} ( o ) > 0, \ pdx.\text{PI} ( x ) > 0, \dots : o.\text{M} ( x, \dots ) = y \}.$$

The different nature of accessor methods and transformation methods induces a different further modelling of possibility distributions of literal objects and of possibility distributions of non-literal objects. For modelling possibility distributions of literal objects, the modelling is complete at this point.

### 4.2 Uncertain Non-Literal Attribute Values

The previous section completely discussed the modelling of uncertain and imprecise literal attribute values. Uncertain and imprecise non-literal values are also modelled as possibility distributions, by means of the generic class POSS. However, for modelling possibility distributions of non-literal objects, uncertain invocations of transformation methods need to be accounted for : if a non-literal object $o$ occurs in an uncertain or imprecise context, such as described by a POSS-object $pd$, the modifications, made as a result of the invocation of a transformation method M on $o$ by the iterator over $pd$, are also uncertain. The object $o$ appears here in an uncertain role, created by the uncertain context, and the behaviour invoked within the uncertain context should only be a tentative behaviour.

An uncertain role of a CL-object $o$ is modelled in the UFO database model by means of one or more *role objects*, which are created by the POSS-object $pd$ and associated with $o$, and in which the uncertain modifications of the internal state of $o$ are made. Role objects are modelled by a generic system class ROLE : by supplying a class CL as an argument, a new class ROLE ( CL ) is instantiated, which models role objects associated with CL-objects. Each class instantiation ROLE ( CL ) is defined as a subclass of CL, so that the structure and behaviour defined by CL are inherited by ROLE ( CL ). Each role object associated with $o$ therefore is a perfect reflection of $o$ in an uncertain context.

The role objects created by different POSS-objects and associated with $o$, called the *main object* of the role objects, follow $o$ like shadows, that are created by different light sources :
- role objects reflect the main object in an uncertain context,
- a change in the main object affects the role objects (but not the other way around),
- different POSS-objects create different role objects, and

■ different POSS-objects have a combined effect on the role objects associated with $o$.

As role objects are reflections of the main object they are associated with, changes made to the internal state of $o$, should also be reflected in its associated role objects : whenever a message is sent to $o$, and the message is not sent from within an uncertain context, the message invokes a method on $o$, and is forwarded to all role objects associated with $o$, invoking the same method on the role objects. However, tentative behaviour is not to affect the main object $o$ itself, but is only to affect the role objects that are created by the uncertain context that invoked the tentative behaviour : a message sent from within an uncertain context, such as from a POSS-object $pd$, is not sent to $o$ itself, but is sent to the role objects that were created by $pd$ and associated with $o$. Therefore, for every class CL of non-literal objects, a possibility distribution of CL-objects actually is modelled by the system class POSS ( ROLE ( CL ) ). The POSS-object $pd$ that models this possibility distribution then actually is an instance of POSS ( ROLE ( CL ) ); $pd$ creates ROLE ( CL )-objects and associates the corresponding possibility degrees with the role objects (instead of with the main objects).

When a CL-object $o$ is referenced from within several uncertain contexts, $o$ appears in several uncertain roles, which are not necessarily mutual exclusive and which therefore may influence each other. The combined effect of different uncertain roles of one main object $o$ is also modelled by role objects. The role objects that model only one uncertain role are called *direct* role objects, the ones that model combinations of uncertain roles are called *further* role objects. In this way, a hypercube of role objects is created and associated with $o$. Each new uncertain role defines a new dimension in this hypercube of role objects : it creates one new direct role object to model the new uncertain role, and, for each already existing role object associated with $o$, one new further role object to model the combined effects with other uncertain roles.

To tie together the role objects associated with $o$, the following attributes are defined by each class instantiation ROLE ( CL ) :

■ the optional attribute MAIN-OBJ, with domain defined as the extent of the parameter class CL. The attribute is defined for every direct role object $o$-$dr$ and its value is the main object $o$, which $o$-$dr$ is associated with. This attribute is not defined for further role objects.

■ the attribute MAIN-ROLES, with domain defined as the maximal extent of the class SET ( ROLE ( CL ) ). For a direct role object $o$-$dr$, its value is the singleton { $o$-$dr$ }. The combined effect of several uncertain roles, each of them modelled by the direct role objects { $o$-$dr$, ... }, is modelled by a further role object $o$-$fr$, which is said to *depend* on each of the involved direct role objects *o-dr*. For a further role object, the value *o-fr*.MAIN-ROLES is the non-empty set of direct role objects that *o-fr* depends on : { *o-dr*, ... }.

To link the direct role objects to their main object *o*, an additional system attribute ROLES is defined by each non-literal class CL appearing within the database scheme (but not for the system class ROLE). Its value *o*.ROLES represents a (not necessarily normalized) possibility distribution of direct ROLE ( CL )-objects, in which the possibility degree associated with a direct role object *o-r*, created by the POSS-object *pd*, equals the possibility degree associated with *o-r* by *pd*. The value *o*.ROLES is not necessarily normalized, because it may be happen that, in the end, when all uncertainty is resolved, none of the uncertain roles in which *o* appears, correspond with reality.

The following methods are also defined by every class instantiation POSS ( ROLE ( CL ) ) :

- CREATE-DIRECT ( *o*:CL, p:UNITINTERVAL ) → *o-dr*:ROLE ( CL )

    Creates an uncertain role of *o*. The method creates one new direct role object *o-dr*,
    with :     *o-dr*.MAIN-OBJ = *o*,

              *o-dr*.MAIN-ROLES = { *o-dr* },

              *o-dr* copies the internal state of *o*,

    and associates possibility degree p with it :

              *o*.ROLES.CHANGE-PI ( *o-dr*, p )

    For each ROLE ( CL )-object *o-r*, not having *o-dr* as an element of *o-r*.MAIN-ROLES, the method also creates a new further role object *o-fr*, with :

              *o-fr*.MAIN-OBJ is not defined,

              *o-fr*.MAIN-ROLES = *o-r*.MAIN-ROLES ∪ { *o-dr* }, and

              *o-fr* copies the internal state of *o-r*.

- DEL-DIRECT ( *o-dr*:ROLE ( CL ) )

    Removes an uncertain role of *o*. This method removes the direct role object *o-dr*, originally associated with *o* by the POSS-object, and all further role objects *o-fr* having *o-dr* as an element of *o-fr*.MAIN-ROLES.

- MERGE ( *o*:CL, *o-dr*:ROLE ( CL ) ) → *o*:CL

    Merges *o* with its uncertain role *o-dr*. This method is invoked when the POSS-object is certainly to be replaced by *o*. It deletes all further role objects *o-fr*, associated with *o*, that do not have *o-dr* as an element of *o-fr*.MAIN-ROLES; *o* copies the internal state of *o-dr*, and *o-dr* is deleted.

The methods are outlined in [Van Gyseghem & De Caluwe, 1996b]. When a POSS-object *pd* receives a message to invoke a method defined by CL, the iterator, defined by each class instantiation POSS ( ROLE ( CL ) ), iterates over the direct role objects *o1-dr*, *o2-dr*, ... that have a non-zero possibility degree associated with by *pd*, and forwards the message to all ROLE ( CL )-objects *o-r* for which *o1-dr* or *o2-dr* or ... is an element of *o-r*.MAIN-ROLES. In this way, the tentative behaviour invoked by *pd* is reflected in all role objects that model the uncertain role given by *pd*.

Message handling is also extended to account for uncertain roles of objects : every message sent to a CL-object *o*, is automatically forwarded to the POSS-object *o*.ROLES. The iterator then iterates over the direct role objects *o-dr1*, *o-dr2*, ... that have a non-zero possibility degree associated with by *o*.ROLES, and forwards the message to all ROLE ( CL )-objects *o-r* for which *o-dr1* or *o-dr2* or ... is an element of *o-r*.MAIN-ROLES, so that the certain behaviour of *o* is reflected in all role objects associated with *o*, and thus in all uncertain roles of *o*.

For example, assume that the value *John*.SPOUSE is not exactly known for the PERSON-object *John*; it is assigned a POSS ( PERSON )-object, *pd1*, modelling the possibility distribution { 1 / *Jane*, 0.5 / *Susan*, 0.4 / *Lucy* }$_\pi$. Because of this uncertain context, the PERSON-objects *Jane*, *Susan* and *Lucy* appear in an uncertain role, and the following messages are sent :

*pd1*.CREATE-DIRECT ( *Jane*, 1 ), creating the ROLE ( PERSON )-object *Jane-1*, with :
    *Jane-1* copies the internal state of *Jane*,
    *Jane-1*.MAIN-OBJ = *Jane*,
    *Jane-1*.MAIN-ROLES = { *Jane-1* }, and
    *Jane*.ROLES = { 1 / *Jane-1* }$_\pi$ ;
*pd1*.CREATE-DIRECT ( *Susan*, 0.5 ), creating the ROLE ( PERSON )-object *Susan-1*, with :
    *Susan-1* copies the internal state of *Susan*,
    *Susan-1*.MAIN-OBJ = *Susan*,
    *Susan-1*.MAIN-ROLES = { *Susan-1* }, and
    *Susan*.ROLES = { 0.5 / *Susan-1* }$_\pi$ ;
*pd1*.CREATE-DIRECT ( *Lucy*, 0.4 ), creating the ROLE ( PERSON )-object *Lucy-1*, with :
    *Lucy-1* copies the internal state of *Lucy*,
    *Lucy-1*.MAIN-OBJ = *Lucy*,
    *Lucy-1*.MAIN-ROLES = { *Lucy-1* }, and
    *Lucy*.ROLES = { 0.4 / *Lucy-1* }$_\pi$ .

The POSS-object *pd1* actually represents { 1 / *Jane-1*, 0.5 / *Susan-1*, 0.4 / *Lucy-1* }$_\pi$ .

The message *Jane*.ADD-AGE ( 5 ), to (certainly) add 5 years to the age of *Jane*, results in changing the value *Jane*.AGE, and is forwarded to all ROLE ( PERSON )-objects having *Jane* as main object, i.e. the message *Jane-1*.ADD-AGE ( 5 ) is sent, resulting in changing the value *Jane-1*.AGE. When a similar message is sent to an uncertain value, for instance when the message *John*.SPOUSE.ADD-AGE ( 5 ) is sent, the iterator defined for the POSS-object *pd1* (representing *John*.SPOUSE ) takes care of this tentative behaviour, and sends the following messages :

*Jane-1*.ADD-AGE ( 5 ), *Susan-1*.ADD-AGE ( 5 ), and *Lucy-1*.ADD-AGE ( 5 ),

changing the values *Jane-1*.AGE, *Susan-1*.AGE, and *Lucy-1*.AGE only.

Assume now that the uncertain value of *Maria*.MOTHER is modelled by a POSS ( PERSON )-object *pd2*, which models the possibility distribution :

{ 1 / *Beth*, 0.8 / *Jane* }$_\pi$.

The messages *pd2*.CREATE-DIRECT ( *Beth*, 1 ) and *pd2*.CREATE-DIRECT ( *Jane*, 0.8 ) are then sent. For the object *Jane*, this results in the creation of two ROLE ( PERSON )-objects *Jane-2* and *Jane-1-2*, with :

*Jane-2* is a direct role object; it copies the internal state of *Jane*,

*Jane-2*.MAIN-OBJ = *Jane*,

*Jane-2*.MAIN-ROLES = { *Jane-2* };

*Jane*.ROLES = { 1 / *Jane-1*, 0.8 / *Jane-2* }$_\pi$ ;

*Jane-1-2* is a further role object; it copies the internal state of *Jane-1*,

*Jane-1-2*.MAIN-OBJ = *Jane*,

*Jane-1-2*.MAIN-ROLES = { *Jane-1*, *Jane-2* }.

The POSS-object *pd2* actually represents { 1 / *Beth-2*, 0.8 / *Jane-2* }$_\pi$ .

The message *Jane*.ADD-AGE ( 5 ) still results in changing the value *Jane*.AGE, and is forwarded to *Jane*.ROLES; the iterator then sends the messages :

*Jane-1*.ADD-AGE ( 5 ), *Jane-2*.ADD-AGE ( 5 ) and *Jane-1-2*.ADD-AGE ( 5 )

(because *Jane-1*, *Jane-2* and *Jane-1-2* have *Jane-1* or *Jane-2* as element of the value of their attribute MAIN-ROLES), resulting in changing the values *Jane-1*.AGE, *Jane-2*.AGE and *Jane-1-2*.AGE.

Similarly, when receiving a message *John*.SPOUSE.ADD-AGE ( 5 ), the iterator defined for the POSS-object *pd1* now sends the messages :

*Jane-1*.ADD-AGE ( 5 ), *Jane-1-2*.ADD-AGE ( 5 ),

*Susan-1*.ADD-AGE ( 5 ), and *Lucy-1*.ADD-AGE ( 5 )

(because *Jane-1*, *Jane-1-2*, *Susan-1* and *Lucy-1* have *Jane-1* or *Susan-1* or *Lucy-1* as element of the value of their attribute MAIN-ROLES), changing the values *Jane-1*.AGE, *Jane-1-2*.AGE, *Susan-1*.AGE, and *Lucy-1*.AGE.

Assume then that the value *Alice*.MOTHER equals the uncertain value *John*.SPOUSE. The object *Jane* is then seen by the object *Alice* within the same (uncertain) context as by the object *John*. No new uncertain role is imposed here and, therefore, no new role objects are created.

Figure 6 shows the result of adding a third uncertain role to the object *Jane*; it is created from an uncertain context given by a POSS ( PERSON )-object *pd3*, which associates the possibility degree 0.4 with *Jane*. The uncertain role is added by sending the message *pd3*.CREATE-DIRECT ( *Jane*, 0.4 ).

Figure 7 shows the result of merging the third uncertain role of *Jane* with the object *Jane*. This happens when additional information in the database application states that *pd3* certainly corresponds with *Jane*. The corresponding message *pd3*.MERGE ( *Jane*, *Jane-3* ) has the following effect :

- all further role objects *Jane-r*, having *Jane-1* or *Jane-2* as element of *Jane-r*.MAIN-ROLES, but not having *Jane-3* as element of *Jane-r*.MAIN-ROLES, are deleted.
- *Jane-1* copies the internal state of *Jane-1-3* (i.e. the further role object for which :
    *Jane-1-3*.MAIN-ROLES = { *Jane-1*, *Jane-3* }.)
  Similarly for *Jane-2* and *Jane-2-3*.
- *Jane-1-3* and *Jane-2-3* are deleted.
- for the remaining further role objects *Jane-r-3* having *Jane-3* as element of *Jane-r-3*.MAIN-ROLES, the direct role object *Jane-3* is removed from *Jane-r-3*.MAIN-ROLES.
- *Jane* copies the internal state of *Jane-3*
- *Jane-3* is deleted.                                                                      ■

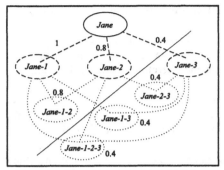

Figure 6: *pd3* creates an uncertain role of *Jane*.

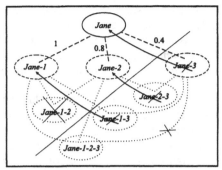

Figure 7: Merging the uncertain role *Jane-3* with *Jane*.

The methods CREATE-DIRECT, DEL-DIRECT and MERGE are outlined in [Van Gyseghem & De Caluwe, 1996b]. To analyze their complexity, suppose that the hypercube of role objects associated with $o$ contains a total of $n = 2^m-1$ role objects, i.e. m direct role objects and n-m further role objects. Then :

- CREATE-DIRECT creates n+1 new role objects, i.e. one direct role object and $n = 2^m-1$ further role objects. This exponential increase in the number of role objects does not necessarily have a permanent effect, because uncertain roles are removed when uncertain information is replaced with certain information.
- DEL-DIRECT deletes $(n+1)/2 = 2^{m-1}$ role objects, i.e. one direct role object and $(n-1)/2 = 2^{m-1}-1$ further role objects; $(n-1)/2 = 2^{m-1}-1$ role objects remain in the hypercube.
- MERGE also deletes $(n+1)/2 = 2^{m-1}$ role objects, i.e. one direct role object and $(n-1)/2 = 2^{m-1}-1$ further role objects; $(n-1)/2 = 2^{m-1}-1$ role objects remain in the hypercube.

Of course, these methods can be optimized, for instance, by only creating role objects when a modification of the internal state is actually requested by a POSS-object.

POSS-objects themselves can also appear in an uncertain role, created by an uncertain context. When this happens, higher level possibility distributions of non-literal objects are to be modelled. This is also done using the concept of role objects, which, in this case, are associated with POSS-objects : the generic class ROLE accepts a class instantiation POSS ( CL ) as argument for its class parameter, defining class instantiations ROLE ( POSS ( CL ) ).

Formally, if *pd* is a POSS-object *pd*, which models the possibility distribution { p / *o*,

... $\}_\pi$ and actually represents { p / *o-pd*, ... $\}_\pi$ , and *pd'* is a POSS-object, which models the higher level possibility distribution { p' / *pd*, ... $\}_\pi$ , then, just as with regular objects, *pd'* creates a direct role object *pd-dr* and associates it with *pd*. The POSS-object *pd'* then actually represents the higher level possibility distribution { p' / *pd-dr*, ... $\}_\pi$ .

What is different from regular objects, is that a direct role object *pd-dr*, in turn, models a possibility distribution (because a role object, *pd-dr*, defines the same structure as its main object, *pd*); *pd-dr* therefore defines an uncertain context, now for the role objects *o-pd*. The role object *pd-dr* defines an uncertain role of *o-pd*, which is called an uncertain *dependent* role of *o*. It creates new direct role objects *o-pd-dr*, and associates them with their "main role object" *o-pd*; the "direct" role object *o-pd-dr* is said to *depend* on the role object *o-pd*. The role object *pd-dr* actually represents the possibility distribution { p / *o-pd-dr*, ... $\}_\pi$ . The dependent roles model the combined effect of "the uncertain context given by *pd*, appearing in the uncertain context given by *pd'* ".

What is also different is that only direct role objects but no further role objects are created or associated with a POSS-object *pd*, because the combined effect of several uncertain roles of *pd* is already modelled by the further role objects that are created by each of the uncertain roles *pd-dr* of *pd* and associated with regular objects.

Dependent direct role objects are like direct role objects, because they are immediately referenced from a POSS-object, and at the same time are like further role objects, because they depend on other direct objects.

The class-instantiations POSS ( CL ) define extra methods to handle role objects of POSS ( CL )-objects and dependent direct role objects :

- for creating role objects of POSS ( CL )-objects, creating dependent direct role objects of POSS ( CL )-objects and creating dependent direct role objects of CL-objects :
  - CREATE-ROLES ( *pd*:POSS ( CL ), p:UNITINTERVAL ) → *pd-dr*:ROLE ( POSS ( CL ) )
  - CREATE-DEP-ROLES ( *pd-dr*:ROLE ( POSS ( CL ) ), p:UNITINTERVAL )
  
    → *pd-ddr*:ROLE ( POSS ( CL ) )
  - CREATE-DEPENDENT ( *o-dr*:ROLE ( CL ), p:UNITINTERVAL ) → *o-ddr*:ROLE ( CL ).
- for deleting direct role objects (dependent or not) of POSS ( CL )-objects :
  - DEL-ROLES ( *pd-dr*:ROLE ( POSS ( CL ) ) ).
  
  Deleting a dependent direct role object of a CL-object is already defined by the class instantiations included in the method DEL-DIRECT.
- for merging direct role objects with POSS ( CL )-objects, merging dependent direct role

objects with direct role objects of POSS ( CL )-objects and merging dependent direct role objects with direct role objects of CL-objects :

- MERGE-ROLES ( $pd$:POSS ( CL ), $pd$-$dr$:ROLE ( POSS ( CL ) ) ) → $pd$:POSS ( CL )
- MERGE-DEP-ROLES ( $pd$-$dr$:ROLE ( POSS ( CL ) ), $pd$-$ddr$:ROLE ( POSS ( CL ) ) )
  $$→ pd\text{-}dr\text{:ROLE ( POSS ( CL ) )}$$
- MERGE-DEPENDENT ( $o$-$dr$:ROLE ( CL ), $o$-$ddr$:ROLE ( CL ) ) → $o$-$dr$:ROLE ( CL ).

The methods are outlined in [Van Gyseghem & De Caluwe, 1996b].

For example, the POSS-object $pd1$ models *John*.SPOUSE, and $pd4$ models the uncertain value of *Alice*.MOTHER, which is given as the possibility distribution { 1 / *Beth*, 0.8 / $pd1$ }$_\pi$ . The direct role objects *Beth-3* and $pd1$-$4$ are created by $pd4$, so that $pd4$ actually represents the possibility distribution { 1 / *Beth-3*, 0.8 / $pd1$-$4$ }$_\pi$ . The direct role object $pd1$-$4$ itself represents a possibility distribution, because the same structure is defined for a role object as for its main object. The POSS-object $pd1$ created the direct role objects *Jane-1*, *Susan-1* and *Lucy-1* and actually represents { 1 / *Jane-1*, 0.5 / *Susan-1*, 0.4 / *Lucy-1* }$_\pi$ . Its direct role object $pd1$-$4$, however, creates dependent direct role objects *Jane-1-4*, *Susan-1-4* and *Lucy-1-4*, which are associated with their respective "main role objects" *Jane-1*, *Susan-1* and *Lucy-1*, and which model the uncertain context "SPOUSE of *John* and MOTHER of *Alice*" :

*Jane-1-4*.MAIN-OBJ = *Jane*,

*Jane-1-4*.MAIN-ROLES = { *Jane-1*, *Jane-1-4* }

*Jane-1-4* copies the internal state of *Jane-1*

For each role object *Jane-r*, having *Jane-1* as an element of *Jane-r*.MAIN-ROLES, a
further role object *Jane-r-4* is created, with :

*Jane-r-4*.MAIN-ROLES = *Jane-r*.MAIN-ROLES ∪ { *Jane-1-4* }

*Jane-r-4* copies the internal state of *Jane-r*

(similar for the other role objects)

$pd1$-$4$.MAIN-OBJ = $pd1$,

$pd1$-$4$.MAIN-ROLES = { $pdo$-$4$ }.

$pd1$-$4$ actually represents { 1 / *Jane-1-4*, 0.5 / *Susan-1-4*, 0.4 / *Lucy-1-4* }$_\pi$ .

Assume in addition that the POSS-object $pd5$ models the uncertain value *Peter*.MOTHER, which is given as the possibility distribution { 0.5 / *Beth*, 1 / $pd1$ }$_\pi$. A direct role object $pd1$-$5$ is created by $pd5$ and associated with $pd1$. The direct role object $pd1$-$5$ creates dependent direct role objects *Jane-1-5*, *Susan-1-5* and *Lucy-1-5*, which are associated with their respective "main role objects" *Jane-1*, *Susan-1* and *Lucy-1*, and which model the uncertain context "SPOUSE of *John* and MOTHER of *Peter*" :

*Jane-1-5*.MAIN-OBJ = *Jane*,

*Jane-1-5*.MAIN-ROLES = { *Jane-1, Jane-1-5* }

*Jane-1-5* copies the internal state of *Jane-1*

For each role object *Jane-r*, having *Jane-1* as an element of *Jane-r*.MAIN-ROLES, e.g.

    *Jane-1-4*, a further role object *Jane-r-5* is created, with :

        *Jane-r-5*.MAIN-ROLES = *Jane-r*.MAIN-ROLES $\cup$ { *Jane-1-5* },

        *Jane-r-5* copies the internal state of *Jane-r*

    e.g. *Jane-1-4-5* is created, with :

        *Jane-1-4-5*.MAIN-ROLES = { *Jane-1, Jane-1-4, Jane-1-5* },

        *Jane-1-4-5* copies the internal state of *Jane-1-4*

(similar for the other role objects)

*pd1-5*.MAIN-OBJ = *pd1*,

*pd1-5*.MAIN-ROLES = { *pd1-5* }

*pd1-5* actually represents { 1 / *Jane-1-5*, 0.5 / *Susan-1-5*, 0.4 / *Lucy-1-5* }$_\pi$ , and the combined effect of the uncertain context "SPOUSE of *John* and MOTHER of *Alice* and MOTHER of *Peter*" is modelled a.o. by the further role objects *Jane-1-4-5*, *Susan-1-5* and *Lucy-1-5*.            ■

As it is the aim of the UFO database model to model uncertain attribute values in a "to the user" implicit way, the management of ROLE-objects is concealed from users of a UFO database. The class instantiations of the generic class ROLE are considered not to be a part of the database scheme, but are considered built-in. Regular objects cannot create, delete or reference role objects, nor can they explicitly invoke any behaviour of role objects, except through their system attribute ROLES, which is automatically maintained. In order to avoid regular objects from referencing role objects, the UFO database model maintains role objects in a separate part of the database system.

Also, the existence of any role object is only justified as long as it represents an uncertain role of a regular object; its existence therefore is always tied to one regular object. The UFO database model achieves concealing role objects from the user, and connecting role objects to regular objects, by using special ID's for role objects : a "role object identity" (ROID) is a combination of a regular OID (from the regular object it is associated with) and a specific ID which is unique within the set of role objects associated with the regular object. ROID's are modelled by a system class ROID, which is different from the system class OID of regular OID's. Both classes are subclass of the system class of all identities, ID. Within the database scheme, only OID-objects are used.

Role objects are completely managed from the class instantiations of the generic class POSS. The methods defined by POSS to manage role objects, are only visible in the class POSS and are invoked by the "visible" methods of the class POSS, i.e. the methods discussed in Sec. 4.1, such as the method CHANGE-PI and the methods defined for its parameter class.

This completes the modelling of uncertain and imprecise non-literal attribute values in the UFO database model.

Although fuzziness was not explicitly considered in Sec. 4.1 or Sec. 4.2, the proposed modelling of uncertain and imprecise values is also valid for an uncertain or imprecise, fuzzy value of a multivalued attribute. If the domain of such attribute is the class instantiation FUZZYSET ( CL ), an uncertain or imprecise value of this attribute then is modelled by the class instantiation POSS ( FUZZYSET ( CL ) ), which models possibility distributions of fuzzy sets. Modelling role objects of fuzzy instances, which have a fuzzy set of immediate classes : { m / CL, ... }, also is straightforward : the role objects then are fuzzy role objects, and are instances of a fuzzy set of class instantiations of ROLE : { m / ROLE ( CL ), ... ).

## 4.3 Uncertain Applicability of Properties

The previous sections discussed one form of uncertainty and imprecision at the data level of the UFO database model : uncertain and imprecise values are given as possibility distributions and modelled by the generic system classes POSS and ROLE. Another form of uncertainty at the data level is discussed in this section : uncertain or imprecise degrees of applicability of properties for objects.

The degree of applicability was introduced in Sec. 3.2; it indicates the degree with which a property P is applicable for an object $o$, and is expressed by the membership degrees in the fuzzy set $o.\tau$ of properties defined for the CL-object $o$ :

$o.\tau.\text{MU} ( P ) = 1$   means that P is completely defined and fully applicable for $o$,

$o.\tau.\text{MU} ( P ) = 0$   means that P is not defined, and therefore not applicable for $o$,

$0 < o.\tau.\text{MU} ( P ) < 1$   means that P is defined for $o$, but that it is only partially applicable.

When an uncertain or imprecise degree of applicability is given for some object $o$, it implies that there exists uncertainty about the definition of this particular object $o$. It does not affect the definition of other objects, though, and therefore is an issue of the data level.

The case in which the properties are assumed to be "crisp", which means that the degrees of applicability are either 1 (i.e. a required property) or 0 (an optional property) and that $o.\tau$ is a crisp set of properties, is discussed in detail in [Van Gyseghem & De Caluwe, 1996b]. Uncertainty in this case is modelled by a possibility distribution of possible sets of properties defined for $o$. The UFO database model uses the concept of role objects, introduced in Sec. 4.2, to model this kind of uncertainty. Possible optional properties are not applicable for the object itself, but for specially created role objects.

Formally, the properties that are applicable for the CL-object $o$ are given by a possibility distribution of sets of properties (also called an *uncertain set* of properties) : { p / sp, ... $\}_\pi$ , in which each set $sp$ of properties includes a.o. all required properties defined by CL. Only the properties which are certainly applicable for $o$, are defined for $o$ itself. For every set of properties with a non-zero possibility degree associated, a direct ROLE ( CL )-object $o$-$sp$ is created, with :

$o$-$sp.\tau = sp$,          $o$-$sp$.MAIN-OBJ $= o$,          $o$-$sp$.MAIN-ROLES $= \{$ $o$-$sp$ $\}$
$o$.ROLES.CHANGE-PI ( $o$-$sp$, p ).

All direct role objects created in this way include at least the structure and behaviour certainly defined for $o$. However, this is not a redundancy, because different uncertain behaviour may affect the certainly defined structure differently. Further role objects that depend on more than one of these direct role objects $o$-$sp$, need not be created, because the sets of properties with non-zero possibility degree associated, are mutually independent.

This approach is easily extended for fuzzy properties, by replacing the concept of a "set of properties" with the concept of a "fuzzy set of properties".

Formally, the properties that are applicable for the CL-object $o$ are given by a possibility distribution of fuzzy sets of properties (also called an *uncertain fuzzy set* of properties) : { p / *fsp*, ... $\}_\pi$ , where the membership degrees associated by each fuzzy set *fsp* of properties are restricted by the "conditional" set of properties, CL.$\wp$, defined by CL:

- $\blacksquare_1$  if CL.$\wp = \{$ CL.$\theta$ ( P ) / P, ... $\}$, with CL.$\theta$ ( P ) a threshold for the degree of applicability associated with P, then :
  $$fsp.\text{MU} ( \text{P} ) \geq \text{CL}.\theta ( \text{P} )$$
- $\blacksquare_2$  if CL.$\wp = \{$ CL.$\Theta$ ( P )./ P, ... $\}$, with CL.$\Theta$ ( P ) a non-empty set of possible degrees of applicability associated with P, then :
  $$fsp.\text{MU} ( \text{P} ) \in \text{CL}.\Theta ( \text{P} )$$

For every fuzzy set *fsp* of properties with a non-zero possibility degree associated, a direct ROLE ( CL )-object $o$-*fsp* is created, with :

$o$-*fsp*.$\tau$ = *fsp*,          $o$-*fsp*.MAIN-OBJ $= o$,          $o$-*fsp*.MAIN-ROLES $= \{$ $o$-*fsp* $\}$

$o$.ROLES.CHANGE-PI ( $o$-fsp, p ).

Again, only the properties about which there is no uncertainty for $o$, are defined for $o$ itself; all direct role objects created in this way, include at least these properties; and further role objects that depend on more than one of these direct role objects $o$-fsp, need not be created.

For example, there is doubt about whether or not the PERSON-object *Pete* has a MAIN-JOB, but in the case he has one (with possibility degree 0.7), it is a part-time job. The properties applicable for *Pete* are given as the possibility distribution :

$\{ 1 / fsp1, 0.7 / fsp2 \}_\pi$ ,

in which *fsp1* and *fsp2* are fuzzy sets of properties defined by the class PERSON, with *fsp1*.MU ( MAIN-JOB ) = 0 and *fsp2*.MU ( MAIN-JOB ) = 0.5. A direct ROLE ( PERSON )-object *Pete-fsp2* is created, with :

*Pete-fsp2*.MAIN-OBJ = *Pete*,     *Pete-fsp2*.MAIN-ROLES = { *Pete-fsp2* }

*Pete-fsp2*.$\tau$ = *fsp2*,     *Pete-fsp2*.$\tau$.MU ( MAIN-JOB ) = 0.5.     ■

### 4.4  Uncertain Instances

The UFO database model handles three forms of uncertainty and imprecision at the data level : uncertain and imprecise attribute values, uncertain degrees of applicability of properties, and, discussed in this section, uncertain classification of objects.

An uncertain classification of a (non-literal) object $o$ occurs when uncertain information about $o$ prevents a precise classification of $o$ : assigning one class as the immediate class of $o$ is not possible in this case. Such object $o$ is called an *uncertain instance*.

In an OODBM, every object has to belong to at least one class, and always is an instance of some class. Therefore, for each uncertain instance $o$, at least one class is to be indicated for which it is completely possible that it is the immediate class of $o$. In this situation, a possibility distribution of possible immediate classes is given, and the uncertain instance $o$ is an instance of a possibility distribution of classes.

In the crisp case, with only crisp instance degrees and crisp membership degrees, the possibility distribution of immediate classes of an uncertain object $o$, maintained in the system attribute $o$.IMM-CLASS, determines uncertain instance degrees and membership degrees of $o$ in a class CL : [Van Gyseghem & De Caluwe, 1996b]

CL.ι $( o ) = \{$ p $/ 1,$ f $/ 0 \}_\pi,$
        where : p $= o$.IMM-CLASS.PI $($ CL $)$
               f $=$ max $\{$ $o$.IMM-CLASS.PI $($ CLX $)$ $\mid$ CLX $\neq$ CL $\}$
CL.μ $( o ) = \{$ p' $/ 1,$ f '$/ 0 \}_\pi,$
        where : p' $=$ max $\{$ $o$.IMM-CLASS.PI $($ CLX $)$ $\mid$ CLX $\preceq$ CL $\}$
             f ' $=$ max $\{$ $o$.IMM-CLASS.PI $($ CLX $)$ $\mid$ CLX $\npreceq$ CL $\}$

The extent and maximal extent of a class CL is an uncertain set of objects (i.e. a possibility distribution of sets of objects).

When fuzzy instance degrees and fuzzy membership degrees are allowed, as discussed in Sec. 3.3, the immediate class of each fuzzy instance $o$ is a unimodal fuzzy set of immediate classes, and is maintained in the system attribute $o$.IMM-CLASS. Uncertainty about the immediate class of a fuzzy instance $o$, then is modelled by an uncertain "unimodal" fuzzy set of immediate classes, i.e. a possibility distribution of unimodal fuzzy sets of immediate classes. The value of the system attribute $o$.IMM-CLASS is an uncertain fuzzy set of immediate classes : $\{$ p $/ fsc,$ ... $\}_\pi$ . It determines uncertain fuzzy instance degrees and membership degrees of $o$ in a class CL, which associate the following possibility degrees with each possible fuzzy instance degree or fuzzy membership degree m :

CL.ι $( o )$.PI $($ m $)$ $=$ max $\{$ $o$.IMM-CLASS.PI $( fsc' )$ $\mid$
                        $\forall$ fuzzy set $fsc'$ of classes : $fsc'$.μ $($ CL $) =$ m $\}$
CL.μ $( o )$.PI $($ m $)$ $=$ max $\{$ $o$.IMM-CLASS.PI $( fsc' )$ $\mid$
                        $\forall$ fuzzy set $fsc'$ of classes, $\forall$ class CLY,
                        $\exists$ class CLX : $fsc'$.μ $($ CLX $) =$ m, CLX $\preceq$ CL,
                                  $fsc'$.μ $($ CLY $) >$ m, CLY $\npreceq$ CL $\}$

The extent and maximal extent of a class CL is an uncertain fuzzy set of objects (i.e. a possibility distribution of fuzzy sets of objects).

For instance, if it is uncertain whether or not *Jane* is a student, nor whether or not *Jane* is a part-time student, then *Jane* is defined as an uncertain instance, shown in figure 8, for which *Jane*.IMM-CLASS is an uncertain fuzzy set of immediate classes :

$\{$ 0.5 $/ \{$ 1 $/$ PERSON $\}$, 0.7 $/ \{$ 1 $/$ PERSON, 0.5 $/$ STUDENT $\}$, 1$/ \{$ 1 $/$ STUDENT $\}$ $\}_\pi.$

The (maximal) extents of the classes PERSON and STUDENT are possibility distributions of fuzzy sets of objects, and the following uncertain instance degrees are defined :

PERSON.ι $($ *Jane* $) = \{$ 0.7 $/ 1,$ 1 $/ 0 \}_\pi$         PERSON.μ $($ *Jane* $) = \{$ 1 $/ 1 \}_\pi$
STUDENT.ι $($ *Jane* $) =$ STUDENT.μ $($ *Jane* $) = \{$ 1 $/ 1,$ 0.7 $/ 0.5,$ 0.5 $/ 0 \}_\pi.$     ■

164

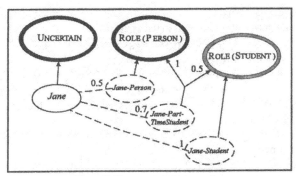

Figure 8: The uncertain instance *Jane*.

Uncertainty about the immediate class of an object imposes uncertainty on the applicability of properties for the uncertain instance, because each of the different possible immediate classes define their own properties. The UFO database model also uses the introduced concept of role objects here.

An uncertain instance is modelled by creating a temporary object with associated (fuzzy) role objects, one for each possible fuzzy set of immediate classes, and therefore for each possible structure and behaviour of the uncertain instance. The temporary object is modelled by a system class UNCERTAIN, which also defines the system attribute ROLES to tie the role objects and the temporary object together.

Formally, for each UNCERTAIN-instance $o$, for which the value of the system attribute $o$.IMM-CLASS is an uncertain fuzzy set of immediate classes : $\{ p / fsc, ... \}_\pi$ , the value of $o$.ROLES is a (normalized) possibility distribution of role objects, which are members of different class instantiations of the generic class ROLE. Assume that $o$-$fsc$ is a (fuzzy) role object having a non-zero possibility degree in $o$.ROLES, then :

$o$.ROLES.PI ( $o$-$fsc$ ) = $o$.IMM-CLASS.PI ( $fsc$ )

If $fsc$ is a fuzzy set of classes $\{ m / CL, ... \}$, then :

$o$-$fsc$.IMM-CLASS = $\{ m / ROLE( CL ), ... )$.

$o$-$fsc$.MAIN-OBJ is not defined

$o$-$fsc$.MAIN-ROLES = $\{ o$-$fsc \}$

The (fuzzy) role object $o$-$fsc$ defines a possible internal state of the object $o$ and is called an *instance-role object*. No further role objects, that would depend on more than one instance-role object, are created, because the different instance-role objects model mutually independent possibilities of the uncertain object.

To model uncertain roles of UNCERTAIN-objects, an optional system attribute ROLES is defined by the generic class ROLE. This attribute is applicable only for instance-role objects and serves the same purpose as the system attribute ROLES for regular objects : its value is a (not necessarily normalized) possibility distribution of ROLE-objects, which model the uncertain roles of the instance-role object.

The following methods are defined by the class UNCERTAIN :

- CREATE-INSTANCE ( *fsc*:FUZZYSET ( METACLASS ), p:UNITINTERVAL )

$$\rightarrow o\text{-}fsc\text{:ROLEFSC}$$

   Creates an instance-role object of $o$. The method creates one instance-role object $o\text{-}fsc$, with :

   $o\text{-}fsc$.MAIN-ROLES = { $o\text{-}fsc$ },
   $o\text{-}fsc$.MAIN-OBJ is not defined,
   If *fsc* is a fuzzy set of classes { m / CL, ... }, then :
         $o\text{-}fsc$.IMM-CLASS = ROLEFSC = { m / ROLE ( CL ), ... },
   $o$.ROLES.CHANGE-PI ( $o\text{-}fsc$, p ).

- DEL-INSTANCE ( $o\text{-}fsc$:ROLEFSC )

   Removes the instance-role object *fsc* of the uncertain instance $o$. The method removes the (fuzzy) role object $o\text{-}fsc$, and all other role objects $o\text{-}r$ having $o\text{-}fsc$ as an element of $o\text{-}r$.MAIN-ROLES.

- MERGE ( $o\text{-}fsc$:ROLEFSC ) $\rightarrow$ $o$:*fsc*

   Merges $o$ with its instance-role object $o\text{-}fsc$. The method is invoked when the UNCERTAIN-object is certainly to be replaced by $o\text{-}fsc$. It deletes all role objects and instance-role objects $o\text{-}r$, associated with $o$, that do not have $o\text{-}fsc$ as an element of $o\text{-}r$.MAIN-ROLES; $o$.IMM-CLASS = $o\text{-}fsc$.IMM-CLASS and $o$ copies the internal state of $o\text{-}fsc$.

The methods are outlined in [Van Gyseghem & De Caluwe, 1996b].

The modelling of uncertain instances as explained in this section, concludes the discussion of uncertainty and imprecision at the data level in the UFO database model. Handling uncertainty and imprecision at the database scheme level is discussed in the next section.

## 4.5 Hypothetic Modelling : Uncertain Properties and Uncertain Inheritance

Uncertain information about a database application is reflected in uncertainties in the database scheme of the application. The term *hypothetic modelling* for databases means that such (temporary) uncertainties are not avoided but are modelled appropriately by defining a database scheme capable of handling hypothetical information. Two forms of hypothetical information, or uncertainty at the database scheme level, are discussed here: uncertainty about the existence of properties defined by a class, and uncertainty about the inheritance relationship between two or more classes.

The first form of hypothetic modelling concerns uncertainty about whether or not to include some properties in the definition of a class, in other words, it is about an uncertain intention of a class CL. The properties defined by CL, and maintained in the system attribute CL.$\rho$, then are given as a possibility distribution of "conditional" sets of properties. Every possible "conditional" set of properties, having a non-zero possibility degree in CL.$\rho$, causes the creation of corresponding role objects associated with every CL-object. The CL-objects are handled further according to the procedure explained in Sec. 4.3, uncertain applicability of properties.

The second form of hypothetic modelling concerns uncertainty in the inheritance relationship, which has a twofold effect : both the inheritance of properties and the membership of members of the subclass, into the superclass, are uncertain. Therefore, modelling an uncertain inheritance relationship is based on the proposed modelling of an uncertain intention of a class, and the proposed modelling of uncertain members of a class.

## 4.6 Summary of the "Uncertainty Part" of the UFO Database Model

The previous sections gave a detailed overview of the uncertainty part of the UFO database model. They discussed the handling of uncertainty and imprecision at several layers of the model :

- Properties : fuzzy or crisp attributes and methods

  The uncertain value of an attribute is modelled as a possibility distribution, i.e. an object of a class instantiation of the introduced generic system class POSS. This class instantiation is a subclass of its parameter class, and thus of the domain of the attribute.

A possibility distribution of non-literal objects usually expresses an uncertain relationship between objects; such uncertain context causes the creation of role objects, i.e. instances of class instantiations of the generic system class ROLE, which is also a subclass of its parameter class. Role objects model the uncertain roles of the involved objects in the uncertain context; an extra system attribute ROLES is defined for each regular object to keep track of its uncertain roles. Messages sent to a possibility distribution of objects, instead of on a single object, are forwarded only to the role objects created by the uncertain context; the invoked methods express a tentative behaviour, which should not immediately affect regular objects.

The uncertain applicability of (crisp or fuzzy) properties for an object is expressed by an uncertain (crisp or fuzzy) set of properties defined for the object. Uncertainty also causes the creation of corresponding role objects.

- Objects :

  The classification of an object may be "uncertain", which means that there is uncertainty about which class the object is a (crisp or fuzzy) instance of. The "immediate class" of the object is an uncertain (unimodal) fuzzy set of classes; the classes involved have uncertain fuzzy sets of objects as extent and/or maximal extent. The object is called an uncertain instance. As its definition itself is uncertain, an uncertain instance is modelled by the introduced system class UNCERTAIN, and has role objects associated to model the different possible definitions of the uncertain instance.

- Classes :

  Uncertainty in the definition of a class is a form of hypothetical information. Defining a database scheme that can handle hypothetical information is called hypothetic modelling. Two forms of hypothetical information are defined in the UFO database model : uncertainty about whether or not some properties are to be defined by the class, and uncertainty in the inheritance relationship between classes. An uncertain inheritance relationship leads to uncertainty about the inheritance of properties in the possible subclass and to uncertainty about the membership degree in the "superclass" of members of the "subclass". These forms of hypothetical information are also modelled by means of role objects.

## 5 The "Interface" of the UFO Database Model to an Extended Relational Database

The UFO database model is an extension of an OODBM which is able to handle and maintain fuzzy and uncertain (imprecise) information, expressed by means of fuzzy sets, fuzzy degrees and possibility distributions. Similar extensions of the relational database model (RDBM) have been defined for a long time, and prototypes of such extended relational databases already exist. [Bosc & Kacprzyk, 1995] [Petry 1996] It therefore seems interesting to define a mapping from the UFO database model onto an extended relational database model : this will show that a UFO database system can be realized as an interface to an existing extended relational database system, and the advantages of the currently available relational database systems with regard to data management are then combined with the improved modelling facilities of the UFO database system.

The interface is designed in three steps : first, a mapping is defined between the underlying OODBM and the RDBM, which also maps methods, generic classes and the inheritance relationship, adhering to SQL-92 [Melton & Simon, 1993] and the SQL3 working draft; [Gallagher, 1994] then, the "fuzziness part" of the UFO database model is mapped onto a "fuzzy" RDBM (or the "fuzziness part" of an extended RDBM); and last, its "uncertainty part" is mapped onto an "uncertainty" RDBM (or the "uncertainty part" of an extended RDBM).

### 5.1 From the Underlying OODBM to the RDBM

Since the emergence of OODBM's, numerous methods have been proposed to map concepts from an OODBM to concepts in the RDBM. However, most proposals rely too much on features that are specific to one relational database product but not yet agreed upon in a standard proposal, [Burleson, 1994] or handle only the mapping of literal classes onto (user-defined) domains in the RDBM, [Date, 1995] or do not map more recent object-oriented concepts such as a generic class, [Premerlani et al., 1990] or restrict themselves to the static aspect. [Lebastard, 1993] The "interface part" of the UFO database model therefore includes a mapping of its underlying OODBM to the RDBM.

In general, the mapping between an OODBM and the RDBM is based on the natural resemblance between the following concepts :

OODBM :   attribute, object, class, method
RDBM :    column, tuple, table, stored procedure.

Both objects and tuples are used to model real-world entities. However, a tuple in the RDBM represents a flat structure, while an object represents a complex structure. An object therefore is mapped onto one or several tuples, generally belonging to different relational tables (but each tuple corresponds with only one object).

Similarly, a class defines the (complex) structure of its instances, while a table definition determines the (flat) structure of the tuples in the table extent. Therefore, a class is mapped onto one or several tables, which are related through foreign keys. A view is then defined over this relational subscheme, such that the structural part of the intention of the class is mapped onto the intention of the view (and thus the intentions of the underlying tables), and that each object is mapped onto a tuple of a view.

The class of OID's is mapped onto a domain of OID's in the RDBM; all tables in the RDBM define a column OID, with this domain, as their primary key, and all tuples corresponding with one object, have the same value for OID. Because of this, the uniqueness and value-indenpendence of the OID's are preserved, and the defined views are updatable. An additional column with a UNIQUE-constraint is defined for user-defined object names.

Some literal classes are mapped onto domains in the relational database model; for instance, the class UNITINTERVAL, defined in the UFO database model, is mapped onto a user-defined relational domain that is derived from the built-in relational domain REAL by adding the following CHECK-clause (for the syntax of a domain definition in SQL-92, cf. [Melton & Simon, 1993] ) :

CREATE DOMAIN UNITINTERVAL$^R$ REAL$^R$
CHECK ( VALUE$^R$ >= 0 AND VALUE$^R$ <= 1 ).

Instances of these literal classes are mapped onto the values of the corresponding domains. For such classes and objects, the "is-an-instance-of" relationship is mapped onto the relationship "is-a-value-of" in the RDBM. The other objects are mapped onto several tuples within the RDBM, and their classes are mapped onto several tables; for these classes and objects, the "is-an-instance-of" relationship is mapped onto several occurrences of the relationship "is-a-tuple-of" in the RDBM.

The mapping of the inheritance relationship is similar to the mapping of the subclass-superclass relationship of the Enhanced Entity-Relationship model to the RDBM. [Elmasri

& Navathe, 1989] The option for overlapping subclasses is not included here, because the UFO database model does not allow overlapping subclasses. The mapping of the inheritance relationship also adds an extra system class "subsup" to the RDBM, defining the columns SUB and SUP as foreign keys to the "views system table".

A formal description of the mapping algorithm for crisp objects and crisp classes in a crisp inheritance relationship is given in Appendix A. The two options in the mapping algorithm can be intermingled when mapping a UFO database scheme to a RDBM scheme. With the first option, a new table is created for each subclass to map the specific (or inherited, but redefined) attributes of the subclass; this table is the *principal* table onto which the subclass is mapped. With the second option, a subclass is mapped onto the table corresponding with a superclass, which then also is the principal table onto which the subclass is mapped. With each option, a view is defined over the principal table and all other tables corresponding with the superclasses. Each table, created by this mapping algorithm and corresponding with a superclass, contains a tuple for each member of the superclass, allowing the proposed mapping of attributes to columns; for each tuple, the column TYPE references the view corresponding with the immediate class of the object that corresponds with the tuple. Redefined inherited attributes are handled by the mapping algorithm as specific attributes of the subclass; with the second option, they have to be renamed in the mapping process, while with the first option, the same name can be used. The second option defines a smaller number of joins within the view definition corresponding to a class, but it is prone to the emergence of more null-values within the table extents.

Methods and stored procedures both model operations in the database. However, methods are defined by a class, while stored procedures are defined by the database and are not associated with a specific table. Therefore, methods with the same name, but (re)defined in several classes, cannot be mapped onto stored procedures with the same name. The mapping of methods therefore adds a system table "sysprocmap", defining the following system columns :

- OONAME, for the name of the method,
- TYPE, as a foreign key to the "views system table" to reference the view corresponding to the class defining the method,
- PROCNAME, for the name of the corresponding stored procedure.

The columns OONAME and TYPE define the primary key of the "sysprocmap system table". Sometimes, the mapping of methods defines additional columns (for instance when a method models an implicit attribute), which are only to be addressed by the corresponding stored procedures.

A generic class is initially mapped onto two principal tables : one table for class instantiations for which the parameter class corresponds with a (built-in or user-defined) domain, the other table for class instantiations for which the parameter class corresponds with a view of tables. Each of the generated class instantiations are then mapped onto separate tables. The methods defined by a generic class are partially mapped onto triggers, defined for the two tables which the generic class is initially mapped onto, and partially mapped onto stored procedures. The mapping of the built-in generic classes defined in ODMG-93 are given in [Van Gyseghem, 1995]. An example of the mapping of a generic class is given in Appendix B.

### 5.2  From the "Fuzziness Part" of the UFO Database Model to a "Fuzzy" RDBM

In this section, a mapping is defined between the "fuzziness part" of the UFO database model and a "fuzzy" RDBM. The "fuzziness part" of the UFO database model is summarized in Sec. 3.5. In a "fuzzy" RDBM, "fuzzy set domains" are defined, such as a domain for fuzzy numbers, and each table represents a fuzzy relationship, associating a membership degree with each tuple. [Bosc & Kacprzyk, 1995] [Petry, 1996] In addition, a "fuzzy" non-first-normal-form RDBM allows multivalued attributes, i.e. it also defines "set domains". A "fuzzy" data definition and data manipulation language is also defined.

The class instantiations of the generic class FUZZYSET that have corresponding "fuzzy set" domains defined in the "fuzzy" RDBM, are mapped onto these "fuzzy set" domains. For the other class instantiations, the generic class FUZZYSET is mapped following the mapping algorithm for generic classes, and is given in Appendix B. The methods defined by FUZZYSET are mapped onto corresponding stored procedures.

To map fuzzy attributes, a column THRESH, with domain UNITINTERVAL$^R$, is added to the "syscolumns system table" (i.e. the system table of which each tuple defines a column of a table within the RDBM scheme). For each (fuzzy) attribute P, defined by a class CL, which are respectively mapped onto a column and onto a principal table T, the extra column THRESH contains the (set of) thresholds associated with P by CL : CL.$\theta$ ( P ) or CL.$\Theta$ ( P ). Each fuzzy attribute P itself is actually mapped onto two columns : one column P to contain the value of the fuzzy attribute, as explained in Appendix A, and one system column DEGREE-P to contain the degree in which P is applicable, and for which the following

CHECK-clause is defined :

■₁  CHECK ( DEGREE-P >= (   SELECT THRESH
                           FROM syscolumns
                           WHERE NAME = P  AND TBNAME = $T$   ) )

■₂  CHECK ( DEGREE-P IN (   SELECT THRESH
                           FROM syscolumns
                           WHERE NAME = P  AND TBNAME = $T$   ) ).

When different (sets of) thresholds are associated with P by subclasses of CL, P is treated as a redefined inherited fuzzy attribute by the subclasses.

Likewise, to map fuzzy methods, an extra column THRESH, with domain UNITINTERVAL$^R$, is added to the "sysprocmap system table". The fuzzy set of methods applicable for an object are stored in a new system table "sysapplproc". This new system table defines a column OID for the OID of each object, the columns OONAME and TYPE, both as a foreign key referencing the "sysprocmap system table", and a column DEGREE-M, containing the degree in which a method is applicable, and for which a similar CHECK-clause is defined. Every stored procedure needs to be adjusted to take the value of the column DEGREE-M into account.

A crisp class is mapped onto several tables, grouped within a view. Each of these tables is a partial mapping of the structure defined for the class. The membership degree of an object in a class CL (which is mapped onto the principal table T) is mapped onto the membership degree DEGREE-T, associated with the corresponding tuple of T in the "fuzzy" RDBM. The CHECK-clause defined for the mapping of a fuzzy property P is then adjusted to take fuzzy instances into account :

■₁  CHECK ( DEGREE-P >= (   SELECT THRESH
                           FROM syscolumns
                           WHERE NAME = P  AND TBNAME = $T$  ) )
       OR (    DEGREE-P $\geq$ 0
               AND DEGREE-T > (  SELECT 1 - THRESH
                                 FROM syscolumns
                                 WHERE NAME = P  AND TBNAME = $T$  ) ) )

$\blacksquare_2$  CHECK ( DEGREE-P IN (   SELECT  THRESH
                        FROM  syscolumns
                        WHERE  NAME = P  AND TBNAME = T  ) )
     OR (   DEGREE-P $\geq$ 0
                AND DEGREE-T > (   SELECT  1 - MIN ( THRESH )
                                FROM  syscolumns
                                WHERE  NAME = P  AND TBNAME = T  ) ) )

A similar CHECK-clause is defined for the "sysapplproc system table".

For the mapping of a fuzzy inheritance relationship, a column INH-PROC is added to the "subsup system table", as a foreign key to the "sysprocmap system table". For each tuple in the "subsup system table", with SUB = VCL and SUP = VSPCL (the views corresponding with the classes CL and SPCL, which are mapped onto the principal tables T and TSPCL), the value of INH-PROC references the stored procedure onto which the extended inheritance method between CL and SPCL is mapped. The stored procedure is used to calculate the membership degree DEGREE-T of tuples of TSPCL that correspond with members of CL. If only partial inheritance is used, the column INH-PROC in the "subsup system table" is replaced by a column INH-DEGREE, to contain the fuzzy inheritance degree between two classes (which defines an upper limit for the membership degree DEGREE-T of tuples of TSPCL that correspond with members of CL).

### 5.3 From the "Uncertainty Part" of the UFO Database Model to an "Uncertainty" RDBM

In this section, a mapping is defined between the "uncertainty part" of the UFO database model and an "uncertainty" RDBM. The "uncertainty part" of the UFO database model is summarized in Sec. 4.6. An "uncertainty" RDBM models uncertainty at the level of the column values, i.e. it allows possibility distributions as column values, as well as uncertainty at the level of the tuples in the tables, i.e. each table represents an uncertain relationship, associating a possibility distribution with each tuple. [Bosc & Kacprzyk, 1995] [Petry, 1996] [Unano & Fukami, 1991] In addition, an "uncertainty" non-first-normal-form RDBM allows multivalued attributes, i.e. it also defines "set domains". A data definition and data manipulation language which can handle uncertainty is also defined.

The modelling of possibility distributions of literal objects and of non-literal objects differs in the UFO database model, and so does their mapping to the "uncertainty" RDBM.

A class instantiation POSS ( CL ) and its literal "parameter class and superclass" CL, which corresponds with a domain D for which possibility distributions are defined in the "uncertainty" RDBM, are both mapped onto D. For instance, both classes UNITINTERVAL and POSS ( UNITINTERVAL ) are mapped onto the relational domain UNITINTERVAL$^R$, for which the "uncertainty" RDBM defines possibility distributions. However, for non-literal classes CL, which are mapped onto a principal table, the UFO database model defines two system subclasses, POSS ( CL ) and ROLE ( CL ), to model possibility distributions of CL-objects. Both subclasses are generally mapped following the mapping algorithm for subclasses, option 2, as given in Appendix A.

However, the system subclass ROLE ( CL ) is special in it that it does not define regular objects, but role objects, which are associated with regular objects and which have special ROID's. The ROID's themselves are not immediately mapped here; for the "interface" of the UFO database model, it is assumed that ROID's are defined as a combination of a regular OID (from the regular object it is associated with) and a specific ID which is unique within the set of role objects associated with the regular object. The specific ID's then are modelled by a class RID, so that the system class of all identities is defined as a structure of OID's and RID's :

ID = STRUCTURE ( OID, RID ).

An ID-object [ oid, nil ] defines a regular OID, an ID-object [ oid, rid ] defines a ROID. The class ID is mapped to a structured relational domain for all ID's : ID[ OID, RID ]. The mapping algorithms defined thus far for the interface of the UFO database model, then are modified as follows :

- the primary key columns OID with domain OID are replaced by primary key (nested) columns : ID[ OID, RID ] with domain ID.
- columns with domain OID are replaced by columns with domain ID
- the foreign key constraints are replaced by more complex CHECK-clauses, to ensure that regular objects do not reference role objects through regular attributes. For instance, the foreign key constraint on the column AB, with domain ID and referencing the table T, is replaced by :

```
CHECK ( ( AB IS NULL )
        OR ( ( ID[ RID ] IS NULL )
             AND ( AB[ RID ] IS NULL )
             AND ( AB[ OID ] IN ( SELECT ID[ OID ] FROM T ) ) )
        OR ( ( ID[ RID ] IS NOT NULL )
             AND ( AB IN ( SELECT ID FROM T ) ) ) )
```

The mapping algorithm for the system subclasses POSS ( CL ) and ROLE ( CL ) are given in Appendix C. The methods defined by POSS ( CL ) and ROLE ( CL ) are mapped onto corresponding stored procedures.

In the previous section, it is explained that the degree of applicability of properties is mapped onto extra columns DEGREE-P, associated with columns P onto which (fuzzy) properties are mapped, and onto the extra column DEGREE-M of the extra "sysapplproc system table", associated with stored procedures onto which (fuzzy) methods are mapped. The extra columns have domain UNITINTERVAL$^R$, and therefore, in the "uncertainty" RDBM, also accept possibility distributions of UNITINTERVAL$^R$-values as a value. However, modelling an uncertain degree of applicability in the UFO database model is not primarily based upon such possibility distributions associated with each property, but instead is based on possibility distributions of (fuzzy) sets of properties associated with an object, which causes the creation of several role objects for which a (fuzzy) set of properties is certainly applicable. The created role objects are then mapped in the "interface part" following the mapping algorithms as previously outlined.

To map uncertain instances, the "interface part" of the UFO database model does not map the class UNCERTAIN itself onto the "uncertainty" RDBM. Only the instance-role objects of an uncertain instance are considered, and mapped onto tuples in the different tables corresponding with the possible immediate classes. Within the "uncertainty" RDBM, all tables associate a possibility distribution with each of their tuples; the uncertain (fuzzy) membership degrees defined in the UFO database model are mapped onto the possibility distributions associated with the tuples of a table.

If there exists a common superclass SPCL of all possible immediate classes of an uncertain instance, a tuple with the ID of the uncertain instance is inserted into the view corresponding with SPCL, allowing other regular objects to reference the uncertain instance as a SPCL-object. The value of the column TYPE for these tuples is a possibility distribution of references to the "views system table", in particular to the views corresponding with the possible immediate classes of the uncertain instance.

Hypothetic modelling is handled in the UFO database model by creating more role objects, and therefore is mapped in the "interface part" following the mapping algorithms previously outlined.

## 6    Further Research On the UFO Database Model

The current UFO database model is to be situated within the "earliest" period of "fuzzy" extensions of an OODBM. Further research will refine the UFO database model, e.g. by investigating alternatives for the principle of immediate fuzzification, or by introducing other semantic forms of "fuzzy" degrees, such as a degree of typicality, [Dubois et al., 1991], a similarity degree [George et al., 1993] or a degree of relevance or importance. [Mouaddib & Subtil, 1995]

The design of a "predefined ad hoc query language" for the UFO database model also is a topic for further investigation. Its foundation has already been laid, because objects should only be accessed in such a query language by means of their methods, and the UFO database model already includes this behavioural aspect.

## 7    Conclusion

Two types of imperfect information, appearing in database applications, are discussed in this paper : fuzzy information, representing information with inherent gradations, for which it is impossible to define sharp or precise borders, and uncertain or imprecise information, representing information which is (temporarily) incomplete due to a lack of sufficient or more precise knowledge. Dealing with this kind of imperfect information within the formal and crisp environment of a computer, is based in this paper upon the fuzzy set theory and its related possibility theory, which offers a formal framework to model imperfect information, and upon the object-oriented paradigm, which offers flexible modelling capabilities. The result is the UFO database model, a "fuzzy" extension of a full-fledged object-oriented database model.

This paper discusses the UFO database model in detail in three steps. First, it is shown how fuzzy information is handled : meaningful fuzzifications of several object-oriented concepts are introduced in order to store and maintain fuzzy information, and to allow a flexible or "soft" modelling of database applications. Then, it is discussed how uncertainty and imprecision in the information are handled : possible alternatives for the information are stored and maintained by introducing role objects, which are tied like shadows to regular objects in the database; they allow the processing of uncertainty and imprecision in a, to the user, implicit and transparent way, and they also allow the modelling of tentative behaviour and of hypothetical information in the database application. Both the static and the dynamic aspects of (imperfect) information are developed in the UFO database model, and imperfect information is considered at the data level as well as at the metalevel of a database application. The process of "extending" an object-oriented database model to the UFO database model, as discussed here, adheres, as closely as possible, to the original principles of the object-oriented paradigm, to allow a flexible and transparent, but semantically sound modelling of imperfect information. The object-oriented database model which the extension process starts off from, adheres to the standard proposal ODMG-93, to allow for practical implementations of the UFO database model. For the same purpose, this paper also discusses an interface of the UFO database model to an extended relational database model, capable of handling some imperfect information, and for which some prototypes are already available.

Although further research will improve and extend the capabilities of the UFO database model, this version of the UFO database model, proposed in this paper, already proves that it is possible and advantageous to design a true object-oriented database model in which imperfect information can be appropriately processed.

**Acknowledgments**

The authors are very grateful to Ms. R. Vandenberghe and to the other members of the Computer Science Laboratory from the University of Ghent for the helpful discussions and for their support to this work. Our gratitude also extends to the Fund for Scientific Research - Flanders, which made this research financially possible, and to Mr. J. Meister, who helped improving the language in this text.

## Appendix A

The mapping algorithm for crisp objects and crisp classes in a crisp subclass-superclass relationship is given here (concepts and names used in the UFO database model are denoted with superscript $^O$, concepts and names used in the extended RDBM are denoted with superscript $^R$) :

→  All superclasses $\text{SPCL}^O$ are mapped following the mapping algorithm given below.

■  For each subclass $\text{SBCL}^O$ :

    ■  If $\text{SBCL}_i^O$ is a literal class with corresponding (built-in or user-defined) domain $D_i^R$ :

    →  $\text{SBCL}_i^O$ is mapped onto $D_i^R$.

    ■  Otherwise, OPTION 1 :

        →  A table $\text{TB}^R$ is created, defining a column $\text{OID}^R$, with domain $\text{OID}^R$, as its primary key; $\text{OID}^R$ is also a foreign key referencing all tables corresponding with superclasses of $\text{SBCL}^O$.

        ■  For each specific attribute $\text{AB}_i^O$ with domain determined by $\text{CL}_i^O$ :

            ■  If $\text{CL}_i^O$ corresponds with the domain $D_i^R$ :

            →  A column $\text{AB}_i^R$ with domain $D_i^R$ is added to $\text{TB}^R$.

            ■  Otherwise :

            →  $\text{CL}_i^O$ is mapped onto the principal table$_i$ $T^R$ following this mapping algorithm, if $\text{CL}_i^O$ is not already mapped.

            →  A column $\text{AB}_i^R$ with domain $\text{OID}^R$ is added to $\text{TB}^R$, as a foreign key referencing $T_i^R$.

        →  A column $\text{TYPE}^R$ is added to $\text{TB}^R$ as a foreign key referencing the "views system table".

        →  Constraints defined by $\text{SBCL}^O$ are mapped onto CHECK-clauses defined for $\text{TP}^R$.

        →  A view $\text{VSBCL}^R$ is created to relate $\text{SBCL}^O$ to its principal table $\text{TB}^R$ and to all other tables corresponding with superclasses of $\text{SBCL}^O$.

- If $\text{SBCL}^\circ$ is an abstract class :
  - ↦ A constraint is added on the column $\text{TYPE}^R$ that it may not reference $\text{VSBCL}^R$.
- Otherwise :
  - ↦ Instances of $\text{SBCL}^\circ$ are mapped on tuples with $\text{TYPE}^R = \text{VSBCL}^R$.
- For each immediate superclass $\text{SPCL}_i^\circ$ of $\text{SBCL}^\circ$, with corresponding view $\text{VSPCL}^R$ :
  - ↦ Insert a tuple ( $\text{SUB}^R = \text{VSBCL}^R$, $\text{SUP}^R = \text{VSPCL}^R$ ) in the "subsup system table".
- If $\text{SBCL}^\circ$ is a literal class :
  - ↦ The privilege to update $\text{TB}^R$ is revoked for all users.
- Otherwise, OPTION 2 :
  - ↦ Choose an immediate superclass $\text{SPCL}^\circ$, with principal table $\text{TP}^R$.
  - For each specific attribute $\text{AB}_i^\circ$ of $\text{SBCL}^\circ$, with a domain determined by $\text{CL}_i^\circ$ :
    - If $\text{CL}_i^\circ$ corresponds with a domain $\text{D}_i^R$ :
      - ↦ A column $\text{AB}_i^R$ with domain $\text{D}_i^R$ is added to $\text{TP}^R$.
    - Otherwise :
      - ↦ $\text{CL}_i^\circ$ is mapped onto the principal table $\text{T}_i^R$ following this algorithm, if $\text{CL}_i^\circ$ is not already mapped
      - ↦ A column $\text{AB}_i^R$ with domain $\text{OID}^R$ is added to $\text{TP}^R$ as a foreign key referencing $\text{T}_i^R$.
  - ↦ Constraints defined by $\text{SBCL}^\circ$ are mapped onto CHECK-clauses defined for $\text{TP}^R$.
  - ↦ A view $\text{VSBCL}^R$ is created to relate $\text{SBCL}^\circ$ to its principal table $\text{TP}^R$ and to all other tables corresponding with $\text{SPCL}^\circ$.
  - ↦ Instances of $\text{SBCL}^\circ$ are mapped onto tuples with $\text{TYPE}^R = \text{VSBCL}^R$.
  - For each immediate superclass $\text{SPCL}^\circ$ of $\text{SBCL}^\circ$, with corresponding view $\text{VSPCL}^R$ :
    - ↦ Insert a tuple ( $\text{SUB}^R = \text{VSBCL}^R$, $\text{SUP}^R = \text{VSPCL}^R$ ) in the "subsup system table".

□

**Appendix B**

The mapping algorithm for the generic class $\text{FUZZYSET}^o$ is given here :

→ A table $\text{FUZZYSET-V}^R$ is created, defining a column $\text{OID}^R$, with domain $\text{OID}^R$, as its primary key.

→ A table $\text{FUZZYSET-D}^R$ is created, defining a column $\text{OID}^R$, with domain $\text{OID}^R$, as its primary key.

→ A column $\text{NAME}^R$ is added to both tables, which contains the user-defined name or linguistic description of the fuzzy concept.

→ A column $\text{TYPE}^R$ is added to $\text{FUZZYSET-V}^R$ as a foreign key referencing the "views system table". It contains a reference to the view corresponding with the parameter class. The column $\text{NAME}^R$ (when not empty), together with the column $\text{TYPE}^R$, contains the unique user-defined name of the mapped $\text{FUZZYSET}^o$-object.

→ A column $\text{TYPE}^R$ is added to $\text{FUZZYSET-D}^R$; it indicates the domain corresponding with the parameter class. The column $\text{NAME}^R$ (when not empty), together with the column $\text{TYPE}^R$, contains the unique user-defined name of the mapped $\text{FUZZYSET}^o$-object.

→ An "after insert trigger" is defined for $\text{FUZZYSET-V}^R$, to invoke the stored procedure $\text{TO-INSERT-V}^R$.

→ An "after insert trigger" is defined for $\text{FUZZYSET-D}^R$, to invoke the stored procedure $\text{TO-INSERT-D}^R$.

→ Similar update triggers and delete triggers are defined for both tables.

→ A view $\text{VFUZZYSET}^R$ is defined as the union of projections of both $\text{FUZZYSET-V}^R$ and $\text{FUZZYSET-D}^R$ onto their common columns.

■ If the generic class $\text{COLLECTION}^o$ corresponds with the view $\text{VCOLLECTION}^R$, then :

→ Insert a tuple ( $\text{SUB}^R = \text{VFUZZYSET}^R$, $\text{SUP}^R = \text{VCOLLECTION}^R$ ) in the "subsup system table".

□

The trigger $\text{TO-INSERT-V}^R$ creates a corresponding table with every class instantiation $\text{FUZZYSET}^o$ ( $\text{CL}^o$ ); assume that $\text{CL}^o$ is mapped onto the principal table $T^R$ and the view $\text{VCL}^R$ :

■ If a table $\text{FUZZYSETCL}^R$ has not yet been created :

→ A table $\text{FUZZYSETCL}^R$ is created, defining a column $\text{OID}^R$, with domain $\text{OID}^R$, as its primary key and a foreign key referencing $\text{FUZZYSET-V}^R$.

→ A column ELEMENT$^R$ is added to FUZZYSETCL$^R$, as a foreign key referencing T$^R$. This column contains references to the different (fuzzy) members of a fuzzy set.
The primary key of FUZZYSETCL$^R$ is formed by these two columns.

→ A column MU$^R$, with domain UNITINTERVAL$^R$, is added to FUZZYSETCL$^R$. It contains the membership degree of the fuzzy member, which is to be referenced by the column ELEMENT$^R$, in the fuzzy set, which is to be inserted into FUZZYSET$^R$.

■ For each CL$^O$-object (with OID $o$) having a non-zero membership degree m in a FUZZYSET$^O$-object (with OID $fs$) :

→ Insert the tuple ( OID$^R$ = $fs$, ELEMENT$^R$ = $o$, MU$^R$ = m) into FUZZYSETCL$^R$.

□

The trigger TO-INSERT-D$^R$ creates a corresponding table with every class instantiation FUZZYSET$^O$ ( CL$^O$ ); assume that CL$^O$ is mapped onto the domain D$^R$ :

■ If a table FUZZYSETD$^R$ has not yet been created :
→ A table FUZZYSETD$^R$ is created, defining a column OID$^R$, with domain OID$^R$, as its primary key and a foreign key referencing FUZZYSET-D$^R$.
→ A column ELEMENT$^R$, with domain D$^R$, is added to FUZZYSETD$^R$. This column contains references to the different (fuzzy) members of a fuzzy set.
The primary key of FUZZYSETD$^R$ is formed by these two columns.
→ A column MU$^R$, with domain UNITINTERVAL$^R$, is added to FUZZYSETD$^R$. It contains the membership degree of the fuzzy member, which is to be referenced by the column ELEMENT$^R$, in the fuzzy set, which is to be inserted into FUZZYSET$^R$.

■ If no ordering is defined for CL$^O$-objects (as for instance for the class EUROPEANCOINS$^O$) :
■ For each CL$^O$-object (with OID $o$) having a non-zero membership degree m in a FUZZYSET$^O$-object (with OID $fs$) :
→ Insert the tuple ( OID$^R$ = $fs$, ELEMENT$^R$ = $o$, MU$^R$ = m) into FUZZYSETD$^R$.

■ If an ordering is defined for CL$^O$-objects (as for instance for the class REAL$^O$), a fuzzy set is stored by means of a piecewise linear membership function :
→ The columns LEFT-LIMIT$^R$ and RIGHT-LIMIT$^R$, both with domain UNITINTERVAL$^R$, are added to FUZZYSETD$^R$, respectively representing the left limit and right limit of the membership function in a breaking point.

- For each breaking point (with OID $o$ and left limit l, right limit r and membership degree m) of a $\text{FUZZYSET}^{O}$-object (with OID $fs$) :
  → Insert into $\text{FUZZYSETD}^{R}$ the following tuple :
  ( $\text{OID}^{R} = fs$, $\text{ELEMENT}^{R} = o$, $\text{MU}^{R} = m$, $\text{LEFT-LIMIT}^{R} = l$, $\text{RIGHT-LIMIT}^{R} = r$).

  □

## Appendix C

The mapping algorithm for the system subclass $\text{POSS}(\text{CL})^{O}$ is given here; assume that $\text{CL}^{O}$ is mapped onto its principal table $T^{R}$ and corresponding view $\text{VCL}^{R}$ :

→ A column $\text{POSS-DISTR}^{R}$ with domain $\text{ID}^{R}$ (and all possibility distributions of ID's) is added to $T^{R}$.

→ The following foreign key constraint is defined on $\text{POSS-DISTR}^{R}$ to reference (tuples corresponding with role objects mapped in) $T^{R}$ :

$\text{CHECK}$ ( ( $\text{POSS-DISTR}^{R}$ IS NULL )

OR ( $\text{POSS-DISTR}^{R}$ IN ( SELECT $\text{ID}^{R}$ FROM $T^{R}$

WHERE $\text{ID}^{R}[\text{RID}^{R}]$ IS NOT NULL ) ) )

→ A view $\text{VPOSSCL}^{R}$ is created to relate $\text{POSS}(\text{CL})^{O}$ to $T^{R}$ and to all other tables corresponding with $\text{CL}^{O}$.

→ Instances of $\text{POSS}(\text{CL})^{O}$ are mapped on tuples with $\text{TYPE}^{R} = \text{VPOSSCL}^{R}$.

The mapping algorithm for the system subclass $\text{ROLE}(\text{CL})^{O}$ is given here; assume that $\text{CL}^{O}$ is mapped onto its principal table $T^{R}$ and corresponding view $\text{VCL}^{R}$ :

- Mapping the attribute $\text{MAIN-OBJ}^{O}$ :
  → A column $\text{MAIN-OBJ}^{R}$ with domain $\text{OID}^{R}$ is added to $T^{R}$
  → The following foreign key constraint is defined on $\text{MAIN-OBJ}^{R}$ to reference $T^{R}$ :
  $\text{CHECK}$ ( ( $\text{MAIN-OBJ}^{R}$ IS NULL )

  OR ( $\text{MAIN-OBJ}^{R}$ IN ( SELECT $\text{ID}^{R}[\text{OID}^{R}]$ FROM $T^{R}$ ) ) )
- Mapping the attribute $\text{MAIN-ROLES}^{O}$ :

→ A multivalued column MAIN-ROLES$^R$ with domain SET OF ID$^R$ is added to T$^R$

→ The following CHECK-clause is defined on MAIN-ROLES$^R$ to reference T$^R$ :

CHECK ( ( MAIN-ROLES$^R$ IS NULL )

OR ( MAIN-ROLES$^R$ IN ( SELECT ID$^R$ FROM T$^R$

WHERE ID$^R$[ RID$^R$ ] IS NOT NULL ) ) )

- All stored procedures are adjusted according to the adjusted methods in the "uncertainty part" of the UFO database model, for instance :

- Every update of a tuple with ID$^R$[ OID$^R$, RID$^R$ ] = $id$ [ $o$, null ] triggers updates of the tuples found by the following selection :

SELECT * FROM T$^R$ WHERE ( ID$^R$[ OID$^R$ ] = $o$ )

- Every update of a tuple with ID$^R$[ OID$^R$, RID$^R$ ] = $id$ [ $o$, $r$ ] triggers updates of the tuples found by hte following selection :

SELECT * FROM T$^R$ WHERE ( ID$^R$[ OID$^R$ ] = $o$ ) AND ( $id$ IN MAIN-ROLES )

The mapping algorithm for the system attribute ROLES$^o$ of every regular CL-object is given here; assume that CL$^o$ is mapped onto its principal table T$^R$ and corresponding view VCL$^R$ :

→ A column ROLE-DEGREE$^R$ with domain UNITINTERVAL$^R$ is added to T$^R$.

→ The following CHECK-clause is defined on ROLE-DEGREE$^R$ :

CHECK ( ( ( ID$^R$[ RID$^R$ ] IS NULL ) AND ( ROLE-DEGREE$^R$ IS NULL ) )

OR ( ID$^R$[ RID$^R$ ] IS NOT NULL ) )

For each tuple onto which direct a role object is mapped, ROLE-DEGREE$^R$ contains the possibility degree of the direct role object in the attribute ROLES$^o$ of its main object.

□

# References

[Bertino & Martino, 1991] E. Bertino, L. Martino, "Object-Oriented Database Management Systems : Concepts and Issues", *IEEE Computer*, **24 (4)**, 33-47 (1991).

[Bosc & Kacprzyk, 1995] P. Bosc, J. Kacprzyk, *Fuzzy Sets and Possibility Theory in Database Management Systems* (Physica-Verlag, Heidelberg, Germany, 1995).

[Burleson, 1994] D.K. Burleson, *Practical Application of Object-Oriented Techniques to Relational Databases* (John Wiley & Sons Inc, New York, NY USA, 1994).

[Cattell, 1996] R.G.G. Cattell, *The Object Database Standard : ODMG-93* (Morgan Kaufmann Publishers, San Mateo, CA USA, 1996).

[Date, 1995] C.J. Date, *Relational Database Writings 1991-1994* (Addison-Wesley Publishing Company, Reading, Massachusetts, 1995).

[Dubois et al., 1991] D. Dubois, H. Prade, J.-P. Rossazza, "Vagueness, Typicality and Uncertainty in Class Hierarchies", *International Journal of Intelligent Systems*, **6**, 167-183 (1991).

[Elmasri & Navathe, 1989] R. Elmasri, S.B. Navathe, *Fundamentals of Database Systems* (The Benjamin Cummings Publishing Company, Redwood City, CA USA, 1989).

[Gallagher, 1994] L. Gallagher, "Influencing Database Language Standards", *ACM Sigmod Record*, **23-1**, 122-127 (1994).

[George et al., 1993] R. George, B.P. Buckles, F.E. Petry, "Modeling Class Hierarchies in the Fuzzy Object-Oriented Data Model", *Fuzzy Sets and Systems*, **60 (3)**, 259-272 (1993).

[Lebastard, 1993] F. Lebastard, *Une couche object virtuelle persistante pour le raisonnement sur les bases de données relationelles* {Ph.D. Dissertation, l'Institut National de Sciences Appliquées de Lyon, France, 1993).

[Melton & Simon] J. Melton, A.R. Simon, *Understanding the New SQL : A Complete Guide* (Morgan Kaufmann Publishers Inc., San Francisco, CA USA, 1993).

[Mouaddib & Subtil, 1995] N. Mouaddib, P. Subtil, "Fuzzy Thesaurus and Fuzzy Semantic Network", *Proceedings of the Workshop on Fuzzy Database Systems and Information Retrieval*, FUZZ-IEEE/IFES95, Yokohama, Japan, 37-42 (1995).

[OFTA, 1994] l'Observatoire Français des Techniques Avancées, *Logique Flous* (Masson, Paris, 1994).

[Petry, 1996] F.E. Petry, *Fuzzy Databases: Principles and Applications* (Kluwer Academic Publishers, Norwell, MA USA, 1996).

[Premerlani et al., 1990] W.J. Premerlani, M.R. Blaha, J.E. Rumbaugh, T.A. Varwig, "An Object-Oriented Relational Database", *Communications of the ACM*, **33** (11), 99-109 (1990).

[Unano & Fukami, 1991] M. Unano, S. Fukami, "Perspectives of Fuzzy Databases", *Japanese Journal of Fuzzy Theory and Systems*, **3** (1), 75-91 (1991).

[Van Gyseghem & De Caluwe, 1995] N. Van Gyseghem, R. De Caluwe, "Fuzzy Behaviour and Relationships in a Fuzzy OODB-Model", *Proceedings of the Tenth Annual ACM Symposium on Applied Computing*, Nashville, TN USA, 503-507 (1995).

[Van Gyseghem, 1995] N. Van Gyseghem, *A Fuzzy and Uncertain Object-Oriented Database Model* (Ph.D. Dissertation, University of Ghent, Belgium, 1995).

[Van Gyseghem & De Caluwe, 1996] N. Van Gyseghem, R. De Caluwe, "Fuzzy Inheritance in the UFO Database Model", *Proceedings of the IEEE International Conference on Fuzzy Systems*, New Orleans, LA USA, 1365-1370 (1996).

[Van Gyseghem & De Caluwe, 1996b] N. Van Gyseghem, R. De Caluwe, "Imprecision and Uncertainty in the UFO Database Model", *Journal of the American Society for Information Science* (to appear).

[Yager, 1987] R.R. Yager, "Set-Based Representations of Conjunctive and Disjunctive Knowledge", *Information Sciences*, **41**, 1-22 (1987).

# FUZZY OBJECT-ORIENTED DATA MODEL AND FUZZY ASSOCIATION ALGEBRA

SELEE NA

*Department of Computer Science, Hanyang Women's Junior College., Mount 17, Haengdang-dong, Sungdong-gu, Seoul ,133-793, Korea*

SEOG PARK

*Department of Computer Science, Sogang University, 1, Sinsu-dong, Mapo-gu, Seoul, 121-742, Korea*

The complexity of real world applications in the fields of intelligent information systems has required fuzzy data models for the representation and the processing of uncertain and imprecise data. In this paper, we propose a new Fuzzy Object Oriented Data model (F-model) and a Fuzzy Association algebra (FA-algebra) for the F-model as a query algebra. The F-model is investigated as a fuzzy extension of an Object Oriented data model which allows fuzzy classes and fuzzy associations. Databases are represented by a fuzzy schema graph at schema level and a fuzzy object graph at object instance level. The FA-algebra operators can operate on the fuzzy association patterns of homogeneous and heterogeneous structures. As the results of fuzzy association operations, the truth values of patterns are returned with the patterns. The completeness of the FA-algebra is shown. In the F-model, we describe the management of fuzzy objects with fuzzy attribute values. Objects representing linguistic terms are proposed for the representation of fuzzy attribute values. The fuzzy objects and the linguistic term objects are uniformly represented by the fuzzy association patterns which are manipulated by the FA-algebra operators. By the FA-algebra, the fuzzy queries involving fuzzy values can be processed easily.

## 1 Introduction

We propose a new Fuzzy Object Oriented Data model (F- model) and a Fuzzy Association algebra (FA-algebra) for the F-model. The F-model is defined as an extended Object Oriented data model which allows fuzzy classes and fuzzy associations. Fuzzy classes are classes having uncertain boundaries of semantics. Fuzzy associations are characterized by the fact that the relationships can be stronger or weaker. The databases are represented at two levels, schema level and object instance level. At the schema level, classes and associations between classes can be labelled with fuzzy linguistic terms like 'highly_educated_person' or 'rich_person' for classes and 'may_be' or 'well_defined' for the associations. At the object instance level, each object of a fuzzy class has a degree of membership of the fuzzy class and each association between two objects has a

187

degree of relationship for the fuzzy association. The domain of the FA-algebra is a set of fuzzy association patterns. Database retrieval is based on a pattern matching a query pattern. The FA-algebra manipulates the fuzzy association patterns of homogeneous as well as of heterogeneous patterns of object associations and evaluates the truth values of patterns. By the truth values, the degrees of suitability of patterns as answers for the queries are specified. The FA-algebra allows very complex fuzzy patterns of object associations to be directly manipulated. The completeness of the FA-algebra is proved.

## 2 The F-Model

### 2.1 Main Concepts

The F-model is defined on the essential characteristics of the OO paradigm. It allows fuzzy classes and fuzzy relationships between two classes at the schema level and fuzzy objects having fuzzy attribute values and fuzzy associations with other objects, which are characterized by their membership degrees at the object level.

### 2.1.1 Fuzzy Object

Objects represent physical entities, abstract concepts, events, processes and so on. Each object is assigned a system-defined, unique object identifier(OID). *Fuzzy objects* are objects that have an uncertain structure or behaviour. This implies that they may have fuzzy attribute values or fuzzy associations between objects.

### 2.1.2 Fuzzy Class

The objects having the same structural and behavioural properties are grouped together to form an object class. Object classes can be either primitive classes or nonprimitive classes. A primitive class represents a class of self-named objects serving as a domain for defining other object classes, such as a class of symbols or numerical values. A nonprimitive class represents a set of objects, each of which is assigned an OID. The structural properties of an object class are represented by descriptive data which define states of objects and by associations which specify relationships between the objects of the related classes.

A fuzzy class is a class which has an uncertain boundary. For example, the class 'person' has a certain boundary and the class 'highly_educated_person' has an uncertain boundary. A *fuzzy class* (FC) is defined as follows:

$$FC_i = \{(o_{ij}, \mu(o_{ij})) \mid o_{ij} \text{ is an object and } 0 < \mu(o_{ij}) \leq 1\}$$

where $\mu(o_{ij})$ is the degree of membership of the $j^{th}$ object $o_{ij}$ in the fuzzy class $FC_i$. We call a pair $(o_{ij}, \mu(o_{ij}))$ a fuzzy object.

### 2.1.3 Fuzzy Association

Associations specify the relationships between the objects of a class and the objects of some related class. There are different types of associations, such as aggregation, generalization, etc.

A fuzzy association is a relationship with fuzzy semantics. For example, the 'may_be' association, the 'well_defined' association and the 'fluent' association are fuzzy associations. At the object level, a fuzzy association is defined as an association between to objects with a degree of relationship. A *fuzzy association* (FA) is defined as follows:

$$FA_{im}(k) = \{((o_{ij}, o_{mn}), R_{(k)}(o_{ij}, o_{mn})) \mid \text{for all } j \text{ and } n,$$
$$(o_{ij}, \mu(o_{ij})) \in FC_i, (o_{mn}, \mu(o_{mn})) \in FC_m$$
$$\text{and } 0 \leq R_{(k)}(o_{ij}, o_{mn}) \leq 1\}$$

where $R_{(k)}(o_{ij}, o_{mn})$ is the degree of relationship between the two objects $o_{ij}$ and $o_{mn}$ and $k$ is the identifier of the association. Identifiers are not needed if no confusion is possible. $FC_i$ and $FC_n$ are fuzzy classes. There is no need to represent the associations which have a degree of relationship with value 0, i.e., $R_{(k)}(o_{ij}, o_{mn}) = 0$. The traditional association, in an OO database corresponds with the degree 1.

### 2.2 Representations of Databases

A fuzzy digraph $FD = (V, R)$ consists of a finite set $V = \{v_1, v_2, ..., v_n\}$ and a fuzzy relation $R$ on $V$. If the relation $R$ satisfies the condition of symmetry $R(v, w) = R(w, v)$, $\forall v, m \in V$, and the condition of reflexivity $R(v, v) = 1$, $\forall v \in V$, then we call it a fuzzy graph. We indicate a fuzzy graph as $FG = (V, R)$.

Consider a fuzzy relation $R$ defined on a finite set $V$. The relation $R$ is interpreted in terms of a fuzzy graph. That is, for $v, w \in V$, $R(v, w)$ is the grade of adjacency from $v$ to $w$. If $R$ is reflexive and symmetric, then $R(v, w)$ is the grade of adjacency between the vertices $v$ and $w$. At the same time, a fuzzy digraph FD or a fuzzy graph FG is considered to be a collection of its $\alpha$-cuts.

The fuzzy OO database is represented by two extended fuzzy graphs, one for the extensional and one for the intensional databases.

*Fuzzy Schema Graph (FSG)* The FSG is defined by FSG(FC,FA), where $FC = \{FC_i \mid$ For all $i\}$, is a set of vertices representing fuzzy classes and $FA = \{FA_{im}(k) \mid$ For all $i$ and $m\}$ is a set of edges of fuzzy associations between two classes. Based on the FSG, users can query the database by specifying patterns of object associations as search conditions. The pattern is called an intensional pattern.

*Fuzzy Object Graph (FOG)* The FOG is defined by FOG(FO,FE), where $FO = \{(o_{ij}, \mu(o_{ij}))\}$ is a set of vertices with truth values representing fuzzy object instances, and $FE = \{(k) : o_{ij} - o_{mn}, R(o_{ij}, o_{mn})\}$ is a set of edges with truth values representing fuzzy associations between two fuzzy object instances. Based on the FOG, the operations of the query algebra are processed by selecting the patterns that match the intensional patterns. The pattern on the FOG is called an extensional pattern.

The relationship between a FOG(FO,FE) and its corresponding FSG(FC, FA) is a morphism. The mapping function F is defined as:

$$F_1 : FC_i \Rightarrow \{(o_{ij}, \mu(o_{ij}))\}, \text{ and}$$

$$F_2 : FA_{im}(k) \Rightarrow \{(k) : o_{ij} - o_{mn}, R(o_{ij}, o_{mn})\}$$

The mapping between FSG and FOG is one-to-many, since a database is dynamically changing and may have different instances at different times for the same fuzzy schema graph.

The examples of FSG and FOG for a human resource database are illustrated in Figure 1 and Figure 2. In Figure 1, the classes 'highly_educated _person' and 'high_level_technician' are fuzzy classes. Class 'person' has a crisp boundary, but as we would like to process the classes uniformly, we extend nonfuzzy classes to fuzzy classes with all objects having degrees of membership 1. Class 'person' has four attributes ss#, name, age and position. 'fluent', 'well_defined' and 'may_be' are fuzzy associations. By the association 'fluent', the statement "a 'highly_educated_person' has a fluent knowledge of a 'spoken_language' " is represented. By the association 'well_defined', the statement "a 'highly_educated_person' has a 'well_defined' speciality" is represented. By the association 'may_be', "a 'faculty' (member) may be a 'highly_educated_person' ", "a 'researcher' may be a 'highly_educated_person' " and "an 'engineer' may be a 'high_level_technician' " are represented. By the association 'employed', "a 'person' is employed in an 'organization' " is

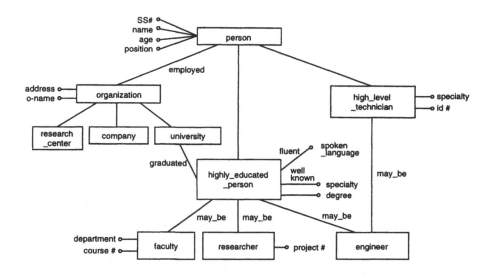

Figure 1: A Fuzzy Schema Graph of A Human Resources Database fuzzy classes.

represented. The non labelled associations are 'is_a' relationships. The 'is_a' relationship is a special case of the association 'may_be' in which every association between objects has degree of relationship 1. By the association 'is_a', "a 'highly_educated_person' is a 'person' " and "a 'high_level_technician' is a 'person' " are represented. The associations are called by their identifiers, but if no confusion is possible, the associations can be called by their two related classes. In Figure 2, for example, object 'p3' in 'person' has the name 'Kim' with a degree of relationship 1, and 'e3' is 'p3' with a degree of relationship 1, 'e3' is a 'highly_educated_person' with a degree of membership 0.5, and 'e3' has 'English' as a fluently 'spoken_language' with a degree of relationship 1, 'p3' is employed in 'o3' and has the name 'Hanyang' with a degree of relationship 1.

## 3 The FA-algebra

An FA-algebra is defined for the F-model as illustrated in section 2. In the FA- algebra, all operators are defined to operate on fuzzy association patterns of homogeneous as well as on heterogeneous structures.

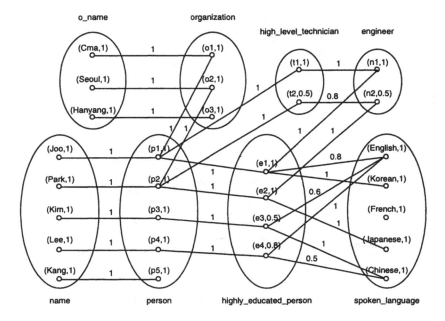

Figure 2: An Example of Fuzzy Object Graph.

### 3.1 Fuzzy Association Pattern

A domain of an FA-algebra is a set of fuzzy association patterns. A connected subgraph of a FOG is a fuzzy association pattern. There are five types of primitive patterns and one complex pattern type that is composed of primitive patterns. A fuzzy association pattern is a pair containing a pattern and a truth value associated with this pattern, algebraically represented by $(P, T(P))$. We define the primitive patterns as follows:

The *Fuzzy Inner Association Pattern* (or f-inner pattern) is a single vertex (or fuzzy object) in the FOG represented by $((a_i), T(a_i))$ for a vertex of the fuzzy class A in FSG. The truth value should be replaced with a membership value, $T(a_i) = \mu(a_i)$. Thus fuzzy object instances in fuzzy classes are treated as fuzzy inner patterns.

The *Fuzzy Inter Association Pattern* (or f-inter pattern) is composed of two vertices and an edge between the two vertices represented by $((a_i b_j), T(a_i b_j))$. The truth value should be the minimum of $T(a_i), T(b_j)$ and $R(a_i, b_j)$ , i.e. , $T(a_i b_j) = \min(T(a_i), T(b_j), R(a_i, b_j))$. This pattern states that the two objects

$a_i$ and $b_j$ are associated with each other in the FOG with the degree of the truth value.

The *Fuzzy Complement Association Pattern* (or f-complement pattern) is composed of two vertices and a complement edge between two vertices, represented by $((a_ib_j)', T(a_ib_j)')$ where $T(a_ib_j)' = \min(T(a_i), T(b_j), R(a_i, b_j)')$. $R(a_i, b_j)'$ is the complement relation of $R(a_i, b_j)$. Thus $R(a_i, b_j)' = 1 - R(a_i, b_j)$. This pattern states that $a_i$ and $b_j$ are not associated with each other in the FOG with the degree of the truth value.

The *Fuzzy Derived Inter Association Pattern* (or f-d-inter pattern) is composed of two nonadjacent vertices and a derived edge between the two vertices, represented by $((a_ib_j) \sim, T(a_ib_j) \sim)$. It is possible that there exist many sequences between $a_i$ and $b_j$. Let $c_{1k}, c_{2k}, \ldots, c_{nk}$ be the $k^{th}$ sequence of adjacent vertices between $a_i$ and $b_j$, $T_k(a_ib_j) \sim$ be the truth value of the sequence. Then $T_k(a_ib_j) \sim = \min(T(a_ic_{1k}), T(c_{1k}c_{2k}), \ldots, T(c_{nk}b_j))$. $T(a_ib_j) \sim$ is the supreme of $T_k(a_ib_j) \sim$, for all $k$, i.e. $T(a_ib_j) \sim = Sup_k(T_k(a_ib_j) \sim)$. This pattern states that two nonadjacent objects $a_i$ and $b_j$ are indirectly associated with each other by a path that consists of only regular edges, with the degree of the truth value.

The *Fuzzy Derived Complement Association Pattern* (or f-d-complement pattern) is composed of two nonadjacent vertices and a derived complement edge between the two vertices, represented by $((a_ib_j) \sim', T(a_ib_j) \sim')$. For all the sequences with more than one complement edge between $a_i$ and $b_j$, the truth value $T(a_ib_j) \sim' = Sup_k(T_k(a_ib_j) \sim')$ for all $k$. This pattern states that the two adjacent objects not associated by a path that consists of at least one complement edge with the degree of the truth value.

The above five types of patterns are the primitive patterns, with the latter four being binary patterns. All other connected subgraphs are called complex fuzzy patterns. *Complex patterns* are composed of a set of primitive patterns. We represent the fuzzy association patterns by a graphical representation and an algebraic representation as illustrated in Figure 3. For example, the complex fuzzy pattern shown in Figure 3 contains three primitive patterns: two inner patterns$((a_1, b_1), T_1)$ and $((b_1, d_1), T_2)$, and a complement-pattern $((b_1, c_1)', T_3)$. The truth value for a complex fuzzy pattern will be evaluated by using FA operations.

A special type of fuzzy association sets is called a homogeneous fuzzy association set if all fuzzy association patterns in the set have the same class

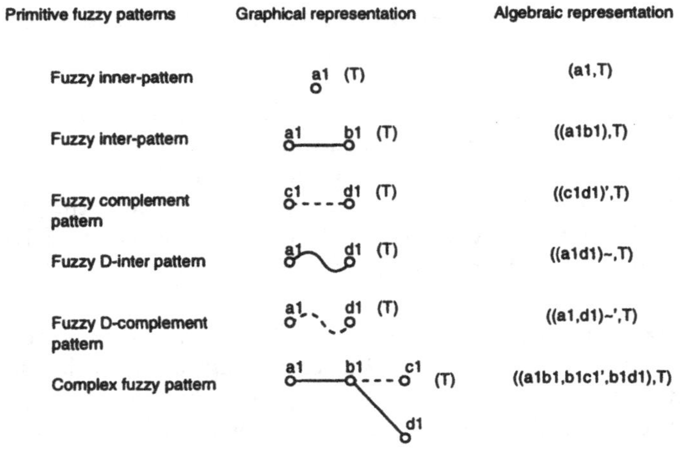

| Primitive fuzzy patterns | Graphical representation | Algebraic representation |
|---|---|---|
| Fuzzy inner-pattern | a1 (T) | (a1,T) |
| Fuzzy inter-pattern | a1 b1 (T) | ((a1b1),T) |
| Fuzzy complement pattern | c1 --- d1 (T) | ((c1d1)',T) |
| Fuzzy D-inter pattern | a1 d1 (T) | ((a1d1)~,T) |
| Fuzzy D-complement pattern | a1 d1 (T) | ((a1,d1)~',T) |
| Complex fuzzy pattern | a1 b1 c1 (T) d1 | ((a1b1,b1c1',b1d1),T) |

Figure 3: Representation of fuzzy patterns

structure and are formed by the same primitive pattern types. In other words, all the fuzzy association patterns in the homogeneous fuzzy association set are formed by object instances of the same set of fuzzy object classes. They also have the same number of instances from each of the involved classes, and the corresponding links among all the patterns are of the same primitive pattern types. Otherwise, it is a heterogeneous fuzzy association set.

### 3.2 Operators

First of all, we describe the notations that will be used in the definition of the operators. $A, B, \ldots, K$ denote fuzzy classes. $FC_i$ denotes a variable for a fuzzy class, which can be explicitly named by an attribute. $[R(FC_i, FC_j)]$ denotes the fuzzy association between two classes. $\{[R(FC_i, FC_j)]\}$ denotes the fuzzy set of f-inter patterns having the association denoted by $[R(FC_i, FC_j)]$. $a_i$ denotes $i^{th}$ fuzzy pattern of fuzzy class $A$. $P(a_i)$ denotes the pattern of fuzzy pattern $a_i$. $T(a_i)$ denotes the truth value of fuzzy pattern $a_i$. @ denotes a f-inner pattern variable. $\alpha, \beta, \gamma, \ldots$ denote sets of fuzzy associations. $\alpha_i$ denotes $i^{th}$ fuzzy pattern of the fuzzy association set. $P(\alpha)$ denotes a set of primitive patterns in $\alpha$. $\{W\}, \{X\}, \{Y\}, \ldots$ denote sets of fuzzy classes. $\alpha_{\{X\}}$ represents the fuzzy association set $\alpha$ which has f-inner patterns from the classes in $\{X\}$. The notations for fuzzy patterns are the same as those in the previous section.

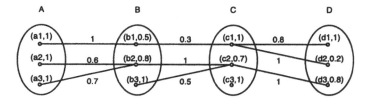

Figure 4: Sample fuzzy object graph.

### (1) Associate (*)

The associate operator constructs a fuzzy association set of complex patterns by concatenating the fuzzy patterns represented by the fuzzy association set operands of the two operands. The definition is as follows:

$$
\begin{aligned}
\gamma \;=\;& \alpha * [R(A,B)]\beta \\
=\;& \{(P(\gamma_k), T(\gamma_k)) \mid P(\gamma_k) = (P(\alpha_i), P(\beta_j), a_m b_n), \\
& T(\gamma_k) = \min(T(\alpha_i), T(\beta_j), T(a_m b_n)) \\
& \text{where } a_m \in P(\alpha_i), b_n \in P(\beta_j) \text{ and } T(\gamma_k) > 0\}
\end{aligned}
$$

The result of an Associate operation is a fuzzy association set containing no duplicates. Each of its patterns is the concatenation of two patterns with an inner pattern.

A general example of the Associate operation is shown in Figure 5(a). In the example, $\alpha_1$ is concatenated with $\beta_1$ with truth value 0.3, which is the minimum of $T(\alpha_1), T(\beta_1)$ and $T(b_1 c_1)$, due to the existence of $(b_1 c_1, (0.3))$ in Figure 4.

### (2) Complement (\)

The complement operator constructs a fuzzy association set of complex patterns by concatenating the fuzzy patterns represented by the two fuzzy association set operands over the fuzzy complement patterns. The definition is as follows:

$$
\begin{aligned}
\gamma \;=\;& \alpha \mid [R(A,B)]\beta \\
=\;& \{(P(\gamma_k), T(\gamma_k)) \mid P(\gamma_k) = (P(\alpha_i), P(\beta_j), a_m b'_n), \\
& T(\gamma_k) = \min(T(\alpha_i), T(\beta_j), T(a_m b_n)') \\
& \text{where } a_m \in P(\alpha_i), b_n \in P(\beta_j) \text{ and } T(\gamma_k) > 0\}
\end{aligned}
$$

The result of a Complement operation is a fuzzy association set. Each of its patterns is formed by concatenating two patterns via a fuzzy complement pattern. A general example of the Complement operation is shown in Figure 5(b). $\alpha_1$ and $\beta_1$ can be connected by a complement edge because in Figure 4, $b_1$ and $c_1$ are associated with the complement value of 0.3 by the complement relationship. The minimum of the two truth values of the patterns and the degree of the complement relationship is taken as the truth value. The result is 0.5. Between $b_1$ and $c_2$, between $b_1$ and $c_3$, between $b_2$ and $c_1$, and between $b_2$ and $c_3$, there exist complement relationships. Between $b_2$ and $c_2$ there is no complement relationship. So five fuzzy association patterns with complement edges are returned.

### (3) Select($\sigma$)

The select operator produces a subset of fuzzy patterns which satisfy two specified predicates $\hat{P}$ and $\hat{C}$. The $\hat{P}$ and $\hat{C}$ are optional but it is not allowed to skip both.

When both $\hat{P}$ and $\hat{C}$ are specified :

$$
\begin{aligned}
\gamma &= \sigma(\alpha)[\hat{P}, \hat{C}] \\
&= \{(P(\gamma_k), T(\gamma_k)) \mid P(\gamma_k) = P(\alpha_i) \text{ and } T(\gamma_k) = 1, \\
&\quad \text{where } \hat{P}(P(\alpha_i)) = \text{true and } \hat{C}(T(\alpha_i)) = \text{true}\}
\end{aligned}
$$

When only $\hat{P}$ is specified :

$$
\begin{aligned}
\gamma &= \sigma(\alpha)[\hat{P}] \\
&= \{(P(\gamma_k), T(\gamma_k)) \mid P(\gamma_k) = P(\alpha_i) \text{ and } T(\gamma_k) = T(\alpha_i), \\
&\quad \text{where } \hat{P}(P(\alpha_i)) = \text{true and } T(\alpha_i) > 0\}
\end{aligned}
$$

When only $\hat{C}$ is specified :

$$
\begin{aligned}
\gamma &= \sigma(\alpha)[\hat{C}] \\
&= \{(P(\gamma_k), T(\gamma_k)) \mid P(\gamma_k) = P(\alpha_i) \text{ and } T(\gamma_k) = 1, \\
&\quad \text{where } \hat{C}(T(\alpha_i)) = \text{true}\}
\end{aligned}
$$

The predicate $\hat{C} = T \, \theta \, c$. $T$ is a truth variable. $\theta$ is one of the comparison operators, $=, >, <, \leq, \geq$ and $\neq$. $c$ is a value in [0,1]. The predicate $\hat{P} = T_1 \, \theta_1 \, T_2 \, \theta_2 \, \ldots \, \theta_{n-1} \, T_n$. $\theta_i (i = 1, \ldots, n-1)$ is a boolean operator ('$\wedge$' or '$\vee$'). $T_i(i = 1, \ldots, n)$ is a term. Three kinds of terms, comparison terms, connectivity terms and existence terms are available. A term $T_i$ consists of two operands $o_1$ and $o_2$ and an operator $op$, with syntax $T_i = o_1\ op\ o_2$. $o_1$ and $o_2$ must have the same type. In comparison terms, $o_1$ and $o_2$ can be constants or object instances, at most one of them being a constant. The operator can be either $=$, $>$, $<$, $\geq$, $\leq$, $\neq$ for numerical type operands, or $=$, $\neq$ for character type, string type and OID type operands or $=$, $\subset$, $\supset$, $\subseteq$, $\supseteq$, $\neq$ for fuzzy set type operands. In connectivity terms, $o_1$ and $o_2$ can be object instances. The operator can be either $*$ or $|$, but here, $*$ and $|$ are not algebraic operators, they are merely symbols which denote the connections of objects. In existence terms, $o_1$ can be a fuzzy class and $o_2$ can be $\phi$. The operator can be either $=$ or $\neq$, i.e., for a fuzzy classA , A$=\phi$ and A$\neq$ $\phi$ are all existence terms. Figure 5(c) shows an example of the Select operation. There are two conditions. The condition for the pattern is '$A*B \wedge D = 7$' , and the condition for the truth value is 'the Truth value is greater than 0.5'. For $\alpha_3$ and $\alpha_4$ the two conditions are satisfied. The truth value of the result patterns is 1.

*(4) Project($\pi$)*
The project operation is used to eliminate the subpatterns of the heterogeneous pattern it operates on. The definition is as follows:

$$\pi(\alpha)[\hat{E},\hat{D}] = \{(P(\gamma_k), T(\gamma_k)) \mid P(\gamma_k) = P(\alpha_i^s),$$
$$T(\gamma_k) = \max(T(\alpha_i), T(\alpha_j), \ldots, T(\alpha_n))$$
$$\text{where } P(\alpha_i), P(\alpha_j), \ldots, P(\alpha_n) \text{ are projected to}$$
$$\text{an identical pattern } P(\gamma_k)\}$$

$\hat{E}$ is a set of expressions that specifies the subpatterns of $\alpha$ with syntax $\hat{E} = (e_1,\ e_2,\ ...,\ e_n)$ where $e_1, e_2, ..., e_n$ are the expressions of the patterns which are included in the set of the result patterns against a query. $\hat{D}$ is the set of the pairs of the classes with syntax $\hat{D} = (d_1,\ d_2,\ ...,\ d_n)$ where $d_1, d_2, ..., d_n$ are the pairs of the classes. For $d_i$ with syntax(A:B), A and B must be the classes which have appeared in $\hat{E}$ and the result patterns will include the derived edge between the objects in A and B whenever possible. $\hat{D}$ is optional.

In Figure 5(d), $\hat{E}$ is given by $(A*B, D)$ and $\hat{D}$ is given by $(B:D)$. This means that the result pattern is one of the three different types, $((a_ib_j),T)$, $((d_k),T)$ or $((a_ib_j, b_jd_k \sim),T)$. $\alpha_1$ is projected to two subpatterns - an inter pattern with $a_1$ and $b_1$ and an inner pattern $d_1$. The two subpatterns are connected by the derived edge from $b_1$ to $d_1$. From $\alpha_1$ and $\alpha_2$, the same projected patterns are constructed, and the maximum truth value 0.7 is taken for the pattern. Duplicate patterns are eliminated. From $\alpha_3$, only the inner pattern $d_3$ is returned because there is no subpattern such as $A$ associate $B$, but there is subpattern $d_3$.

### (5) Intersect(•)

The intersect operation constructs a pattern with a branch, a lattice or a network structure since a pattern in such a structure can be seen as the intersection of two patterns. The definition is as follows:

$$\begin{aligned}
\gamma &= \alpha_{\{X\}} \bullet \{W\}\beta_{\{Y\}} \\
&= \{(P(\gamma_k), T(\gamma_k)) \mid P(\gamma_k) = (P(\alpha_i), P(\beta_j)), \\
&\quad T(\gamma_k) = \min(T(\alpha_i), T(\beta_j)), \\
&\quad \text{where for all } P(@) \text{ such that } FC_n \in \{W\}, P(@) \in P(FC_n) \\
&\quad \text{and } P(@) \in P(\alpha_i), P(@) \in P(\beta_j) \text{ is satisfied.}\}
\end{aligned}$$

The intersect operator is similar to the JOIN operator in the relational algebra. Two patterns are combined into one if they contain the same set of inner-patterns for each specified class.

In Figure 5(e), $\alpha_1$ and $\beta_1$ are combined with minimum truth value 0.3 because the two patterns intersect at class $B$ and $C$. In the result set, three fuzzy object patterns are included.

### (6) Union(+)

The union operation combines two fuzzy association sets which are homogeneous or heterogeneous, with the maximum truth value associated with identical patterns. The definition is as follows:

$$\begin{aligned}
\gamma &= \alpha + \beta \\
&= \{(P(\gamma_k), T(\gamma_k)) \mid \gamma_k = \alpha_i, \text{ or } \gamma_k = \beta_j \text{ or } P(\gamma_k) = P(\alpha_i) \\
&\quad \text{and } T(\gamma_k) = \max(T(\alpha_i), T(\beta_j)) \text{ where } P(\alpha_i) = P((\beta_j))\}
\end{aligned}$$

In Figure 5(f), for $\alpha_1$ and $\beta_1$, there is an identical pattern $(a_1, b_1)$, with different truth values 0.5 and 0.8. The result set includes only $((a_1, b_1), 0.8)$ with the maximum value of $T(\alpha_1)$ and $T(\beta_1)$. Only one pattern is in the result set with the maximum value 0.5 as the truth value. In the result set, there is only one pattern $(a_1, b_1)$, which has the maximum value 0.8 as the truth value. The remaining patterns are included.

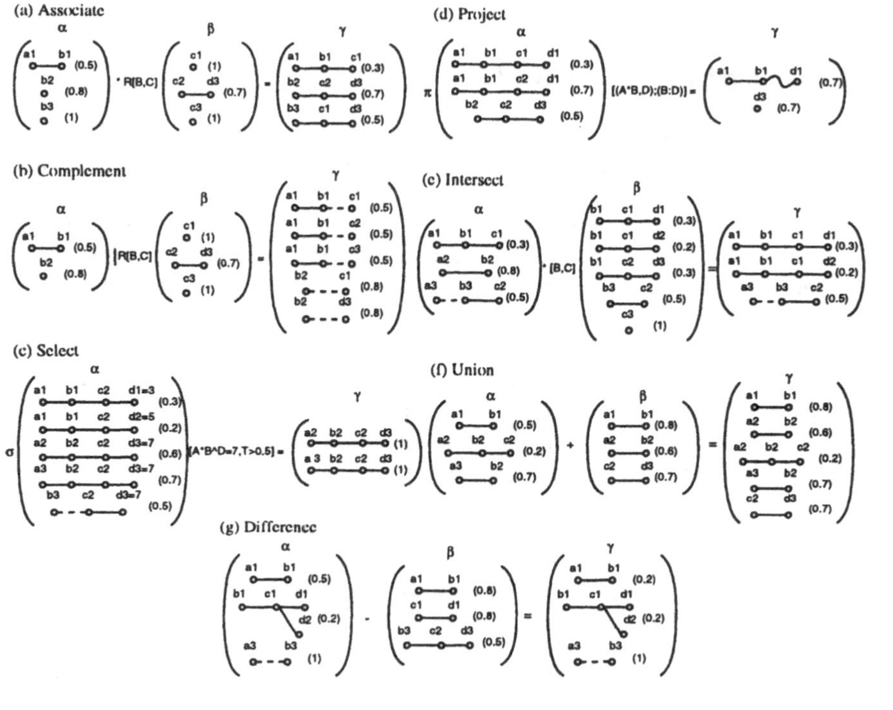

Figure 5: Examples of operations.

## (7) Difference(-)

The difference operation is defined on two homogeneous or heterogeneous association sets with the minimum value of the truth values of $T(\alpha_i)$ and $1 - T(\beta_j)$ between identical patterns. The definition is as follows:

$$\gamma = \alpha - \beta$$
$$= \{(P(\gamma_k), T(\gamma_k)) \mid \gamma_k = \alpha_i, \text{ or } P(\gamma_k) = P(\alpha_i),$$
$$T(\gamma_k) = \min(T(\alpha_i), 1 - T(\beta_j)) \text{where } P(\alpha_i) = P(\beta_j)\}$$

In Figure 5(g), because $\alpha_1$ and $\beta_1$ have the same pattern $(a_1, b_1)$ and different truth values 0.5 and 0.8, the result set includes $((a_1, b_1), 0.2)$. The truth value 0.2 is the minimum of 0.5 and 1-0.8. There are no more identical patterns in $\alpha$ and $\beta$, so $\alpha_2$ and $\beta_3$ are included in the result set.

*3.3 Query Examples*

The following query is illustrated by Figure 1 and Figure 2.

*Query : List the o_names of the organizations and the names of the persons who are highly educated, high level technicians and speak English fluently.*

The answer to this query requires the construction of those patterns which are composed of the two nodes, 'o_name' and name of person, and the link between these two nodes. The person should be a member of the class 'highly _educated_person' and a member of the class 'high_level_technician'. Because the class 'highly_educated_person' has the attribute 'spoken_language' represented with the membership degree representing fluency for the condition of 'speak English fluently', the person as a member of the class 'highly_educated _person' should be linked with the attribute value 'English'. The query pattern is shown in Figure 6 and the algebraic representation is:

$\pi$ ( $\sigma$ ( (o_name * organization * person * name)
    &bull; (person * highly_educated_person * spoken_language)
    &bull; (person * high_level_technician) ) [spoken_language = 'English'] )
[o_name, name, o_name: name]

Four steps can be distinguished. The construction of the corresponding fuzzy patterns is shown step by step in Figure 6.

Step 1: The three subpatterns are processed by the associate operator.

    subpattern_1 = o_name * organization * person * name
    subpattern_2 = person * highly_educated_person * spoken_language
    subpattern_3 = person * high_level_technician

Step 2: The three subpatterns are combined to total patterns by the intersect operator.

    Total pattern = subpattern_1 &bull; subpattern_2 &bull; subpattern_3

Step 3: The patterns satisfying the condition are selected, person is associated with 'spoken_language = 'English' ' and the resulting pattern is processed.

    selected_pattern =$\sigma$ (total_pattern)[spoken_language = 'English']

Step 4: The 'selected_pattern' is projected into two subpatterns 'o_name' and 'name' and then the pattern from the node 'o_name' to the node 'name' is derived.

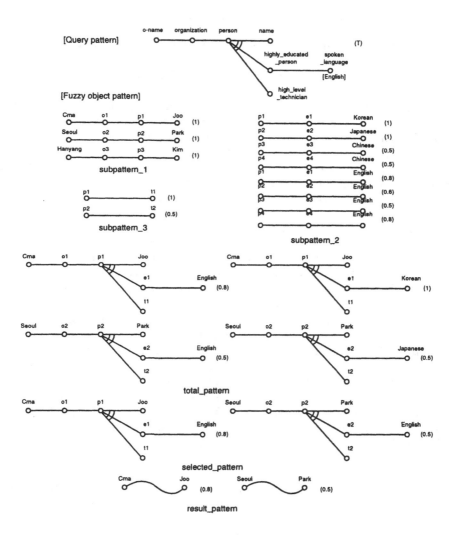

Figure 6: Fuzzy patterns for Query.

$\pi$ (selected_pattern)[o_name, name, o_name : name]

The result patterns are represented in an algebraic way as follows:

$$((cma, Joo)\sim, 0.8), ((seoul, Park)\sim, 0.5)$$

For the query, the result fuzzy pattern $((cma, Joo)\sim, 0.8)$ means that the proposition *'Joo employed in cma is highly educated, high level technician and speaks English fluently'* is true with degree 0.8. The result fuzzy pattern $((seoul, Park)\sim, 0.5)$ means that the proposition *'Park employed in Seoul is highly educated, a high level technician and speaks English fluently'* is true with degree 0.5. By comparing the truth values of the two result patterns, we know that $((cma, Joo)\sim, 0.8)$ is the best available answer to the query.

### 3.4 The Completeness of the FA-algebra

In the preceding sections, we have illustrated that a query issued against the F-model database can be specified by a fuzzy association pattern, and that the FA-algebra provides a useful mathematical method for specifying and manipulating the fuzzy association patterns to produce the result for a query. However, for the algebra to be truly useful, the completeness of the algebra needs to be addressed. To show the completeness of the FA-algebra, we need to explain its closure property. The closure property is very useful to construct a complex query because it certifies that the result of a query can be further operated on, uniformly using the same query operators to produce a new result. The operands of the FA-algebra are sets of fuzzy association patterns and the result of the operations is also a set of fuzzy association patterns. This means that the FA-algebra has the closure property. Before defining the completeness of a fuzzy algebra, we give the formal definition of the completeness of the algebra of an object oriented database.

***Definition of Completeness of an algebra*** An algebra is complete if it can be used to specify all possible subdatabases of an OO database.

Since the fuzzy object oriented database is a collection of fuzzy association patterns, the definition of the completeness of a fuzzy algebra can be restated as follows.

***Definition of Completeness of a fuzzy algebra*** A fuzzy algebra is complete if there exists an algebraic expression for every fuzzy association pattern in the FOG of a fuzzy OO database.

We can give the completeness theorem as follows.

*Completeness Theorem* The FA-algebra is complete.

Before proving the completeness of the FA-algebra, we must indicate the similarity and the difference between the A-algebra and the FA-algebra. The A-algebra has been established on a nonfuzzy schema graph and a nonfuzzy object graph, i.e., the concepts of membership degree and of relationship degree have not been considered. The operands of the A-algebra are sets of association patterns and the result of an A-operation is also a set of association patterns. We know that a fuzzy association pattern is composed of two parts, the pattern part and the truth value part. The fuzzy association patterns are manipulated by the FA-algebra and differ from the association patterns in the truth value part. The operations of the FA-algebra are the extensions of the operations of the A-algebra, which have the ability to manipulate the truth value part. In [10], the completeness of the A-algebra has been proved. The same method can be used to prove the completeness of the FA-algebra. Hence, we indicate how the proof of the completeness of the A-algebra can be extended to prove the completeness of the FA-algebra.

*Proof by induction:* Base: We can show that there is an expression for the case that a fuzzy inner pattern contains a single fuzzy object. Since the name of a fuzzy class, say $FC_1$, represents all the object instances of the class, a fuzzy association pattern containing a single fuzzy object instance of that class can be represented by a select operation over the object instances of $FC_1$ to select a particular one of interest, as shown below:

$$\sigma(FC_1)[\hat{P}, \hat{C}] \text{ or } \sigma(FC_1)[\hat{P}] \text{ or } \sigma(FC_1)[\hat{C}]$$

where $\hat{P}$ is the condition to be satisfied by the pattern and $\hat{C}$ is the condition to be satisfied by the truth value.

*Hypothesis:* Assume that there exists an expression for every fuzzy association pattern that contains $n-1$ object instances. These $n-1$ object instances must form a connected graph, i.e., there must exist at least one path between any two object instances in the graph.

*Induction:* Suppose there exists an expression for a fuzzy association pattern $FP^{n-1}$ which contains $n-1$ object instances. When adding the $n$th fuzzy object instance to this pattern, $FP^n$ containing $n$ object instances can be formed in one of the following two ways: (a) the $n$th object instance belongs to a fuzzy class $FC_k$ and the object instances of $FC_k$ are not participating in $FP^{n-1}$, (b) the $n$th object instance belongs to a fuzzy class $FC_j$, which has some object instance participating in $FP^{n-1}$. In the proof for the A-algebra, the two cases (a) and (b) are discussed. To prove the completeness of the FA-algebra, we only have to replace the operations of the A-algebra with the operations of the FA-algebra. Remember that the truth value part of a fuzzy association pattern is defined only depending on the definitions of fuzzy set and fuzzy set operations. The calculations of the truth value parts are independent of the calculations of the pattern matching parts. The completeness of the A-algebra guarantees that in the FA-algebra every pattern can be expressed by a FOG. As to the truth values, they are calculated in the FA-algebra by using MAX or MIN operations corresponding to T-norms and T-conorms. Hence, we can conclude that the FA-algebra is complete.

## 5. Conclusion

In this chapter, we have proposed a Fuzzy Object Oriented Data model (F-model) and a Fuzzy Association algebra (FA-algebra) which can serve as a basis for the definition of database query languages.

The proposed concepts are especially interesting as a support for the development of graphical query interfaces based on the fuzzy schema graphs in which the patterns can be directly processed. Further investigations will be made on the use of fuzzy comparison operators such as 'much greater than'.

## References

1. G.Bordogna, D.Lucarella, G.Pasi, "A Fuzzy Object Oriented Data Model" In Proc. of Third IEEE Int. Conf. on Fuzzy Systems, 313-318 (1994).

2. K.Tanaka, S.Kobayashi, T.Sakanoue, "Uncertainty Management in Object- Oriented Database Systems" In Proc. of DEXA, 251-256 (1991).

3. N.Van Gyseghem, R.De Caluwe, R.Vanderberghe, "UFO:Uncertainty and Fuzziness in an Object-Oriented Model" Second IEEE Int. Conf. on Fuzzy Systems, 1, 489-495, San Francisco (1993).

4. B.P.Buckles, R.George and F.E.Petry," Toward a Fuzzy Object-Oriented Data Model" In NAFIPS, 73-77 (1991).

5. D.Dubois, H.Prade, J.P.Rossazza, "Vagueness, Typicality, and Uncertainty in Class Hierachies" Int. J. of Intelligent Systems, 6, 167-183 (1991).

6. M.Carey, D.Dewitt, S.Vandenberg, "A data model and query language for EXODUX" In Proc. ACM SIGMODE Int. Conf on Management of Data, pp.413-423 (1988).

7. S.L.Vandenberg, D.Dewitt, " Algebraic support for complex object with array, identity, and inheritance" In Proc. ACM SIGMODE Int. Conf. on anagement of Data, 158-167 (1991).

8. S.Cluet, C.Delobel, "A general framework for the optimization of Object-Oriented queries" In Proc. ACM SIGMOD Int. Conf. on Management of Data, 383-392 (1992).

9. C.Lecluse, P.Richard, F.Velez," O2, an Object-Oriented data model" ACM- SIGMODE Conf. 1988, 425-433 (1988).

10. S.Y.W.Su, M.Guo, H.Lam," Association Algebra : A Mathematical Foundation for Object-Oriented Databases" IEEE Tran. on Knowledge and Data Engineering, 5, 5, 775-798 (1993).

11. S.Y.W.Su, V.Krishnamurthy, H.Lam, "An Object-Oriented semantic association model(OSAM*)" AI in Industrial Engineering and anufacturing: Theoretical Issues and Applications, S.Kumara, A.L.Soyster, and .L.Kashyap, Eds. American Institute of Industrial Engineering (1989).

12. G.Shaw, S.Zdonic, "A object algebra for Object-Oriente databases" In Proc. 6th Int. Conf. on Data Engineering, 154-162 (1990).

13. S.L. Na, S. Park, "Management of fuzzy objects with fuzzy attribute values in new fuzzy object oriented data model" In Proc. 2nd Int. Workshop on FQAS,19-40 (1996).

14. S.L. Na, S. Park, "A fuzzy association algebra based on a fuzzy object oriented data model" In Proc. 20th Int. Conf. on compsac, 624-630 (1996).

15. S.L. Na, S. Park, "A process of fuzzy query on new fuzzy object oriented data model" In 7th Int. DEXA conf. (1996).

16. L.A.Zadeh, "Fuzzy Sets as a Basis for a Theory of Possibility" Fuzzy Sets and Systems, 1, 193-218 (1978).

17. L.A.Zadeh, "The Concept of Linguistic Variable and its Application to Approximate Reasoning" Parts 1 and 2, Information Sciences, 8, 219-327 (1975).

18. L.A.Zadeh, "The Concept of Linguistic Variable and its Application to Approximate Reasoning" Parts 3, Information Sciences, 9, 329-366 (1976).